Henry M. Jackson and World Affairs

Henry M. Jackson and World Affairs

Selected Speeches, 1953–1983

Edited by Dorothy Fosdick
Foreword by James H. Billington

UNIVERSITY OF WASHINGTON PRESS
Seattle and London

Library of Congress Cataloging-in-Publication Data

Jackson, Henry M. (Henry Martin), 1912–1983.
　Henry M. Jackson and world affairs : selected speeches,
　1953–1983 / edited by Dorothy Fosdick : foreword by
　James H. Billington.
　　p.　cm.
　Includes bibliographical references.
　ISBN 0–295–96947–4 (cloth: alk. paper)
　ISBN 0–295–97016–2 (pbk.: alk. paper)
　1. United States—Foreign relations—1945–
I. Fosdick, Dorothy.
II. Title.
E748.J22A5　1990　　　　　　　　　89-70678
327.73—dc20　　　　　　　　　　　　CIP

If we really believe in the cause of freedom,
let us proclaim it, live it, and protect it—
for humanity's future depends upon it.

—Senator Henry M. Jackson

Contents

Foreword

James H. Billington

There was some—but not much—reflection during the 1989 bicentennial year of the Congress of the United States about the neglect by historians of our first branch of government. What studies there are tend to focus largely on negatives. David McCullough noted in his address to the joint session of Congress commemorating the Bicentenary in March 1989 that there have been twelve biographies of Senator Joe McCarthy but none at all of most of the major twentieth-century leaders of the House and Senate. American history tends still to be written in terms of presidential eras, rather the way the English and French used to sort out their past in terms of the reigns of kings and queens.

How welcome, then, to have the concise record in his own words of one of the great statesmen of the Congress in the late twentieth century, Senator Henry Jackson. He was an important leader in America's rise to global responsibility during the age of total war and totalitarian peace. He was also a distinctively American and instinctively democratic man. As much as anyone in our time, he vindicated the Founding Fathers' hope that the Senate might be a place for genuine deliberation about the broad, long-term interest of the Republic. His friend and colleague Senator Daniel Patrick Moynihan in his eulogy to Senator Jackson spoke of "an old belief in the Judaic tradition that at any moment in history goodness in the world is preserved by the deeds of 36 just men who do not know that this is the role the Lord has given them. . . . Henry Jackson was one of those men. There could be no more telling evidence than that this would never have occurred to him."

One of those closest to Scoop Jackson throughout the period encompassed by this volume (1953–83) was the indomitable and much admired Dorothy Fosdick, a key figure on one of the best staffs in Washington. She has gathered here some of his most important speeches, provided an excellent context, and richly supplemented her earlier volume of essays by the Senator's talented aides (*Staying the Course: Henry M. Jackson and National Security*, University of Washington Press, 1987).

An adequate assessment of Jackson's unique contributions to the Republic would require greater knowledge than I possess of both American history and political Washington. But the record that Dorothy Fosdick has assembled and so clearly presents here suggests that this man combined three qualities almost never found in a single statesman: strategic intellect, moral vision, and a sense of practicality.

The fact that his speeches are essentially the working reports of an eminently practical man may make them prosaic reading to some. There are few of either the catchy rhetorical phrases or the broad, utopian visions of other liberal internationalist orators of this era. Nor do the Jackson speeches show much penchant for reorganization schemes as a way of dealing with substantive problems. His pioneering study of our organization for national security begun in the late Eisenhower era was important not just because it influenced the incoming Kennedy administration but also because it did *not* recommend a new structure. It retains validity today precisely because of its practical insistence on the need for better people, on a respected career service, and on a process of policy formation that airs all reasonable alternatives, eliminates excessive committees, and is led by the Secretary of State.

Jackson's characteristic back-to-basics practicality was always at the service both of a tough intellect not afraid to confront the world as it was and of an unrelenting moral determination to push that world closer to where it ought to be. He went against the consensus of a generally complacent foreign policy establishment both during the fifties when he called for more land- and sea-based missiles and during the seventies when he called for real arms reductions rather than symbolic arms control.

His strategic vision remained constant—as Dorothy Fosdick reminds us by reproducing some of his earliest public speeches of the immediate postwar era. He sought to build up both the military strength and the political will that the democratic world needed to deter a totalitarian adversary. At the same time, he sought to reduce the danger of war by mutual and verifiable arms reductions and by promoting the acceptance of human rights that serve to limit the inhuman use of power by authoritarian regimes.

Unlike many other celebrated American strategic thinkers of the postwar era, Jackson was not an academic steeped in abstract geopolitical speculation or amoral behaviorist analysis. His views were rooted in practical experience and moral conviction. He personally saw the horrors of Buchenwald at the end of World War II and lived with the awful realities of atomic weaponry from the time he first joined the Joint Congressional Committee on Atomic Energy in 1949. He sought practical ways to impel the free world to defend itself against a Stalinist empire that was filled with concentration camps and acquiring nuclear weapons, and he believed that America needed to develop alliances with those who shared our values (Western Europe) and relationships with those who shared our fears (China). He established friendly personal relations with many world leaders, but his total lack of pomposity kept him away from the kind of self-congratulatory meetings among the mighty that provide more photo opportunities than substantive accomplishments.

He seems to have established some of his closest ties to two countries that were small in size but strong in moral roots and fortitude: Norway and Israel. Norway, his parents' native land, was a sturdy democracy that had both fought against Hitler and (alone in the European north) signed on with NATO against Stalin. Just as Jackson got his middle name from the Martin Luther whose Protestantism Norway adopted, so he seems to have exemplified the Protestant ethic of hard work and Nordic perseverance in the belief that problems can be solved.

His high regard for the new state of Israel was based on his respect for a democratic enclave in the strategically important, politically volatile, and largely authoritarian Middle East. But there was also clearly a deep moral concern for a people nearly obliterated by Hitler and newly endangered by Stalin—and a special admiration for the new state's commitment both to building a liberal democracy with a strong program for social justice and to defending it strongly against foreign foes. His mixture of admiration and concern for the Jewish people was a major factor in one of his most original acts of legislative statesmanship: the Jackson-Vanik amendment linking the expansion of American trade with nonmarket countries (including the Soviet Union) to the right of free emigration. Reading his speeches on this controversial subject as reproduced in this volume, one sees Jackson both building on an earlier but forgotten moral agenda of United Nations resolutions and anticipating the subsequent acceptance by the U.S.S.R. of the premise that human rights can become international legal obligations. Now that the U.S.S.R. has begun to reveal the full extent of the cynicism and corruption of the Brezhnev era, it may be possible to appreciate anew that only unconventional linkages of this kind could fully establish that moral issues of human rights cannot be disregarded without paying a political price.

A striking personal characteristic of Jackson was his total absence of pretense. As his gifted staff members have repeatedly testified, he believed in the equality of all participants in the many dialogues he sponsored and participated in. As a young Army lieutenant in the midfifties, I first met him when he was already a much-respected congressman but not averse to sitting on the floor for a late-night bull session with graduate students and young government workers, whose views he probed as if they were expert consultants. His nickname suggests both the informality and the good cheer that he always seemed to project. And in his later years he seemed singularly immune from the distractions and vanities of the creeping Versailles culture that began to flourish in social Washington. I doubt if anyone has followed better the advice that James Forrestal once gave to aspiring public servants: "Take your job seriously and yourself lightly."

He may have unconsciously defined his own role during this

era when he noted near the end of his report on organizing for national security in November 1961 that "there is no place in the Congress, short of the floors of the Senate and the House, where the requirements of national security and the resources needed on their behalf are considered in their totality." Senator Jackson became, in effect, that place in the Congress. It is a mark of both the quality of his service and the importance of that role that others who knew and admired him, such as Senator Sam Nunn and Representative Les Aspin, have in many ways sought to follow his model and keep alive this role.

Jackson's global views have been—and will continue to be—criticized in two different ways. First, there are those critics who see both sides bearing equal responsibility for the existence of the cold war; they blame strong advocates of military strength in America for both perpetuating this hostile state of affairs and for distorting our internal economic and social life. For these critics, Jackson has often been a special target, since he was a Democrat with a generally liberal legislative record on issues of concern to environmentalists and trade unionists. One suspects that most elements of this critique will diminish in at least the near term. The Soviets are now revealing more material that shows the extent to which Brezhnev and Khrushchev were continuing aggressors even as Stalin was the original instigator of the cold war. One suspects that increasingly we will look back even on America's traumatic and divisive overseas interventions of the cold war period as contributions to a generally successful attempt at containing what had been a dangerous, immediate postwar expansion of hostile Leninist power—and far preferable to either world war III or a lukewarm retreat into isolationism, which were the only real alternatives. It has been a distortion of the liberal tradition to suggest that continued concern for social welfare in a free society at home requires diminished concern about defending and extending these same values amidst unfree societies abroad.

If questions of overall priorities and "imperial overreach" will no doubt remain controversial among analysts of Jackson and of this cold war era for many years to come, a second, more detailed criticism has also begun to emerge in the seven years since his death in 1983. The growth of debts and deficits has raised questions about the relative neglect of the economic underpinnings of security. Continued turmoil in the Middle East has raised questions about a lack of broader American understanding of Third World problems and aspirations. Deng Xiaoping's brutal repression of the democracy movement may raise some questions about whether the strategic infatuation with China did not involve some sacrifice of the same human rights agenda that Jackson pressed so admirably against the U.S.S.R.

It is a tribute to the stature of Henry Jackson that so many people on and beyond Capitol Hill still ask themselves what he would have said now about these and other developing issues. A hint of how he might naturally have expanded his perspective to the less bipolar, more economic approach that now seems increasingly important is provided by the speech he gave in the last year of his life that led to the formation of the Bipartisan Commission on Central America. In it he calls for a balance of economic development and security assistance. Dorothy Fosdick has happily included this talk to a labor audience and his Senate speech calling for the Commission; they provide an appropriate final statement of his abiding belief in liberal democratic values. His balanced but firm approach was fairly faithfully reflected in the final Commission report, but the report never had much effect. It lacked the vital force that Henry Jackson's unique combination of moral force and practicality might have put behind it.

As political Washington and academic historians alike seek to learn from this record, they will have before them the example of a person for whom saying and doing were all of a piece and always at the service of a higher calling. They will note the continuing contributions to further public service of many who worked for Jackson, such as Thomas Foley, who became Speaker of the House in the bicentennial year of the Congress. And they will benefit from the record that Dorothy

Fosdick has assembled of a deeply humane man who consistently contended throughout a long and difficult period that it was both necessary and possible to prevail in the cold war without getting either cold feet or cold-blooded.

Preface

Dorothy Fosdick

The purpose of this volume is twofold: first, to put in perspective Senator Henry M. Jackson's major speeches on foreign policy and national security as a component of his efforts to influence and shape public policy and, second, to make a number of these addresses readily accessible to students of government, history, and international relations as well as historians, who are only now beginning to make definitive judgments on the events of the post–World War II decades. Throughout that period Jackson was a major participant in the difficult decisions and landmark struggles that determined the present course of this country's role in world affairs. This collection of his speeches will enable readers to comprehend more fully the fateful controversies of that time and the part the Senator played and how he played it.

For those studying the place of Congress and its Members in the foreign policy process, these speeches will contribute to an understanding of how Senator Jackson—as one member of the thousands who sat in Congress in his time—was able to realize so many of his principal objectives.

In July 1983 Jackson's colleagues held a ceremony on the Senate floor as he cast his eleven thousandth Senate roll call vote. There is no such authoritative accounting of the number of speeches made by the Senator over the same period, but it is safe to say that they too numbered in the many thousands.

Faced with an embarrassment of riches how did I make the selections for this volume? In the process I followed one overriding guideline: focus on Jackson's major statements on issues of foreign and defense policy that will help readers understand how the Senator influenced and helped shape United States policy in the post–World War II decades. I gave preference to key addresses that highlight and document the core elements of the Jackson legacy in international affairs. In this

I was undoubtedly influenced by knowing which speeches the Senator himself considered among the most significant of his career.

The collection in this volume spans thirty years. Many are state papers that plow fresh ground, others are explanations and interpretations of policy, and still others emphasize basic policy themes. They illumine Henry Jackson's view of America's proper role in the world, his understanding of the appropriate use of U.S. power—not just military—in the furtherance of national interests, and his grasp of the complex relationship between negotiation and the application of pressure. They also incidentally give a striking portrait of the man as a national leader: his instincts, his motivations, his basic values, his goals.

The Senator delivered his speeches not for the ages but for his period of history. An analysis or statement valid for one era is not necessarily relevant to another. Nevertheless, a good part of what Jackson spelled out in the selections that follow will impress the reader, I believe, as speaking not only to his time but also to our present and our future.

As for the multitude of his speeches not included here, Jackson's papers at the University of Washington Libraries are available to all interested persons. Those papers contain virtually all of the Senator's addresses and statements on foreign affairs and defense for which there is a text or transcription. I am hopeful this present compilation will motivate serious scholars and specialists to consult and study the complete collection.

I have written a short introductory note for each speech to place it in context, to indicate the Senator's purpose, and, as appropriate, to suggest the consequence of the effort. The speeches and the one full press conference appear essentially as delivered, with only the following changes: correcting typographical and punctuation errors, eliminating certain opening salutations when unrelated to substance, and consolidating the parts of an address interrupted in the course of debate.

While I take final responsibility for the selection and arrangement of the speeches and for the introductory comments, I am deeply grateful for the helpful counsel of a number of the Senator's former associates who participated with him in the development of certain of these speeches or who responded to my request to read the full manuscript. I also want to record my thanks to the staff of the University of Washington Press and its director, Donald Ellegood, for their invaluable help in the production of this book.

Above all, a special expression of appreciation is due to Julia Cancio, who gave unstinting encouragement and indispensable professional assistance from the moment the idea for this volume was conceived.

Henry M. Jackson and World Affairs

The Jackson Speeches

Dorothy Fosdick

Henry Jackson was in his first term as Senator when I met him
in 1954. A former student of mine from Smith College days
had invited me to one of those informal dinners so characteristic of life in Washington, D.C. At the time, I was freelancing,
working part-time with NBC News, writing articles for Lester
Markel's *New York Times Magazine*, and finishing a book reflecting on what I had learned from spending some ten years in the
Department of State. In the last four years there I had served
as a member of Secretary of State Dean Acheson's Policy Planning Staff during the chairmanships of George Kennan and
Paul Nitze.

About halfway through the dinner, the Senator said to me:
"I need someone to help on foreign policy. I'm in good shape
for Washington State issues and domestic policy; on the defense side there are the Armed Services and Joint Atomic
Energy Committee staffs; but I have no professional staff on
international affairs. I have a foreign policy speech next week.
I have some ideas, but nothing on paper. Could we have a talk
tomorrow at my office?"

Senator Jackson was known to me as a promising young
Democrat. He was specializing in national defense affairs
and, at the moment, was a major player in the drama of the
McCarthy-Army confrontation. I was aware he had served six
terms in the House representing a district in the State of Washington north of Seattle. He was one of only three Democrats
west of the Mississippi elected to the Senate in the Eisenhower
landslide of 1952.

I had scant knowledge of Capitol Hill and the legislative process. My first-hand experience with Congress was limited to
advising bipartisan American delegations that were involved
in launching the United Nations (UN) and that represented
this country at early UN General Assemblies. These delega-

3

tions had included the colorful Democratic Senator Tom Connally of Texas and Michigan's formidable Republican Senator Arthur Vandenberg.

My professional expertise was in foreign relations, international organization, and international negotiations. On national defense issues—military programs and military budgets—which went to the very heart of an effective American foreign policy, I was an amateur. By the time I arrived at the Senator's office, on the day after the dinner, I was saying to myself: "He may think he needs help. We'll see how it comes out. But, for me, what a providential opportunity."

And that was it. I helped with that initial speech. From volunteer status, it was soon part-time staff, and then it was full-time—for over twenty-eight years until Senator Jackson's death on 1 September 1983.

Jackson's service in the Congress began a year before Pearl Harbor. Rejecting the pacifism and isolationism of many in his generation, he judged that President Roosevelt was the best hope to safeguard the future of the nation and its democratic values. As the son of Norwegian immigrants, Jackson was proud of his ancestry. Norway's subjugation after Hitler's storm-troop invasion of 1940 deeply influenced his growing conviction that ensuring the independence of America and the survival of the values of freedom and human justice was the first and highest responsibility of any administration and any Congress.

Understanding that we needed the assistance of Stalin in defeating Nazi Germany, he accepted the wartime alliance as a mutually useful expedient, well aware that we were cooperating with a powerful despotism. He was not surprised by the emergence of the Kremlin at the end of the war as a formidable adversary that rejected peacetime cooperation and took full advantage of its greatly improved power position in Europe. As Congressman, Jackson joined in President Truman's 1948 effort to save an economically prostrate Europe with the Marshall Plan and then to link the Atlantic area nations in the North Atlantic Treaty Organization (NATO).

At the time I joined the Senator he had teamed up with

Senator Warren G. Magnuson to represent, with singular effectiveness, the varied interests of their Washington State constituents. He was already on his way to an extraordinary record of achievement on domestic matters—a champion of statehood for Alaska and Hawaii, a pioneer in conservation and purposeful use of resources, a promoter of water and electric power development, a leader in protecting the environment, an advocate of public recreation, and a formulator of basic national energy policies. His lasting contribution in these areas is manifest in the series of innovative national programs and laws that he did so much to help create.

By 1954 Jackson was also moving into the middle of debate and controversy on the most critical questions that would engage American foreign policy for the next three decades and beyond. In the years that lay ahead, Senator Jackson would become a major participant—intellectually and politically—in world affairs.

JACKSON'S NATIONAL SECURITY LEGACY

In addressing the Henry M. Jackson School of International Studies at the University of Washington, Seattle, on 5 February 1988, Secretary of State George Shultz said:

> Our relationship with the Soviet Union has preoccupied American foreign policy for nearly half a century. Few public figures in the postwar world have done so much as Scoop Jackson to shape American thinking about that relationship.[1]

The Senator recognized that the Soviet challenge had many aspects. He constantly argued that Moscow's policies and actions that caused concern were interrelated, from building the vast Soviet arsenal of military power, to its thrust of that power beyond its borders, to its refusal to respect the basic rights and freedoms of its citizens.

Calling for realism about the Soviet Union, Senator Jackson helped rally this country and the other Western democracies to rise to Moscow's comprehensive challenge. He believed that if the West maintained its vital strengths, including adequate nuclear and conventional forces for defense and deterrence, and at the same time dealt firmly and skillfully with the geopolitical competition and regional conflicts around the world, a new Soviet-American relationship might be possible that would be more conducive to international stability and a peace based upon respect for human rights. Given the deep differences between the United States and the Soviet Union and the ever-present danger of misinterpretation and miscalculation, the Senator considered it essential to keep open the official channels of communication and discussion between Moscow and Washington.

Senator Jackson's approach to the Soviet Union has stood the test of time and paid historic dividends. The United States and the Western democracies generally, despite many harrowing ups and downs, are strong, economically prosperous, and working together. On the other hand, the Soviet Union is in deep economic crisis, its East European empire is splintered, its communist ideology is discredited, and its leaders are confronting massive complications of governance. Its only hope by the late 1980s was to abandon many failed policies and sue the West for help to rescue its economy, to obtain multiple arms reduction agreements, and to secure at least short-term European stability.

Mikhail Gorbachev's foreign policy reversals—including moves toward a reckoning with the terrible truth about the Soviet past—have been no accident of Russian history. They were a premise and among the aims of the entire effort by Senator Jackson and the others who over long and dangerous years have steadfastly followed through on the "policy of containment."

Looking forward, will the reform movements in Eastern Europe succeed in their drives toward democratic pluralism and free-market economies? Will the process of building a new political order in the heart of Europe proceed largely peacefully? Will East Europe move entirely out of Soviet reach, secure from imperial restoration? How far will the Soviet system evolve toward genuine political pluralism? Will the Kremlin succeed in making the changes essential to reviving its economy? How effectively will Moscow deal with the rising political aspirations of the ethnic and national minorities, as in Estonia, Latvia, Lithuania, Georgia, Armenia, Azerbaijan, and the Ukraine? Will future Soviet governments have less or more will and energy for continuing troublemaking policies in Central America, the Middle East, and other strategic regions around the world?

Andrei Sakharov, who spent six years in internal exile because of his human rights activities, reminded us: "Today it is Gorbachev, but tomorrow it could be somebody else. There are no guarantees that some Stalinist will not succeed him."[2]

As Senator Jackson repeatedly pointed out, the superpower U.S.-Soviet relationship is inescapably ongoing; it calls for unremitting vigilance, a high order of American statesmanship, unflagging national effort, and a "no illusions" approach, generation after generation. To underline this point, he liked to quote the eminent theologian Reinhold Niebuhr:

There has never been a scheme of justice in history which did not have a balance of power at its foundation. If the democratic nations fail, their failure must be partly attributed to the faulty strategy of idealists who have too many illusions when they face realists who have too little conscience.[3]

In due time, scholars and historians will assess Henry Jackson's imprint on the course of world events and his legacy to successive generations. It is not too soon, however, to see the main outlines. As Senator Sam Nunn put it: "Scoop Jackson not only was a great student of history—he made history."[4]

The Jackson legacy includes the influence he brought to bear on the following issues:

Immediately after World War II, the United States adopted the grand strategy of keeping the peace by offsetting Soviet superiority in conventional weapons and numbers of troops with advanced weapons that were technologically superior to Moscow's. Sooner than most of his contemporaries, Congressman Jackson realized that the Soviets were bent on matching, even outstripping, us in these high-technology areas. From the late 1940s on, as Congressman and Senator, he had a leading role in policy decisions to help ensure that Moscow would not win critical races for discovery and deployment of advanced weapons systems, including land-based ballistic missiles of both theater and intercontinental range and the Polaris-Trident submarine-launched ballistic missile system with its near invulnerability to preemptive strike.

In the wake of World War II, with Europe lacking the strength to hold in check the power of Soviet Russia, the power of North America was united with that of Europe in a common endeavor: the organization through NATO of a strong Atlantic defense. Dean Acheson once said, "It takes two to tangle and the Russians have not wanted to tangle with NATO."[5] That was a conviction Jackson shared. Year after year he organized and led winning Senate coalitions that fended off threats to the programs and budgets needed to ensure a continued, responsible American role in the alliance that for over forty years has protected the security of the West. Its aim was not to freeze the status quo but to help create an environment for a genuine European settlement serving the legitimate security interests of all concerned—East and West.

In the 1950s, with the cold war in full gear, there was real doubt whether the free nations would outperform and outlast totalitarian societies. Increasingly concerned about the Eisenhower administration's inability to marshal the key elements of American power and influence to compete effectively with Moscow, the Senator initiated in 1959 the first full-scale review of the policy-making mechanisms that were set up in the National Security Act of 1947. The Jackson-chaired bipartisan study of the National Security Council—followed by studies on the role of the Secretary of State and U.S. ambassadors and the international negotiating process—had an influential impact on national security operations and continues to influence the conduct of national affairs.

Senator Jackson's effort in the 1950s to help ensure a strong, modern Western deterrent was coupled with his parallel effort to test whether the Soviets were willing to engage in serious arms control discussions. In 1950 and again in 1951 and 1953 he introduced congressional resolutions calling upon our government to seek prompt agreement with Moscow and others on across-the-board arms reductions. Jackson had found a path he would follow for the rest of his life: pressing for mutual, verifiable arms reductions in a way to enhance the stability of deterrence. At the center of the U.S. arms control policy process during the 1960s, 1970s, and early 1980s, the Senator is generally recognized as a major architect of the historic U.S.-Soviet shift from negotiating agreements that set higher ceilings, resulting in arms buildups, to negotiating verifiable agreements that set lower equal ceilings, resulting in arms reductions.

For Senator Jackson, the duty of the American government to safeguard and encourage human rights derived not only from ethical considerations but also from concern for world stability and peace. Nations that deny their citizens the basic freedoms, he concluded, deprive themselves of the internal constraints that can regulate and moderate their actions abroad, including their support and encouragement of international terrorism. While Jackson championed the cause of human rights as a national obligation, he was also remarkably aware of the living, breathing human beings struggling for freedom: Anatoly Sharansky, incarcerated in the Gulag by the KGB; Andrei Sakharov and Yelena Bonner, isolated and harassed for saying what they thought; Pastor Georgi Vins, imprisoned because he wished to preach and practice his faith in God; Ida Nudel, "angel of mercy" to countless prisoners of conscience, banished to Siberia; ballet dancers Valery and Galina Panov, denied the chance to perform; Simas Kudirka, seaman from Lithuania, thwarted in his first brave jump to freedom; poet Huber Matos, confined in Cuban jails. As author of the 1974 Jackson-Vanik amendment on freedom of emigration, Jackson, with Senator Daniel Patrick Moynihan and a band of other colleagues, opened the way for hundreds of thousands of Jews, Christians, and others to find freedom in the West; compelled Secretary of State Henry Kissinger and other reluctant Nixon and Ford administration officials to confront the connection between human rights and foreign policy; paved the way for the establishment of human rights as a central focus of U.S. foreign policy; and laid the groundwork for Soviet acceptance of human rights issues on the agenda of superpower summits and of most other bilateral meetings. Moscow discovered that improvements in U.S.-Soviet relations cannot be made without reforms in its approach to freer emigration and other fundamental rights.

A humanitarian concern for the Jewish victims of Buchenwald and the other horrors of totalitarian persecution was the start of Jackson's interest in Jewish refugees and in the national home established to receive them. But his continued support of the democratic State of Israel sprang from more directly political and strategic considerations—his belief in liberal democracy and his conviction, as Elie Wiesel has said, "that only by the collective effort of free humanity can the future of liberty be safeguarded."[6] Convinced that in the rival-ridden, volatile Middle East Israel was an indispensable Western asset, Jackson was in the vanguard of policymakers committed to a close, cooperative U.S.-Israeli relationship. Time and again he assembled the bipartisan coalitions that provided vital support to Israel.

Watchful of the neglect and mismanagement of the transfer of security-sensitive technology to the Soviet Union and its East European allies, the Senator took on this issue in 1963, when he became chairman of the Senate's Permanent Subcommittee on Investigations. (Senator Sam Nunn followed him as chairman in 1977.) The evidence was overwhelming that the loss of our technology was materially improving Moscow's military systems, its economic leverage with other countries, and its intelligence capabilities. The subcommittee's studies, public hearings, and letters to Presidents finally placed this issue on the national agenda. The subcommittee also paved the way for legislation that in the 1970s enhanced the role of the Defense Department in policing strategic trade and ensured that a national security perspective would be present early in the licensing process.

Born and raised on the shores of the Pacific Northwest, Senator Jackson had a long-time interest in China both as a great nation with a distinctive and impressive history and as a modern strategic reality. He recognized that the power and potential of the People's Republic of China made its orientation crucial to world stability. Jackson was among the early advocates of an opening to China—before the initiation of Sino-American "ping-pong diplomacy" in the spring of 1970 and before Kissinger's secret visit of July 1971. In the following decade he became one of the Senate's leading specialists on China, developing a close relationship with its senior leader Deng Xiaoping. Jackson exerted an unusual influence on the development of strategic cooperation with the People's Republic of China in matters of parallel concern, and he promoted a broad-based Sino-American relationship based on mutual and realistic interests.

With the pending economic collapse of Mexico in 1982, Jackson became involved in the growing problems in the strategically vital Central American region. As he saw it, the United States has a steady interest in having near its borders independent, democratic governments that will not allow their countries to be made use of by anti-U.S. foreign powers. He played an important role in developing the August 1982 emergency financial package for Mexico. Seeking to dampen and contain the divisive, partisan congressional debate and move toward a bipartisan consensus on a balanced, long-term U.S. security and economic assistance policy for the region, he proposed the formation of the Bipartisan Commission on Central America; but just as the Commission began its work, the Senator died. His main message stands, as delivered in his 1983 speech to the Sheet Metal Workers Union:

> Security assistance should be an adjunct to our Central American policy, not its foundation. We better face it: the shield will crumble unless we address the serious social and economic injustices in the region.[7]

The great and thorny issues on which the Senator was at work continue on the national agenda, in one form or another. He anticipated this. Major matters of foreign policy span the decades. That is one reason he gave so much attention to young people—teaching them how to think about the problems and dilemmas and how to cope with them courageously.

For Jackson, a respect for the lessons of history and experience was the key to good judgment in the affairs of state. He put it this way:

> In essence, history is what we know about the accountability of human beings before each other and before God, and the repository of what we have learned about how human beings should behave—indeed must behave—if life is to be humane and decent. . . . Therefore, study and comprehend history if you want to shape the future.[8]

"Don't be discouraged," he would add. "What people have messed up, people can straighten out."

George Will says of Senator Jackson:

> He nurtured in this Republic something without which no republic can long endure: a sense that problems are tractable. To be in his presence was to experience the wholesome infection of a reviving spirit. This was especially remarkable because he, more than any contemporary, looked unblinkingly at, and spoke uncomfortingly about, the terrors of our time. He taught less clear-sighted, less brave persons how to combine realism and serenity.[9]

THE JACKSON STYLE

How did this Senator become a leader and powerful participant in developing America's foreign and defense policies? There is no single explanation, but there is substantial, reliable evidence to assist in understanding the part he played and the mark he made.

In our system of government, the Presidency and the Congress are *separated* institutions, *sharing* powers. For example, the President appoints the executive department heads but they are subject to confirmation by a majority of the Senate. The executive departments themselves are created by acts of Congress, they receive their money annually from Congress, and the programs they administer are authorized by Congress and changed by the Congress. And Congress, of course, has the independent power to oversee and investigate their work. Under our Constitution, Senators have a range of options for influencing national policy: confirmation proceedings, authorizing legislation, resolutions, the annual budget review process, oversight and investigation, and appropriations. And always, in conjunction with these activities, there is the opportunity to influence opinion, at home and abroad, by writing, public speaking, and dialogue.

All these avenues were well understood and used by Jackson in bringing to bear his influence on foreign and defense policy. This is true of most Senators. What distinguished Jackson was not the range of the tools available, but the care, manner, and timing of how he used them. What seems to account for his uncommon influence was a rare combination of factors: a basic and consistent point of view; special qualities and skills as a legislator; an effective use of staff; a widespread and responsive network of colleagues, advisers, and allies; his longevity of service; and the deliberate use of major speeches to shape national policy.

THE JACKSON OUTLOOK

Senator Jackson had a world viewpoint. His perspective was essentially that of a Secretary of State: perceiving and acting on problems in the context of our Nation as a whole in its relation to the vast external realm beyond our borders. Moreover, he considered himself no less responsible than a Secretary of State or a President to speak and act for the priority of national-strategic policy over lesser considerations and goals. As a result, he manifested an unusual degree of independent judgment in taking positions that advanced the nation's longer-term interests rather than the shorter-term concerns that so commonly govern congressional decision making.

The Senator believed in the party system and he could be a staunch, partisan Democrat when, in his judgment, the situation called for it. But party lines meant nothing to him when it came to issues concerned with America's fundamental values or with the country's security and survival. On that kind of issue he was impervious to a partisan appeal—often to the dismay of Democratic colleagues and Democratic Presidents. During his association with the redoubtable Speaker Sam Rayburn and other Southern Democratic pillars of the House, Congressman Jackson had found their nonpartisanship in national security policy a style that fitted his assessment of what was required to perpetuate democratic institutions in a world with many totalitarian powers.

An "inner compass" of core values and convictions kept Jackson on a steadfast course in support of American interests and ideals. He was graced with a fortitude lacking in many legislators and other politicians. He stayed with a problem, focusing on the main objective while remaining pragmatically open to adjustments in the light of altered circumstances. Set for the long haul, he was not ready to bow to the conventional analysis or opinion or passion of the moment.

Senator Daniel Patrick Moynihan said it this way:

> He lived in the worst of times; the age of the totalitarian state. . . . He wanted his country strong because he knew the terrible danger of the age in which we live. Where others lurch from one issue to another with the attention span of a 5-year-old, he sustained this understanding and this vision through five of the most awful decades in the history of mankind.[10]

Such constancy is indispensable for the statesman. Jackson called it "a steady hand in an unsteady world" or, using Winston Churchill's phrase, "staying the course." During his years of public service Henry Jackson was the subject of more than his share of raw political caricature: "the hawk," "Senator from Boeing," "cold warrior." This kind of crude and arresting labeling is itself the product and reflection of the gravity of the underlying issues and of the Senator's central role in debating and determining the national response.

PERSONAL QUALITIES AND SKILLS

The Senator approached major questions with deliberation, demanding of himself and his staff rigorous analysis and attention to detail while keeping in mind the interrelationship of issues. He sought to reduce the uncertainties to a minimum before he made his first move.

One good example is his willingness in the 1950s to do his homework on the military and political role of the new, technologically advanced weapons of the nuclear age. Atomic bombs and ballistic weapons were a whole order of magnitude more powerful and complex than weapons previously considered by Congress. And the issues they raised went to the heart of our efforts to contain Soviet power. At one stage, he spent virtually every afternoon in closed-door briefings in the Atomic Energy Committee. He was determined to understand these new highly classified weapons programs early and grasp their momentous implications for world politics. That is exactly what he did.

A second example is the Jackson-chaired bipartisan inquiry conducted by his Subcommittee on National Policy Machinery from 1959 to 1961. The Senator and the staff spent more than six months of intensive, time-consuming preparation interviewing scores of scholars and past and present government officials before a single hearing was held.

However, once the Senator had mastered the history, substance, and procedural aspects of a problem, he was ready to act. Like a Harry Truman, Henry Jackson was willing and able to make decisions, with no going over and over the same ground and no agonizing reappraisals.

As a child, Jackson's older sister Gertrude had nicknamed him Scoop after a little boy in a comic strip who had an innate ability to get others to do what he wanted done. His sister was perspicacious. This gift helps account for the Senator's success as a legislator in gaining support for his views and undertakings.

A Jackson specialty was building bipartisan consensus around a pending bill, an amendment, or a resolution. His membership on the Armed Services Committee allowed him to initiate and shape defense programs and influence budgets before the bills were reported to the Senate floor. But he was not a member of some Senate committees that had jurisdiction in key areas of foreign policy. Therefore, the Senator designed many of his most important foreign affairs initiatives as amendments to be offered to committee bills once they reached the Senate floor.

This was the case with the Jackson-Vanik amendment to the Trade Reform Act of 1974, which used most-favored-nation tariff status and U.S. government credits to increase the numbers of Jews, Christians, and others allowed to emigrate from the Soviet Union and other non-market-economy countries. A turning point in America's arms control policy was achieved through the Jackson equality amendment to the resolution of ratification of the 1972 SALT I (strategic arms limitations talks) Interim Agreement. The amendment put the Congress clearly on record that any future agreement on offensive arms must "not limit the United States to levels of intercontinental strategic forces inferior to the limits provided for the Soviet Union."

Another Jackson specialty was to write a pointed letter or memorandum to the President or some executive department official. The communication might be signed by the Senator alone or by a number of congressional colleagues; it might be prepared as a confidential message or for public release. The moon program is one example. President Kennedy's bold undertaking in early 1961 to land Americans on the moon within a decade can be traced back to a confidential Jackson memorandum sent to the then President-elect urging that he establish this as a national goal. Another example is President Nixon's 1970 proposal for ending the Vietnam War in a stabilizing manner by negotiating a mutual cease-fire. This effort was generated in part by a 1 September 1970 bipartisan letter to Nixon initiated by Jackson and joined in by Hugh Scott, Republican Senator from Pennsylvania, and twenty-eight other Democratic and Republican Senators. The publicly released letter urged the administration to negotiate a mutual, internationally supervised, standstill cease-fire throughout Vietnam, to end the war, to achieve a return of prisoners of war, and to conduct prompt, open, free, and fair elections. Like the related Vietnamization policy of arming and training the South Vietnamese troops, the cease-fire effort did not in the end succeed. The tenacity of the adversary opened the way for a nonnegotiated conclusion on the battlefield as North Vietnam overran South Vietnam and Laos—and then invaded and occupied Cambodia.

In enlisting support for his various initiatives, Jackson was assiduous in working with Democrats and Republicans, one Member after another, using every nook and cranny of the U.S. Capitol. When colleagues think back about their times with Jackson, they are apt to come up with some tale about how he won their vote for a pending measure while they were swaying along on the Senate's antiquated subway cars, or how he gained their support for an amendment or a communication to the President while they were swimming in the small pool of the Senate gymnasium. Senator J. Bennett Johnston recalls:

He simply talked to everyone involved in a particular issue, learned their problems, and found a way to put together a coalition of people interested in resolving the issue . . . [and] he took the time when it was needed. He was a patient man in an impatient institution.[11]

Henry Jackson believed in the essential good sense of the people of the State of Washington he represented in Congress—his true electoral constituency. He had a mistrust of intellectual trendiness and a fundamental respect for the common sense of the average American. One of Jackson's secrets was that, in fact, he listened. Anyone, at least almost anyone, with experience, facts, or informed ideas on a matter that concerned him had an audience and often a friend in Jackson. The Senator was also a great questioner; he could be relentless on subjects he considered important. Some who served with him thought he was too accessible. But when Jackson wanted help or advice, there was a vast reservoir on which to draw.

THE JACKSON STAFF

Like many who serve in the House and Senate, the Senator was able to surround himself with competent staff. But Jackson sought a particular kind of competence. He wanted independent-minded individuals with a feel for history who were endowed with intrinsic common sense. He got the most out of his staff because he counseled with them; and they could argue and disagree with him. In the end, however, he made his own decisions; but, in doing so, he gave staff members abundant opportunity to influence his views and, therefore, to influence policy.

Henry Jackson treated his staff as partners in the enterprise. Once a trusted confidant of the Senator, it was hard to move on. Yet, for some, after having learned his way of analyzing problems, viewing the world, and assessing another's character and judgment, it was natural to go on to other service and put to the test the ethics and the principles that worked so well for him. Even when valuable staff members left for other posts there was a certainty he would see them again, on another full-time Jackson project, in an ad hoc consultative role, or when they sought his opinion on some stubborn problem being faced in the new career.

Peter Jackson says of his father, "I realize that he was not only a generous, caring father, but also an experienced and skillful teacher."[12] As he was to his family and to countless young men and women he encountered, he was to his staff—a consummate teacher. Former member of the Jackson staff, now Speaker of the House of Representatives, Congressman Thomas S. Foley said it best at the 1983 family memorial service for the Senator in Everett, Washington:

> He taught mainly by example. The example of a man of tremendous integrity and commitment, of constancy and courage. A man who infused the profession of a long public service which he had chosen with the greatest dignity. A man who cared for his staff and who received from them in return a fierce loyalty, because for all of us who served him, it will remain to the end of our days a matter of enormous pride.[13]

THE SENATOR'S NETWORK

Senator Jackson never seriously sought membership on the Senate Foreign Relations Committee. Actually, he benefited from not being a member: not only could he exercise more independence in selecting the foreign affairs issues on which he would spend his time, but he could pursue his foreign policy concerns free of the institutional perspectives of the committee and with the advantage of being a ranking member of the Armed Services Committee, the Government Operations Committee, the Joint Committee on Atomic Energy (of which he had been a member in the House), and, in time, the Senate Select Committee on Intelligence. This gave him a number of different perspectives, access to a variety of expert points of view, and the chance to explore policy options free of the constraints that jurisdictional responsibilities often impose.

For his national security/foreign policy support, the Senator relied on a small staff attached to the Subcommittee on National Policy Machinery and the successor Jackson subcommittees of the Government Operations Committee. For additional help he turned to academia and the private sector. The Senator was always scouting and probing for "the best people and the best advice I can find." The subcommittee studies and hearings on national security, which began in 1959, brought him into close and permanent touch with talented scholars, investment bankers, businessmen, generals, and former government officials with special knowledge and experience. This gave him a strong start on what became an extraordinary talent bank of informal advisers and consultants.

As much as any Senator, Jackson was accessible to the news media. He not only dispensed story leads and new angles but reversed the conventional relationships and worked the press for information and trends. He queried and interviewed. Many in the press were drawn to Jackson because he was genuinely interested in their views and judgments. A regular headline guest on Larry Spivak's NBC "Meet the Press" and other in-depth news shows, Jackson knew how to use the major news forums and local and national news coverage to get serious policy messages across to a nationwide, often worldwide, audience.

The Senator also respected the expertise and experience that could be found inside the government. He was continually in touch—in person, by phone, by letter—with key officials, from specialists far down the line in the hierarchy of departments and agencies to admirals and generals, CIA Directors, Secretaries of Defense and State, Special Assistants for National Security Affairs, and Presidents.

In shaping policy in one area after another, Jackson positioned himself at the nexus of the interactions of the private sector, the administration, and the Congress. He knew that this was where the action was. This was the junction where issues were defined, where policy options were developed. This was where debates were shaped and decisions refined.

A 1968 White House meeting is a dramatic case in point. Following Hanoi's devastating Tet offensive against Saigon and other South Vietnamese provincial centers on 30 January 1968, Senator Jackson, Senator Richard Russell, and Senator John Stennis, meeting privately with President Johnson and Clark Clifford, vigorously opposed the President's intent to send a quarter of a million more American troops to Vietnam—and they persuaded the President to withhold any such proposal.

THE SENATOR ABROAD

Jackson planned his overseas trips around policy discussions with top leaders. In 1956 Senator Jackson went to the Soviet Union, exiting through Afghanistan. He always wanted to return. In 1978 he almost made it, but the Kremlin laid down conditions that were unacceptable to him: he was invited for a private meeting with Secretary Leonid Brezhnev but was denied permission to meet privately with Andrei Sakharov or a representative group of other Soviet citizens seeking greater respect for human rights. The Senator did not live long enough to make his return trip to Russia in the Gorbachev period.

From 1956 onward, year after year, Senator Jackson participated in the NATO Parliamentarians' Conference and its successor, the North Atlantic Assembly, sharing and leading in the development of alliance strategies while cultivating ties with his Parliamentary counterparts.

In the Middle East he met with senior officials and heads of state to explore ways to ameliorate the region's poverty and endemic instabilities. In 1972 he visited Saudi Arabia and Crown Prince Fahd, combining this trip with visits to both the Shah of Iran and Prime Minister Golda Meir—all this as a preparation for the North Atlantic Assembly in Bonn, West Germany. On a later trip, he reviewed his initiative for a Marshall Plan for the Middle East with Israel's Prime Minister Menachem Begin and Egypt's President Anwar Sadat.

The classic example of a relationship with a foreign leader that contributed to the Senator's influence is his association with China's senior leader Deng Xiaoping. For almost a decade, starting in 1974, those two historically minded, canny politicians held frank and realistic discussions on geopolitical and bilateral issues. The Senator was a shaper and carrier of Presidential messages to Deng, interpreter for Deng of American policies, and carrier of Deng's understandings and concerns to the President. This special relationship turned out to be invaluable at critical junctures in the development of U.S. relations with the People's Republic of China.

Jackson very clearly understood and honored the constitutional constraints on Members of Congress concerning negotiating with foreign powers. Also, to respect the right of a President and a Secretary of State to know what a Senator was saying to officials of other governments, he included the resident American Ambassador in his meetings, aware, of course, that an ambassador's responsibility included wiring a report to the State Department on what transpired. The Senator had no problem with this arrangement: first-rate ambassadors could be wise counselors. In any case, the reports to home base were one more channel to bring his views before top decision makers in Washington.

LONGEVITY OF SERVICE

Jackson worked on issues not for just the few years that Cabinet officers and Presidents might be on the job. They came and went. He was on duty decade after decade, through the administrations of Roosevelt, Truman, Eisenhower, Kennedy, Johnson, Nixon, Ford, Carter, and into Reagan's first term.

Important national problems commonly carry over from one administration to the next. The accumulation of knowledge, experience, and contacts derived from almost forty-three years in the public arena was an enormous asset. The Senator came to understand more about issues in his areas of interest than most Members of Congress and virtually all Cabinet officers, who are responsible for those matters for only a few years. He learned the procedures of government agencies and how to advance policies through the federal maze better than most agency heads and some Presidents. In hearings with Cabinet members and other witnesses, at White House meetings, and with his congressional colleagues, Jackson represented "the institutional memory"—a strong vantage point from which to ask probing questions and to state arguments.

Given the Senator's long experience near the center of things and his predilection for the big national issues, he had his eye on the office of the Presidency. He missed the prize. His 1972 and 1976 campaigns for the Democratic Party's Presidential nomination ran aground on the shoals of the primaries. Yet, as it turned out, Jackson emerged from his two runs for the Presidency with enhanced influence, widely recognized at home and abroad as a powerful personage who could, if so inclined, set in motion fundamental changes in world and domestic affairs.

THE JACKSON SPEECHES

Jackson made carefully calculated use of the prepared speech. Unlike some of his colleagues, he was not tempted to respond to every issue. He certainly did not set himself the goal of a speech each day or each week on the Senate floor. He typically fashioned his statements as part of a broader strategy to get something done. Would a speech be useful at this stage? How could it help move things forward or prevent the worst from happening? At whom should it be targeted? For the Senator, the development of a major address was a vital part of the serious business of directing and influencing national policy.

Jackson had his own way of going about speech writing. He did not take pen and pad in hand and scratch out a text. Nor did he sit down at a typewriter or dictate to his secretary or use a dictaphone or, thank heaven, experiment with one of those early computers. Nor did he turn to some all-purpose speech writer. Instead, he usually convened a miniseminar. Two or three of the trusted professionals on his personal or committee staff who were knowledgeable about the problem would gather around his desk or at his corner table in the Senate dining room and discuss concepts for the speech's major theme and what he wanted to accomplish. One of them would be assigned to write a first draft.

For Jackson, speech writing was an educational process for all involved. He took delight in the roles of advocate, professor, and commentator and in engaging participants in lively debate, trying out his arguments, directing staff to still another book, scholar, or consultant, and sending a draft back to the drawing board for more facts, better reasoning, more solid justifications, and sharpened recommendations. This painstaking preparation would proceed until he had the text that unambiguously said what he wanted to say.

One example is the evolution of his address to the Senate delivered on 27 May 1957, "Ballistic Seapower—Fourth Dimension of Warfare" (speech 3, this volume). As a member of the Joint Atomic Energy Committee and as chairman of its Military Applications Subcommittee, Senator Jackson had taken a hard look at the prospects of a sea-based missile deterrent. He had become convinced of the great contribution that missiles launched from submarines (with their near invulnerability to a first strike) could make to deterrence of Soviet moves against the West and of nuclear blackmail. A 1956 Jackson-appointed advisory panel of noted scientists and other underseas-warfare experts had confirmed his view and had recommended ways to accelerate the national effort on a sea-based deterrent.

The Senator contemplated his next move. The technology for the system was not fully developed. The United States, for example, had not yet tested its first operational intermediate-range ballistic missile. Were we going to test and produce the missile before moving ahead on other requirements for the system? Would this mean that we would end up with a token ballistic missile fleet years after the Soviets had deployed a bigger fleet? Or should the United States plan ahead, cut down lead times, take some risks, and proceed faster?

He decided to make a major speech on the Senate floor targeted at the decision makers in the Pentagon and the White House. Brought into the initial miniseminar was J. Kenneth Mansfield, who had taught at Yale University and from 1950 to 1956 had worked closely with Jackson on the Joint Atomic Energy Committee. The plan for the speech was outlined. Ken was made responsible for the first draft, and I was to work with him and ensure that the work was progressing on schedule.

Once this speech text neared final form, Jackson decided it should be checked with Admiral Hyman Rickover, the legendary, controversial, irascible father of the nuclear Navy. The Senator wanted to be certain there were no technical flaws, and he asked me to carry a copy to the Admiral and have him read it in my presence. Rickover, of course, questioned my authority to make him read the speech immediately, in my presence. "That was Scoop's instruction," I said. There was a long, low growl and then a barely discernible twinkle in the Admiral's eye. Without more ado, he read the text carefully and gave it his approval. Both the speech and I had survived!

The final sentence of the speech read, "I am deeply convinced that the issue of whether we are giving enough emphasis to the development of ballistic seapower should be reviewed and decided now—not next year or the year thereafter but this year." The Senator thought this diplomatic phrasing would make it possible for Eisenhower's senior people to respond in something like this vein: "Jackson may be right about this. Let's have another good look." And, fortunately for the nation, that is the response the speech received. In the end, the United States acquired a ballistic missile submarine fleet adequate in size and in service on time to reinforce deterrence. The Senator liked good writing, clarity, well-turned phrases, and telling words from a Teddy Roosevelt, a Winston Churchill, or a Reinhold Niebuhr. But he had been trained as a lawyer. He was less concerned with the literary quality of the final product than with building a well-constructed, convincing case designed for a specific audience. The part of his speech that most interested Jackson was usually the action section. Not every speech, of course, included a call for action, policy recommendations, or proposals, but when it did you could be sure he gave those sections special attention. His address "Détente and SALT," delivered before the Overseas Press Club in New York on 22 April 1974, is a case in point (speech 12). Here the intent was to launch a new, original, detailed policy proposal.

Jackson had labored long and hard and successfully in 1972 to amend the interim SALT I authorizing resolution so that any SALT II or other future treaty on offensive strategic arms must provide for equality. At his right hand during those days was Richard Perle, who had joined the staff in October 1969. (Richard had first come to the Senator's attention while he was working with Paul Nitze and Professor Albert Wohlstetter for the Committee to Maintain a Prudent Defense Policy. In that capacity, he had assisted the Senator in achieving the one-vote victory in the Senate for the initial deployment of the limited Safeguard Anti–Ballistic Missile System.)

Once his equality amendment was approved, Jackson voted for the 1972 SALT I Interim Agreement. Over and over again in the debate on his amendment, he had pointed out that SALT I, in effect, authorized a massive Soviet buildup of strategic forces, a buildup that was going forward unabated. The Senator had decided to monitor the SALT II negotiations and increase the pressure on President Nixon to stop negotiating with Moscow for higher ceilings to accommodate future growth and to start negotiating for lower ceilings to encourage reductions. Embarking on an extended set of hearings in the Subcommittee on Arms Control of the Armed Services Committee he urged in hearing after hearing that a SALT II treaty should provide substantial, balanced reductions in strategic arms to equal levels in a way to enhance the stability of deterrence.

Although the Senator was not optimistic that President Nixon (who permitted Secretary of State Henry Kissinger to formulate both arms control policy and the negotiating strategy) would follow his advice, he wanted to ensure that his views were on record and, thus, would contribute to the long-term development of a U.S. arms control policy. The conventional wisdom that the Russians would never agree to any plan of reductions did not impress him. This was one of those challenges the Senator never gave up on, even when the prospects of success seemed remote.

Jackson had been urging administration witnesses to come forward with a concrete proposal for an actual balanced and substantial reduction in strategic arms. Why not push them along by presenting a proposal of his own? The Senator had what amounted to a standing invitation to address the Overseas Press Club in New York City. He chose to use it. Richard and I were called into the miniseminar, and Richard was asked to prepare the first draft of a speech incorporating detailed suggestions.

After the usual discussions with the Senator and the innumerable checks with knowledgeable friends and associates, a text was finalized that proposed a specific schedule of U.S.-Soviet reductions that would diminish strategic forces by a third or more, down to an equal level.

As the text developed, Senator Jackson had in mind that possibly the Nixon administration would not dismiss his proposal out of hand. Perhaps the Defense Department, presided over by James Schlesinger, would be more receptive than the State Department. He asked Richard to make some preliminary soundings at the Pentagon and then sent a copy of his speech to Secretary of Defense Schlesinger with the request for a point-by-point assessment. The response he received was careful and professional and by no means an outright rejection. For Jackson, with his long view of events, this was encouraging.

The Senator could not have known that the sharply reduced, equal ceiling for intercontinental strategic missiles tentatively agreed upon in 1987 by President Reagan and Secretary Mikhail Gorbachev would be almost identical with the reduced ceiling he had proposed in 1974.

Thus, Senator Jackson forged and delivered major speeches as an integral part of his efforts to shape national policies.

I
Military Power:
Balance or Imbalance?

1
Reduction of Armaments
and Extension of Economic Aid
to War-Ravaged Countries

United States Senate
1 May 1953

During his years in the House of Representatives and later, Henry Jackson never believed that American armed forces alone would be sufficient for national survival or to maintain the peace. Yet, as he saw it, adequate military capacity was necessary to deter adventurism, resist blackmail, conduct a wise diplomacy, and rally allies to join in the tasks of peacekeeping. Also, Jackson believed that we should keep talking to adversaries—including the Soviet Union. Building on whatever common or mutual interests might emerge made good sense to him.

As early as 1950, working with Senator Brien McMahon of Connecticut, Congressman Jackson introduced a House resolution calling for speedy U.S.-Soviet negotiations and agreement upon effective and enforceable disarmament that would cover conventional armaments, biological and chemical agents, and atomic and hydrogen bombs. Again in 1951 and yet again in 1953, after winning his seat in the Senate, he sponsored similar arms reduction resolutions.

Jackson had started on an effort he never abandoned: influencing American administrations and the Kremlin to agree on mutual, verifiable arms reductions that would lower the level of military forces in a way that would increase the stability of deterrence and improve the chances for world peace.

MR. PRESIDENT, NOT EVERY MEMBER OF THIS BODY WILL subscribe to every last sentence of the foreign policy address the President of the United States delivered on April 16. But when the President offered the world a plan for the regulation of armaments and the use of the moneys thereby saved for assistance to the economically underdeveloped areas of the world, I believe he spoke for all of us—Republicans and Democrats alike. The President's words were these:

This Government is ready to ask its people to join with all nations in devoting a substantial percentage of any savings achieved by real disarmament to a fund for world aid and reconstruction. The purposes of this great work would be: To help other peoples to develop the underdeveloped areas of the world, to stimulate profitable and fair world trade, to assist all peoples to know the blessings of productive freedom.

The monuments of this new kind of war would be these: Roads and schools, hospitals and homes, food and health.

We are ready, in short, to dedicate our strength to serving the needs, rather than the fears, of the world.

In saying this, the President gave voice to the longings in the heart of every good American. This nation of ours is determined, grimly determined, to build every single tank and plane and atomic bomb needed to punish aggression and prevent world war III. But we do this because the defense of freedom leaves us no alternative. We are a people of peace. We take no satisfaction in channeling the genius of this nation into the building of sterile armaments. We would rather, far rather, be participating in great programs for lifting poverty and disease from the shoulders of decent people everywhere.

It is this down-to-earth truth that the President's speech tried to make known to the world.

You will recall that three years ago, and again in 1951, our late and beloved colleague Senator Brien McMahon sponsored a resolution asking the Senate to go on record as supporting the objectives outlined in the President's speech of April 16— the objectives of rascal-proof regulation of weapons production and the use of resources thereby saved for constructive tasks on a worldwide basis.

Senators from both sides of the aisle joined with Brien McMahon in sponsoring Senate Concurrent Resolution 47. Along with Republicans and other Democrats, I submitted an identical resolution in the House of Representatives at the same time. This resolution proposed:

That the Congress of the United States advocate and recommend an immediate special session of the General Assembly of the United Nations for the single purpose of stopping the armaments race by speeding agreement upon effective and enforceable disarmament and control covering conventional armaments, biological and chemical agents, and atomic and hydrogen bombs;

That the Congress of the United States, as tangible evidence of its good faith, pledge itself to appropriate and to make available to the United Nations—when an effective and enforceable system of worldwide disarmament and control takes effect—a substantial portion of all money saved for a period of 5 years, such sums to be expended by the United Nations for peaceful development of atomic energy, technical-assistance programs to underdeveloped areas, and general economic aid and assistance to all war-ravaged countries.

It may well be that President Eisenhower's words were inspired by recollection of this resolution. But this is of little import; Brien McMahon took no pride of authorship in his plan for peace with justice.

I need not remind this chamber that no person of our generation worked harder to enlarge the armed might of the United States than Senator Brien McMahon. It was my privilege to sit on the Joint Committee on Atomic Energy while he served as its honored chairman. I observed his total dedication to the twin cause of multiplying our atomic strength and, hand in hand with this, finding some way of abolishing these frightful armaments, and all other weapons as well, from the arsenals of the world.

When he peered into the future, Brien McMahon saw what the President of the United States saw. He saw what all of us must see, unless we close our eyes to the meaning of the onrushing arms competition. If the road before us continues without turning, the future promises at best a world living in fear of annihilation—a world in which our treasures are drained away in the manufacture of weapons which cannot feed a single hungry person or ease the pain of a single man or woman racked by disease. And that is the best we can hope for if armaments continue piling up on both sides of the Iron Curtain at an accelerating rate. If history is to be our guide, we must assume that eventually such an armaments race will spill over to outright global war.

In truth, the future holds only two eventual alternatives: atomic war, a war made hideous beyond imagination by the new destroyers of men and all their works; or atomic peace, a peace made rich beyond imagination by the power of modern science and technology freed for peaceful tasks.

Mr. President, I shall now resubmit Senate Concurrent Resolution 47. A resolution of identical wording has already been resubmitted in the House. Senators from both parties are joining with me in this resolution. I am particularly proud to have as one of my cosponsors the chairman of the Foreign Relations Committee, the senior Senator from Wisconsin [Mr. Alexander Wiley].

I would not presume for an instant to predict that the Soviet rulers will be willing to join with us and the other nations of the free world in a plan for carrying on a worldwide crusade against hunger and disease and human squalor. I see nothing in the conduct of the new Soviet regime which would make for confidence on this score. Yet I cannot believe that our nation must be deterred from subscribing to a noble goal simply because our adversaries may continue to act ignobly. This country has prospered and grown great in the service of noble causes, and we can forget this only at our peril.

As a minimum, moreover, the concurrent resolution on behalf of which I now speak, will let men everywhere know who bears the responsibility for the fears and tensions that now beset the world. It tells the Kremlin: Put up or shut up. If this concurrent resolution is adopted by the Congress and if the Soviet rulers refuse to join in a program which will give the world tractors instead of tanks, houses instead of barracks, and medicines in place of explosives—if the Kremlin refuses to become partner to such a program—the Communist slogans of peace and plenty will become a mockery.

I urge with all the power at my command that every Member of the Senate, by supporting this concurrent resolution, now unite behind the President of the United States in our quest for lasting peace.

SENATE CONCURRENT RESOLUTION

Whereas the peoples of the earth are plunged, against their will, in an accelerating armaments race that involves atomic bombs, biological and chemical agents, and conventional weapons; and

Whereas the prospect of the hydrogen bomb propels the peoples of the earth into dangers above and beyond anything heretofore conceived by man; and

Whereas in history, armaments races have always led to war; and

Whereas the United States is unshakably determined to keep strong so long as its strivings to halt the armaments race through just and dependable international agreement are thwarted; and

Whereas United States efforts to achieve international control over all weapons do not flow from craven fear or weakness but rather from the strength of democratic institutions, faith in freedom, belief in the value and worth of the human individual everywhere, and from trust in Almighty God and His laws: Now, therefore, be it

Resolved by the Senate (the House of Representatives concurring)—

That the Congress of the United States appeal to the peoples of the world to join in a great moral crusade for peace and freedom;

That the Congress of the United States advocate and recommend that the next session of the General Assembly of the United Nations devote itself to the purpose of stopping the armaments race by speeding agreement upon effective and enforceable disarmament and control covering conventional armaments, biological and chemical agents, and atomic and hydrogen bombs;

That the Congress of the United States, as tangible evidence of its good faith, pledge itself to appropriate and to make available to the United Nations—when an effective and enforceable system of worldwide disarmament and control takes effect—a substantial portion of all money saved for a period of 5 years, such sums to be expended by the United Nations for peaceful development of atomic energy, technical-assistance programs to underdeveloped areas, and general economic aid and assistance to all war-ravaged countries.

That the Congress of the United States call upon all other governments to make a like pledge; and, therefore,

That copies of this resolution be transmitted to the Secretary General of the United Nations and to each United Nations delegate and also that copies be transmitted to the presiding officer of every national parliament, congress, and deliberative assembly throughout the world.

2
The Race for the Ballistic Missile

United States Senate
1 February 1956

In the postwar years, with Soviet conventional forces towering over those of the United States and its friends, this country adopted the deterrent strategy of offsetting Soviet superiority in conventional weapons and troop levels with advanced weapons superior to those in Moscow's arsenals. The deterrent power of atomic weapons was by far the most important element in this strategy. Congressman Jackson had barely started his service on the Joint Committee on Atomic Energy when the Kremlin broke our atomic monopoly by exploding the first Russian atom bomb. Believing that the Soviets might quite likely achieve a hydrogen bomb before we did, Jackson sided with those who saw no alternative to proceeding with an American program.

On his election to the Senate in 1952, Jackson was assigned a seat on the Senate Armed Services Committee. As a Senator, he also served on the Joint Committee on Atomic Energy and became chairman of its newly established Military Applications Subcommittee. He was thus well positioned not only to work on arms control issues but also increasingly to take a lead in ensuring that we would not lag behind Moscow in the discovery of critical new weapons.

In fact, the Soviets were showing no signs of wanting to join in serious arms control discussions. Rather, while maintaining their superiority in conventional weapons, they were engaged in rapidly catching up with and threatening to pass us in crucial advanced weapons systems.

Among the issues Jackson tackled was the race with the Soviets for the development of land-based intermediate and intercontinental ballistic missiles. To ensure that we did not fall behind Moscow, the Senator held closed hearings in his Subcommittee on Military Applications to explore ways to speed our development program. On 30 June 1955, the subcommittee's top secret recommendations were forwarded to President Eisenhower, causing him to request and receive his first full briefing on the status of our ballistic missile effort.

By early 1956, however, the Senator was still not convinced that we were moving fast or effectively enough. Year after year, Jackson had seen the Soviets challenging the United States more formidably in getting advanced weapons systems into production; and by early 1956 they were well on their way to test-firing a 1,500-mile, land-launched ballistic missile. At that point, Jackson decided to "go public" and make his case to the White House from the floor of the Senate. The message got through. The President gave the land-launched ballistic missile programs a top priority, and the Secretary of Defense appointed a full-time missile coordinator.

SIX MONTHS HAVE PASSED SINCE BRITAIN, FRANCE, THE Soviet Union, and our own nation came together in the summit conference at Geneva. It is now clear that the "Geneva spirit" was never taken seriously by the Soviet rulers. Khrushchev himself publicly ridiculed those who thought the summit conference meant the end of the cold war. Khrushchev said last September: "If anyone believes that our smiles involve abandonment of the teachings of Marx, Engels, and Lenin, he deceives himself poorly. Those who wait for that must wait until a shrimp learns to whistle."

It is now apparent that the honeyed words spoken at Geneva by Khrushchev and Bulganin were merely tactical maneuvers —designed to lull the free world into complacency while the Kremlin continued its military buildup and developed a wide-swinging political and economic offensive. Only this week, in Bulganin's offer of a bilateral friendship treaty, we have seen a classic example of the Soviet technique. Obviously this offer was designed to drive a wedge into the Western alliance on the eve of the Anglo-American conversations. We properly turned the offer down—and now the Kremlin exploits the episode for all its propaganda worth.

On several occasions last summer, I questioned whether the optimism which surrounded the summit conference was justified. The optimism was natural enough and I was not happy about issuing statements of caution. I hoped I was wrong.

I take it, however, that we will agree where America now stands. The flame of the Geneva spirit, which seemingly burned so brightly last August, has dwindled, flickered, and sputtered. Now the flame is out. Soviet Deputy Premier Kaganovich openly boasted in November: "If the nineteenth century was a century of capitalism, the twentieth century is a century of the triumph of socialism and communism."

Far from relaxing its armaments buildup since last summer, Moscow has been intensifying its military preparations. While Khrushchev and Bulganin talked of the peaceful atom, Soviet scientists and engineers worked around the clock to achieve the Russian H-bomb explosion of last November. While Khrushchev and Bulganin spoke soothing words in India, other Kremlin agents roamed the Middle East—offering lures, kindling strife, and stirring hostility against the West.

The basic aim of the Kremlin remains unchanged—a Moscow-dominated world. The Soviet rulers stand ready and able to employ every last weapon in the Communist arsenal of conquest. These weapons are well-known—diplomatic initiative, the smile, psychological pressure, economic warfare, political infiltration, subversion, and military conquest on the installment plan through satellite forces. Beyond this, if the gains appear worth the costs, the Soviets would not even shrink from an all-out nuclear attack against our American homeland.

Let us pay the devil his due: The overlords of the Communist world are not stupid men—they are skillful practitioners of the art of conquest. They have read their Machiavelli and their Clausewitz—just as they have read *Mein Kampf*. Moreover, the Soviets have profited from the mistakes of aggressors in ages past. Unlike Hitler, they might wait for years—or even decades—to achieve their ends. Unlike the rulers of Japan in 1941, they may refrain from acting rashly.

The Kremlin knows that if the opponent can be relaxed, while the Communists are hard at work, time will run in their favor. As Khrushchev said in India last November: "We can wait. The wind is now blowing in our faces. We can wait for better weather."

The ingredients of military power are well known to Moscow. The Kremlin knows that the bases of military power of nations and alliance systems are four in number—land, people, natural resources, and industrial capacity. It knows that the Communist world now surpasses our own nation in at least two of these four factors, and maybe in three.

Land: The Communist landmass is six times as large as the United States.

People: There are eight hundred million people in the Red Empire, and only one hundred and seventy million Americans. The Soviet Union has the largest land army in the world. Red China has the second largest army. The American army is third.

Natural resources: The mineral wealth of the Communist world is vast and largely unexploited. The raw materials within the Communist empire are probably more diversified and more abundant than our own.

Industrial capacity: America now outstrips the Communist world in one ingredient of military power—and one ingredient only—that is, our superior industrial might. This has been our trump card in the struggle with the Soviets. Up to now, at least, our industrial lead has cancelled out the Communist advantage in land and people. The symbol of this lead has been our stockpile of nuclear weapons and our long-range Strategic Air Force.

Up until now, the Soviets have been on notice that all-out Red aggression would be answered by our superior air-atomic strength. Furthermore, the free world alliance system has combined with American industrial supremacy to help offset Communist preponderance in land and people. The assets of the free world, when thus pooled, have been superior to those of the Communist empire. In addition, our network of advanced bases on allied territory has multiplied the effectiveness of our air-atomic power. Our nuclear strength cannot be measured merely by the number of bombs in our atomic stockpile. It is the product of the quantity of bombs, times the destructive force of each bomb, times our ability to deliver them against enemy targets. Without our overseas bases, American atomic might would be reduced to a fraction of its present strength.

None of this comes as news to the Soviets. The Kremlin knows, as well as we know, what Moscow must do to achieve preponderance in national military power. The Kremlin knows, as well as we know, how the balance of world power could be tipped decisively against the United States. The Kremlin knows that our present advantage lies in our industrial supremacy and in the free world alliance system. The Kremlin knows that if the Soviets can overtake our industrial lead and at the same time neutralize our allies, the Communist world will thereby achieve superiority in all four bases of military strength—land, people, raw materials, and industry.

Americans know we have the most productive economy of all history. Many of us think it inconceivable that the Soviets can ever overtake, let alone surpass, us in industry and technology. But before we become complacent, let us examine the record.

Year after year, the Soviets have narrowed the technological gap between the Russian economy and our own. Year after year, they have challenged us more formidably in our one area of superior strength—our ability to design advanced weapon systems sooner, and to put them into production quicker, than any other nation in the world.

Go back to early 1949—a short seven years ago. Then, as now, our conventional armed forces were vastly outnumbered by the Communist legions. But, in contrast, our air-atomic power then stood unchallenged. We alone possessed the only true long-range bomber then existing—the B-36. We alone had flight-tested the world's first jet strategic bomber—the B-47. And above all, we alone possessed atomic weapons. Responsible officials said that it would take ten or twenty years for the Soviets to manufacture an atomic bomb. They informed us also that Moscow would not possess jet bombers for many years to come.

But what happened in fact? The Soviets achieved their first atomic bomb in the summer of 1949—years before the expected date. They tested their first hydrogen bomb in the summer of 1953—less than nine months after the first of our full-scale hydrogen tests.

The development of Soviet aircraft saw the same story repeated. Our experts said the Soviets could not produce jet bombers until 1956 or 1958. In fact, the Soviets flew jet planes comparable to our B-47 and our B-52, not in 1956 or 1958, but in 1954. Moreover, these Russian planes had jet engines more advanced than our own. Some prominent officials argued that these Russian planes were only hand-tooled prototypes—useless for combat and years away from mass production.

Again, what in fact happened? Last spring, the Soviets flew both medium- and long-range jet bombers in operational numbers. These were no laboratory models—these were production-line planes ready for combat units. Furthermore, they flew large numbers of a new fighter plane better than any we had in operational use.

Even more ominous, the Soviets have mass-produced new aircraft faster than we have. Our work on the B-52 bomber began in 1948. It was flight-tested in 1952, and actual production started in the spring of 1954. The comparable Soviet plane, the Bison, was apparently designed in 1950, flight-tested three years later, and produced in quantity in 1954. In short, the Soviets moved two years faster than we did in mass-producing long-range jet bombers.

Seven years ago we had a monopoly of both atomic bombs and planes for delivering them against distant targets. Today, both monopolies are gone. Furthermore, today we cannot even be confident that we are ahead of Moscow in long-range air power.

Up to now we have had one reassurance. So far we have managed to win every race for discovery of crucial new weapons systems. To be sure, we have won these races by smaller and smaller margins, but we have won them.

However, I believe that the Soviet Union may win the next critical race for discovery. I believe that the Soviets may win the race for the intermediate-range 1,500-mile ballistic missile. The intercontinental ballistic missile is the closest thing to an "ultimate weapon" that has ever been projected. Conventional guided missiles, such as our own Regulus or Matador, are merely unmanned versions of jet aircraft—they travel at relatively low altitudes and relatively slow speeds. Defense against such vehicles is relatively easy. But ballistic missiles are ominously different. They travel high in the ionosphere at ten or twenty times the speed of sound. An intercontinental ballistic missile launched from Russian bases against the cities and military installations of our American heartland would arrive in twenty or thirty minutes. An intermediate-range ballistic missile could reach the capitals of our European allies in ten to fifteen minutes. Moreover, an effective defense against ballistic missiles is nowhere in sight. The ballistic missile is the H-bomb of delivery vehicles.

In my judgment there is the danger that the Soviets may fire a 1,500-mile ballistic missile before the end of this year—1956. Some people may minimize the importance of such an achievement. They may say that the Soviets, operating from their present bases, could not reach the American heartland with a 1,500-mile missile. They may contend that ballistic missiles will endanger this country only when the Kremlin achieves a weapon of true intercontinental range. This is not the case. The existence of a 1,500-mile Soviet ballistic missile would cancel out our own vital advantage over Russian air-atomic power—our system of advanced overseas airbases. Virtually all of our overseas SAC bases are within easy striking distance of a 1,500-mile missile. Such a missile could level these bases in a matter of minutes.

Without these bases, our Strategic Air Force would be a shadow of its former self. Without these bases, the effectiveness of the B-47 bomber—the present backbone of our striking force—would be drastically reduced. We would be forced into primary reliance upon the now-obsolete B-36 and the long-range jet B-52—only now beginning to trickle off our production lines.

A Soviet 1,500-mile missile could turn our strategic thinking upside down. It might well compel us to write off our overseas bases as virtually useless. A Russian 1,500-mile ballistic missile could force American air power to retreat 5,000 miles from the Soviet Union.

We need not assume that Moscow would actually use a 1,500-mile missile to start an atomic war. The mere existence of such a weapon in the hands of the Kremlin, at a time when we did not have it ourselves, could radically upset the world balance of power.

We and our free world partners may soon face the threat of ballistic blackmail.

I invite you to put yourself in the place of a governmental leader of France or West Germany or England or Pakistan or Japan. Any of these nations could be devastated by a 1,500-mile missile launched from Communist-controlled bases. Imagine that Soviet Defense Minister Zhukov has just invited the military attachés of the free world to meet at a missile site near Moscow. Imagine Marshal Zhukov then explaining that he is about to press a button which will fire the world's first 1,500-mile ballistic missile. Marshal Zhukov might say that this demonstration missile carried only a TNT warhead. But he would undoubtedly add that a hydrogen warhead could be substituted. Standing in a concrete blockhouse for protection, the military attachés would see the missile launched. Some 1,500 miles away—perhaps in the wastes of Soviet Central Asia —another group of free world observers would be assembled. Mere minutes later, they would witness the crashing explosion of the missile at the end of its journey.

Picture what might happen next. On the wall of the concrete blockhouse would be a huge map, outlining in vivid red the range of the Soviet missile. This range would embrace all of Western Europe, all of North Africa and the Middle East, most of South and Southeast Asia, the Philippines, Formosa, Okinawa, Korea, and Japan.

The demonstration might end amidst assurances of Moscow's peaceful intentions and many Soviet smiles. A few days later, Premier Bulganin might invite the foreign ministers of the NATO powers to a conference in Moscow. While proposing no formal agenda, Bulganin might indicate that the Soviets would advocate dissolving NATO and establishing a new type of defense community. Bulganin would be thinking of a defense arrangement that would not interfere with the Soviet objective—world domination.

Caught in this bind, our most redoubtable supporters might falter. It is well-nigh certain that crucial allies would be forced into neutralism, or even into tacit cooperation with Moscow.

We do not know exactly when the Russians will get the ballistic missile—but there is grave danger that they will get it before we do. We have consistently underestimated the Soviets. We underestimated them on the A-bomb; we underestimated them on the H-bomb; we underestimated them on fighter aircraft; we underestimated them on jet bombers. I believe we are now underestimating the Kremlin on ballistic missiles.

Soviet victory in this race for discovery would be shattering to the morale of our allies and to our own self-confidence. For the first time Moscow would have beaten us in a crucial scientific-industrial race. No longer would America be acknowledged as the unquestioned industrial and technical colossus of the world. Our trump card would have passed to the Kremlin, and the reverberating effects on our relationships abroad would be incalculable.

You will not mistake the meaning of my remarks. I do not maintain for an instant that our own intermediate-range ballistic missile program should take priority over our effort to achieve a true intercontinental missile. In fact, I maintain that while the intermediate-range ballistic missile should be urgently pursued, this effort must not proceed at the cost of jeopardizing progress toward the intercontinental weapon.

Neither do I maintain that superiority in the ballistic missile field will ensure our national survival. In fact, I believe the very opposite. Moscow's economic and political warfare also can be deadly. Over the long run, Communist nibbling tactics and conquests on the installment plan could be as effective as a surprise nuclear assault. Yet American superiority in advanced weapon systems is the minimum prerequisite of peace. Without such superiority all our other programs for staying Soviet power will prove in vain.

In recent months our own ballistic missile program has been accelerated. When the history of our program is some day publicly revealed, the American people will learn that the Joint Committee on Atomic Energy played a major role in accelerating our program—in the form of urgent representations and recommendations to the executive branch of the government.

The history of the race for the ballistic missile dramatizes the need for a basic change in our defense philosophy. Like so many other aspects of our defense program, the ballistic missile program has been plagued in the past by the complacent idea that "we can always increase our efforts if war comes." This archaic idea should be buried once and for all. In an all-out atomic-hydrogen war, the sense of urgency certainly would be with us, but the time and the production facilities would not. In that sort of war, our industrial might would be consigned to a nuclear graveyard. In the event an all-out nuclear war were forced upon us, we would need to have in being, at the start, the weapons and delivery systems essential to ultimate survival.

I am not suggesting that all our weapons programs be placed on a wartime footing. Our defense philosophy must be changed on those projects so crucial in themselves that failure to be first in their completion would cause a tragic shift in the military balance of the free and Communist worlds. Such an overturn will surely follow a Soviet victory in the current race for the intercontinental ballistic missile. The military balance is not likely to change overnight if the free world has a few less jet aircraft than the Kremlin. Nor will that balance shift abruptly if Moscow has a few more fighter aircraft than we do. But the balance will shift if Moscow triumphs in the race for the ballistic missile.

The intercontinental ballistic missile is a clear example of the type of program which demands the new defense philosophy. That philosophy is simply this: all-out work on critical projects today to avoid all-out war tomorrow. The crucial race for ballistic missiles deserves as vigorous an effort as we put into our wartime atomic energy program. This means a three-shift operation, seven days a week. Despite recent progress, we have yet to achieve this momentum.

Today our missile program does not have a single, overall, full-time civilian administrator—and it needs one badly. Today there are distracting interservice rivalries. We do not have an overall, full-time, high-level administrator, even though we know that the success of our wartime atomic program was due largely to the fact that one man, General Leslie Groves, was given full and complete authority.

Likewise, we know that the success of our naval atomic propulsion program has been due to the fact that one man, Admiral Rickover, has been given singular authority.

I most earnestly propose:

1. The ballistic missile project should now proceed with the maximum effort of which this nation is capable, supported by the kind of urgency that heretofore Americans have reserved for wartime conditions.

2. To implement this objective, the ballistic missile program should be placed under a full-time civilian administrator, reporting directly to the Secretary of Defense and to the President.

Obviously, I have been painting a dark picture of our current standing in the ballistic missile race. In my judgment this is an accurate picture. I have presented what I believe to be the factual balance sheet.

But because the outlook is ominous, it does not follow that there is nothing we can do about it. I am confident that if the American people had the necessary facts—if the true peril of our position could be brought home to them—they would support the full marshalling of our resources behind the ballistic missile project.

All the resources of the Soviet Union and its satellites are now directed toward the objective of seizing our trump card of scientific and industrial supremacy, as symbolized in the race for the ballistic missile. We need not give a halfway answer to this all-out Soviet challenge. We need not give a partisan answer to a threat which imperils us all. We face a nationwide peril, which must be met by a concentrated nationwide effort, rooted in our determination that America and its free institutions shall survive.

3

Ballistic Seapower—
Fourth Dimension of Warfare

United States Senate
27 May 1957

By mid-1956 Senator Jackson was becoming convinced that submarine-based missile-launching systems, with their near invulnerability to preemptive assault, could make an indispensable contribution to deterrence and the stability of the strategic balance. To be sure of his ground, Jackson appointed an advisory panel composed of outstanding experts on undersea warfare to review the prospects and problems of getting into service a viable ballistic missile submarine fleet. Meanwhile, he was in constant touch with Navy and Defense Department officials, including Admiral Hyman Rickover.

In this period, the Soviets already had submarines that could fire ballistic missiles with a range of at least 200 miles. It could be presumed that before long they would have submarine-launched ballistic missiles with ranges of 1,000 or 1,500 miles. Was America placing enough emphasis on the development of ballistic seapower? That was the Senator's main question. He concluded that the answer was no.

In the spring of 1957 he felt ready to take the issue to the Senate floor to engage, if he could, the attention of President Eisenhower and his National Security Council. Only at that high level of the government did the Senator believe a matter of such historical import could be resolved.

Jackson got the attention he wanted and the kind of high-level commitment he sought. The United States assembled a ballistic missile submarine fleet sufficient in numbers and in service on time to fortify the American deterrent.

MORE THAN A YEAR HAS GONE BY SINCE I TOOK THIS FLOOR to urge more speed, more effort, and more central direction for our intermediate-range and intercontinental ballistic missiles programs. These missiles will rank with the invention of gun powder and the A-bomb and the H-bomb as among the most revolutionary developments in all military history.

The IRBM—the intermediate-range ballistic missile—could fly from a launching site near Leningrad to London in ten or fifteen minutes. The ICBM—the intercontinental missile —could fly from outside Moscow to Chicago in twenty-five to thirty minutes. Both weapons will travel at speeds and heights making effective interception unlikely—so far as we know today. Both will carry hydrogen warheads. One such missile could destroy the heart of the largest city on earth.

We are now in a neck-and-neck race with the Soviets to see who will get these weapons first. Our own program lagged badly until less than two years ago. The President gave the development of these weapons supreme priority only after urgent pleas from Members of the Congress. The Secretary of Defense appointed a full-time missile program coordinator only after similar urgings.

But the past is behind us. What matters is the present and the future. Today, the development programs we have started are going places—fast. The Air Force is speeding toward the first operational testing of Thor, its intermediate-range missile. It is working around the clock at the same time on Atlas and Titan—alternate versions of the intercontinental ballistic missile. The Army has moved forward rapidly on Jupiter—its version of the IRBM, although statements from the Secretary of Defense have left the outcome of this program in doubt. On a far smaller scale and with a far longer timetable, the Navy is developing Polaris—a sea-launched intermediate-range missile.

We are now taking calculated scientific and technical risks. We are trying to move as quickly as possible from the laboratory and drawing board to the assembly line—from scientific research to large-scale industrial production of operational weapons. We are now cutting down our technological lead time.

But it should be clear that building and testing a missile is not the same as building a missiles force. The technological problem of building accurate and reliable missiles is only half the total problem. The other half is the problem of strategic and military planning. How many intercontinental missiles should we build, and how many intermediate-range missiles? How many of our missile-launching platforms should be on land, and how many on the sea? How many land-based missiles should be deployed in our own country, and how many at advanced overseas bases? How much research and development money should we now put into one missile system, and how much into another? We may have ballistic missiles, but we will not have an effective missiles force, until these questions are answered—and answered correctly.

Some may wonder why I make these points today—when we have yet to test our first operational IRBM. Should we not now concentrate all our energies on testing and building these weapons—and defer until later the problem of military and strategic planning? But technical development and strategic planning must go forward in parallel. One cannot be divorced from the other.

There is a lead time in military and strategic planning just as real as the lead time in technical development. The effectiveness of our missiles force five years from now, and even ten years from now, will depend on strategic planning decisions made in the Pentagon this year—in 1957. Every year's delay in strategic planning means a year's delay in building an effective missiles force.

Recall the history of the B-29—the long-range superfortress which did so much to destroy the Japanese military economy in World War II. The strategic decision to attain long-range bomber capability was made on the eve of World War II—long before the B-29 existed even on paper. Six years of superb technical effort were needed before we secured the B-29 fleets which helped devastate the Japanese Empire in 1944 and 1945.

Our ballistic missiles force will be subject to the same laws of strategic planning. Five or ten years of all-out technical development and industrial production will elapse before strategic planning decisions made this year can be reflected in the actual hardware of a ballistic missiles force. Certain strategic questions are therefore now crucial: Are we now covering every good bet in our strategic planning for the ballistic missile era? Is our planning giving every promising missiles system adequate emphasis? In short: Are we now doing everything possible to cut down the lead time in strategic planning?

I believe that the answer to these questions may be no. I believe that we may now be neglecting one ballistic missile system which could give us a quantum jump upward in our military deterrent power. I refer to a possible future *fourth dimension of warfare*—the intermediate-range ballistic missile fired from ocean-launching platforms. I refer to a delivery system in which the IRBM with a hydrogen warhead could be launched against strategic targets from submerged or surfaced nuclear-propelled submarines.

I call this the fourth dimension of warfare because it would introduce a new element into military strategy and tactics. It would combine nuclear firepower—missiles with H-bomb warheads—with nuclear propulsion, in the form of mobile submarine-launching platforms which could roam anywhere on the high seas without refueling and stay submerged indefinitely.

The Navy is now building Halibut, a nuclear submarine which will fire missiles of relatively slow speed and relatively short range. This will be an excellent ship, but it represents only one very short step toward a true IRBM submarine.

In addition, the Navy now has a long-term, a very long-term, research and development program aimed at ultimately, eventually, firing intermediate-range ballistic missiles from submarines and surface ships. This program, however, commands neither the money, the manpower, nor the priority now assigned to the ICBM and land-based intermediate-range missiles. And yet, an IRBM launched from an ocean platform could have the same target coverage and the same military effect as an ICBM launched from our own country.

It is very probable that we can build submarine-based missile-launching systems. No insurmountable technical obstacles are now foreseen. Nonetheless, special problems are involved in designing, building, and controlling a reliable weapons system in which 1,500-mile missiles could be accurately and reliably fired from ocean platforms. In fact, the technical challenge is far greater than the one of developing Thor or Jupiter—our land-based intermediate-range missiles.

It should not be hard to see why. A land-based launching site is an immovable platform—precisely oriented to our globe's axis. It rests on the bedrock of the earth itself. It is firmly fixed in space. The range to a potential target can be calculated with hairbreadth accuracy long before an emergency occurs. The only real limiting factor would be the accuracy of our guidance systems and maps. A submarine-launching platform would not be fixed in space. Even if anchored, it would be constantly moving because of the ocean's action—and moving in three dimensions. The distance between a patrolling submarine and enemy targets would constantly change. Range calculations could not be easily made.

A land-based missile would fly through only one element— the air. A sea-based missile, if actually fired from under the water, would fly through two elements—water and air. The problem of launching and the problem of accurate guidance would be more difficult.

Land-based launching sites would have a relatively easy logistics problem. Spare parts and replacement depots would be close at hand. Spare parts and replacements for sea-based missiles would be located in the ship itself. But in a crisis, sea-based missiles would be far more difficult to service and replenish than land-based missiles.

The problem of military command—of foolproof control over the operations of our missiles—would be comparatively simple in the case of land-based systems. We would know exactly where every land-based missile platform was, at every instant of time. Land-based sites could be linked with a central headquarters through a jam-proof and instantaneous communications network. Sea-based systems would have to be linked to command headquarters by many communication channels —on the assumption that it would be impossible to jam all the channels at once.

As we see, the difficulties of actually building an effective ocean missile force are numerous. Yet the arguments for a far greater emphasis on the sea-based system are compelling.

Our security clearly lies in convincing the Soviets that even if they strike the first nuclear blow, they cannot prevent an overwhelming and possibly fatal counterattack.

Now a submarine missile base could move in close to the aggressor's shores to launch missiles. It could compete favorably with any land-based system in target coverage. There is this vital difference, however. The Kremlin would know the location of our land-based launching sites—the Kremlin would not know where our ballistic seapower was deployed.

Land-based sites will not be tiny dots on the landscape. They will be relatively large, relatively easy to identify, and fixed in place. It is doubtful whether we or our allies could conceal their location. One cannot discount the future possibility of mobile land-launching sites, as the state of the art improves. This, however, is a possibility of the distant future.

A massive surprise missile attack, skillfully executed by the Soviets, might actually knock out most of our Strategic Air Force and much of our land-based missile capability, before we could retaliate. But the location of our ocean missile force would change constantly. This deterrent fleet, ever-shifting, could be dispersed over the millions of square miles of the Atlantic, the Pacific, and the Arctic oceans. Thanks to nuclear power, it would not have to be refueled. A certain fraction of this force could remain on submerged alert. The surface of the ocean would shield it from hostile search radar. It could be in a state of constant readiness—24 hours a day and 365 days a year.

Steady advances are, of course, being made in submarine detection. Yet finding ships under the sea is vastly more difficult than spotting planes in the air or ships on the surface of the sea, since the scientific laws of radar do not apply.

Hidden, widely deployed, ever on the move, missile submarines would be enormously difficult to locate and even more difficult to destroy. The odds against eliminating such a deterrent fleet before it could strike a counterblow would be a hundred to one or even a thousand to one. The problem faced by an aggressor would be like that of a man trying to find a black cat on a vast and empty plain on a dark, moonless and starless night.

If the enemy launched a surprise missile attack, our only effective reply would be a nuclear counterblow. Yet the aggressor's missiles would strike our homeland within minutes of being launched. Would there be time to strike a counterblow with many of our land-based missiles before they were destroyed? If we rely only on land-based sites, an aggressor's first surprise blow may be the final blow, the blow which makes effective retaliation impossible. This is where the fourth dimension of warfare—ballistic seapower—becomes crucial. No matter how fast the enemy's missiles travel, they could not eliminate this underseas fleet in one massive assault. Enough submarines would remain intact to strike a crushing counterblow.

An additional point needs emphasis. In the IRBM and ICBM era, if the Soviets launched a nuclear war, their first move would be a massive attack on the ballistic retaliatory power of the free world. Failure to destroy this power would leave the Kremlin open to a devastating counterblow—a rain of rockets. In short, our own missile sites and the sites of our allies would be *strategic magnets*. Like a magnet, these sites would draw the fire of an aggressor's ballistic blow.

Note this difference, however. Land-based missile sites, both here and abroad, would be strategic magnets drawing the enemy's missiles *toward* the cities, the towns, the farms, and the factories of the free world. Ocean-based platforms would be strategic magnets drawing the enemy's missiles *away* from our countries. Our missile submarines could be a *save-our-cities* force. This fleet would be stationed far out at sea—thousands of miles from San Francisco or Chicago or New York or London or Paris. The Kremlin, if it started an all-out war, would be forced to attack our ballistic seapower. And every Soviet missile fired against the concealed and shifting submarines would mean one less missile, one less hydrogen warhead, available for use against our cities. Of the Soviet missiles sent against this underseas fleet, almost all would fall harmlessly into the barren and uninhabited seas. The clouds of radioactive spray geysering up from the depths would fall on empty ocean—not on our cities.

In truth, such a force might become the ultimate *save-the-peace* force of the ballistic era. This fleet would confront Soviet military and economic planners with an almost impossible dilemma. Moscow could not make a surprise attack and itself survive if this fleet remained in existence.

But how would the Kremlin's strategists propose to destroy it? The sites of land-based ballistic counterforce would be known in location and immovable. Conceivably, Moscow might calculate that several hundred Soviet missiles, fired in a surprise assault, could break the back of this land-based deterrent. In all probability, however, it would be impossible to locate and attack many of our submarine-based missiles. As long as the submarine was moving it could not be hit with a ballistic missile. The Soviets might require a stockpile of literally tens of thousands of missiles and nuclear warheads and still be unable to destroy our submarine striking power.

Think of the enormous strain on the Soviet economy if Moscow were to prepare for a ballistic Pearl Harbor against the free world. Billions and billions of rubles would be needed to build up the Soviet missile force which could strike against the free world's land-based missile sites and our Strategic Air Command. But these weapons would be nothing compared to the enormous outlays of money, materials, and manpower which would have to be devoted to the attempt to destroy our underseas missile force.

There is a limit to what the Soviet economy can produce. Russia's laboratories and factories might simply prove unequal to the task of building the numbers and types of weapons that would be needed if Moscow were to entertain any serious hope whatsoever of destroying both our land-based and our sea-based missile counterforce. For every million dollars we would spend on a submarine missile fleet, the Soviets might spend 50 million or 100 million and still not be in a position to destroy our underseas fleet.

Nothing I have been saying is any secret to the Soviets. Moscow understands the principles of military strategy. Moscow understands that our system of advanced bases is the greatest single strategic advantage possessed by the free world. Moscow understands that Soviet submarine-launching platforms could cancel out this advantage. Moscow knows that a fleet of underseas missile ships flying the Soviet flag would be the equivalent of Communist bases a few hundred miles from Seattle and Los Angeles and New York.

Today, right now, the Soviets have submarines which can fire ballistic missiles at least 200 miles. We must presume they will soon have submarine-launched ballistic missiles with a 1,000- or 1,500-mile range. No real defense against such weapons is now foreseeable. In fact, our own ballistic seapower may be the one thing above all which will keep Moscow from making a surprise attack with its own sea-based missiles.

I have never been a one-weapon advocate in my approach to defense problems. I do not think for a single moment that a submarine missile-launching system would eliminate the necessity for the land-based ICBM or IRBM. I am sure that we will need a balanced missile force—just as our entire defense effort must be balanced—if we are to be ready to repel military aggression in all its wide variety of forms.

Certainly, for a long time to come, we shall require medium-range and long-range manned bombers. The difference between building a successful test missile and a real missiles force is the difference between day and night. As missiles are perfected they will be added to our arsenal as a supplementary delivery system. I cannot now foresee the day when missiles will completely substitute for manned bombers.

Now as far as missiles are concerned, the real question is not whether we should have a land- *or* sea-based missile system. I am sure we need both. The real issue concerns a tremendously difficult decision in strategic planning. It is the issue of strategic *balance*. It is the issue of how much emphasis we should put on a sea-based system, and how much on land-launched missiles.

It could be that sea-based missiles will be only of very limited military use. If so, one could defend the very leisurely effort we are now making to develop this weapons system. But it could equally be that this weapon will, in fact, introduce a fourth dimension into warfare. If so, one could not defend our existing business-as-usual program.

Which is it? Will the submarine-launching platforms be just another routine weapon? Or will it come to be a supreme deterrent of the ballistic era? This is the issue.

It is no comfort to be told, as I am sure we will be told, that our defense planners are already "studying" this issue. Of course they are. They are "studying" hundreds of issues. The H-bomb was being studied in 1942—but we did not start a real H-bomb program until 1950, eight years later. The ICBM was being studied in 1946—but we did not go all-out to build it until almost ten years later.

Nor is it any comfort to be told, as I am sure we will be told, that the Navy is now "working" on the problem of developing submarine-launched missiles. Of course, the Navy is "working" on this problem. The Navy is "working" on thousands of problems. The real question is *how much* work? How much effort, how much money, and how much priority is now being assigned the sea-based IRBM? Is it the right amount of effort, the right amount of money, and the right priority?

The plain fact is that the money now authorized and appropriated for the Navy is insufficient to support an all-out effort to develop this weapon as quickly as possible, if an all-out effort is now in the national interest. The Navy has just so much money to go around. Its overriding concern is with building the ships and airplanes we need to defend ourselves this year and next year. Further, the law prohibits funds appropriated for the Navy's presently authorized shipbuilding program from being diverted to the development of this new weapons system.

The real point, however, is this: The question of the priority we should now give ballistic seapower is not a question which can be decided wisely among the armed services themselves. Let us be honest about it. Interservice rivalry is a fact. It is a fact also that missile spending may very shortly be the largest military hardware item in our defense budget. Every day common sense argues that each service will try to claim for itself a lion's share of the missiles budget. It is simply unrealistic to expect the three services to answer objectively the question of how much effort should be put on the sea-based IRBM. Any answer given by the services themselves would inevitably reflect interservice logrolling.

There is another reason—even more important—why the issue of the emphasis to be given sea-based missiles should not be decided within the defense establishment. This is not purely a military issue—it is an issue which goes to the roots of our foreign policy as well. The emphasis that is given the ocean-based IRBM affects the very fundamentals of our relations with our allies.

Let us take an example. At the Bermuda conference,* we agreed to give our British friends assistance in securing land-based intermediate-range missiles when these became operational. Sound reasoning lay behind this offer. The IRBM, stationed on British soil, will give our own country the advantage of a counterstrike force located three thousand miles closer to a Eurasian aggressor. In addition, Britain's determination—and ability—to resist an aggressor's threats will no doubt be strengthened if these missiles are added to her arsenals.

At the same time, Britain is a comparatively tiny country. As the British government's own white paper† recently acknowledged, her cities and urban population could not escape from a Soviet air-atomic attack directed against British bases. There is simply not enough real estate to go around. It is a matter of plain geography in the age of weapons of mass destruction.

The problem, however, would be very different if Britain were primarily defended by a force of submarine-based missiles. These weapons would not be dotting the British country-

---

*The Bermuda conference was held in March 1957 and was a series of talks between President Eisenhower and Prime Minister Macmillan, the new British leader. Among other matters, they agreed "in principle that in the interest of mutual defense and mutual economy certain guided missiles will be made available by the United States for the use of British forces" (*New York Times*, 25 March 1957).

†*White Paper on Defense* issued by the British government on 4 April 1957.

side—near London or Manchester or Edinburgh. They would be deployed far out at sea—well beyond direct fallout range of Britain's population. A sneak attack from Moscow, if designed to eliminate this sea-based deterrent, would not fall on the densely populated British countryside—it would fall instead on the empty stretches of the Atlantic and Arctic oceans.

For purposes of defense, Britain would no longer be a tiny country. Tens of thousands of square miles would be added to its defense base. Britain's frontiers would shift from the Hebrides and the cliffs of Dover to the far reaches of the oceans.

A sea-based missiles force should have enormous appeal for our allies, especially in Europe. It could provide a maximum deterrent to Moscow with reduced danger to home territories. It would constitute a rational method of self-defense in the ballistic era.

We and our NATO allies are now reviewing present strategy for the defense of Europe. Might not a water-based missiles force go far to meet our common needs? Is it not possible that the bonds of the NATO alliance could now be strengthened by a cooperative program to develop and support a sea-based missile force?

No further argument should be needed to show why the question of land-based versus sea-based missiles cannot be answered in purely military terms. Neither our men in uniform nor their civilian superiors in the Pentagon should be expected to settle a problem which will affect so vitally the entire future of our relations with our allies.

It is my earnest opinion that only one person is qualified to resolve the question of whether we are placing enough emphasis on the development of ballistic seapower. That person is the President of the United States, acting not only in his capacity of Commander in Chief of our armed forces but also as the one charged under the Constitution with the conduct of our foreign affairs.

I have the highest respect for the dedication, ability, and sincerity of the heads of our armed services and the civilians within the Department of Defense. I simply believe that an issue of this historic import lies beyond their province. It is therefore with the greatest respect that I suggest the following:

First, the President, with the help of the National Security Council, should personally reexamine the question of whether we are now giving enough effort, enough money, and enough priority to the development of sea-based missile-launching systems.

Second, in resolving this issue, the President should give consideration to seeking assistance from a Presidentially appointed Commission on Ballistic Seapower. Such a Commission would of course be completely nonpartisan, both politically and in terms of allegiance to any one of the armed services. Its membership could be made up of a small number of citizens—those best qualified by reason of military, industrial, diplomatic, or scientific attainment to counsel the President most wisely. Its report could be made available to the President in time for his decision to be reflected in next year's budget request.

In conclusion, let me say this. Terrible weapon is being piled on terrible weapon. But a "peace of mutual terror" cannot last forever. I believe that discussions among nations for a sound and safe system for the control and limitation of armaments should be continuous. The statesmen of the free world must never give up in their search for a security system which rests on more than the threat of mutual destruction.

Yet until this quest is successful, we require a balanced military arsenal—with modern weapons to meet both nuclear and limited aggression. And until this quest is successful, we require the most rational and effective deterrent to nuclear war that we can get. If the sea-based missile force is such a deterrent, then we should bend the national effort to achieve it.

I am deeply convinced that the issue of whether we are giving enough emphasis to the development of ballistic seapower should be reviewed and decided now—not next year or the year thereafter but this year.

The American people need not stand in fear. We can welcome the future. We have a great tradition of mastering the

problems that confront us. But no people can escape the laws
of military and strategic planning. Decisions we make—or fail
to make—today determine our chance to deter nuclear war
tomorrow.

II
Organizing
for National Security

4

Forging a National Strategy

Military Government Association, Washington, D.C.
13 June 1959

Senator Jackson was disturbed by what he considered the Eisenhower administration's chronic failure to marshal the elements of national power and influence to compete effectively with the Soviet adversary, not only in advanced weapons but in scientific capability, political influence, and psychological impact as well. He watched the United States losing important ground to the Soviets in one field after another. Just as defeat in war is a possibility, so, he knew, is a defeat without firing a shot if the tides of the cold war went against the free world.

In the spring of 1959, into the seventh year of the Eisenhower presidency, Jackson saw his chance for a Senate-based move to encourage a more purposeful and energetic top leadership. Under Senate rules, the Government Operations Committee, of which he was a member, lacked general jurisdiction to explore the substance of foreign and defense policy but could examine how the processes of government help or hamper effective national action. The timing was good. A new President would be chosen during the coming year—a possible prime consumer of the product of a serious nonpartisan congressional study of national security policy-making at the Presidential level.

Before seeking the Senate's formal authorization, Jackson explored the basic approach for the inquiry and its possible agenda. This preliminary planning led to a number of speeches on the Soviet challenge and the inadequacies of the U.S. response, including the address of 13 June 1959 to the Military Government Association. At that point, the Senator was well along in setting the stage for what became a landmark congressional inquiry.

WHEN A HITLER STRIKES FOR WORLD DOMINATION, FREE men spring to arms in defense of their liberties, and they fight with an irresistible will to victory. Time and again, free men have proven their magnificent ability to unite in response to a military challenge.

Today, free men face a more ingenious foe than the storm trooper. The Soviets confront us with a test of will even more difficult than the battlefield. They are betting that we do not have the staying power to win the long, drawn-out competition of the cold war.

The Soviet rulers think in terms of power. Superior power, they believe, will eventually prevail. In every way, on every occasion, they seek to expand and consolidate their strength, confident that small gains here and there, at the margins of conflict, will determine the fate of the world.

The Kremlin favors settlements that will unsettle things and that will add up, in time, to a Communist world order. By a kind of Gresham's law of politics, bad political currency drives out good. It takes two to make peace, but only one to make trouble. Or, to change the figure of speech, we cannot hope to win the international game of fox and geese if we always allow the Russians to play the role of the fox.

In short, the Russians are determined to play the game of power politics, and we cannot choose not to play. The only course open to us is to play it better or to lose.

The issue that predominates over all others in our national life is this: Can our free society marshal its strength to defend and preserve our way of life against the total challenge of the Communist states? I think you will agree that we cannot take for granted that the answer will be yes.

I hasten to add that this is not a partisan matter. Democracy is on trial for its life. Neither party has a monopoly of wisdom or a monopoly of errors on this great issue. My remarks apply to what is a national problem—a national challenge.

As events have been moving, we are losing the contest. We are on the defensive almost everywhere.

We have been outdistanced *militarily*. We are now not even striving for equality in the advanced weapons systems, although superiority in these weapons was and is the key to maintaining an overall military balance with the Soviet Union. By our own decision, we have accepted second place in the intercontinental ballistic missile race, and the fateful implications of this decision are hardly being discussed publicly.

We are being overtaken *industrially* and *scientifically*, the fields in which our head start seemed to make the contest most one-sided in our favor.

We have been outmaneuvered *politically* in one vital area after another. In the Middle East, for example, which is the arena of our most recent reverses, it takes either a fool or a genius to see anything but disaster ahead.

And finally, we have never been in the same league with the Russians in the *psychological* war of wits and words.

The meaning of all this is clear. Our power, and the power of the free world as a whole, is declining in relation to the power of the Soviet Union and the Communist bloc. The process is cumulative and accelerating. The result of this process can be predicted with something like scientific precision. The cumulative effect of growing Soviet power and declining American power will be a progressive loss of ability to influence events and a chain reaction of defeats for freedom.

Why is our nation falling behind in the contest? We have been repeatedly warned by committees of distinguished citizens that we must pull ourselves together—or fail. Sometimes the warnings are dramatic enough to create a brief stir in the press and public—but they are quickly and quietly forgotten.

The tragedy is that we are not acting upon our knowledge. It is the all-too familiar tragedy of the failure of will. The most important question we face as a nation is, Why? Why are we failing to do what we should do—to survive?

I will not pretend that I can give a full answer in this short speech, tonight. But I would call your attention to what I think may be our fundamental trouble: We lack a coherent and purposeful national strategy to win the cold war. There is no grand plan that sets forth in simple terms what we have to do to survive, and why.

Witness the shotgun approach to weapons problems—doing a little of everything, backing and filling on critical new projects—with no basic plan to guide our effort. Witness the stopgap handling of foreign aid—year after year adopting the familiar program—hoping because it worked once it will work again. Witness the sporadic response to each new crisis—ad hoc committees here, pro tem bureaus there—but no overall plan for a sustained response.

The fact is that few Americans have any idea of what our duty is. It has not been articulated clearly and boldly. Our people are never shown the whole package of effort that is required; their enthusiasms are not aroused nor are their powers engaged.

We could learn from British experience in the nineteenth century. Then every man understood the importance to England of free trade, of freedom of the seas, of a strong navy, and of an able civil service to operate the vast empire. Most young men trained from childhood to contribute to the purposes England had to fulfill. As a result, the British people sustained a prodigious national effort.

We could also learn from our experience in the two World Wars. Then the nation knew what it was trying to do, what was demanded of it, and why. This made possible the marvelous unity, energy, and vitality displayed by free men in time of war.

The nub of the matter is this: Faced with a deadly challenge, a democracy must have a strategy to meet it—a strategy which is the supreme organizer of our strength. Lacking it, our efforts are like Humpty Dumpty after the fall. The wonder is whether all the king's horses and all the king's men can ever put us together again.

Our needs in this respect can be briefly summarized:

First, we must understand that the cold war is a war, the outcome of which will be victory or defeat for the free way of life.

Second, we must understand that we are making our big investment in defense in order to buy time to carry out a positive program for creating a peaceful world. Our real job is to win the cold war.

Third, we must define our short- and long-run goals in meaningful terms. What is the road to the success we seek, and what obstacles stand in the way?

Fourth, we must plan a national policy to move toward our

goals, including a master program of requirements and priorities.

Fifth, we must develop the military, political, economic, scientific, and related capabilities required for success; and

Sixth, we must use these capabilities skillfully and stubbornly until the foundations of a peaceful world order have been securely established.

To do these things would be to forge a national strategy for the cold war and to wield our power as a mighty sword in the cause of freedom. I believe the effort to develop such a strategy, and the public discussion accompanying the effort, would do much to create the unity of purpose and the national will needed for success.

How can we get such a grand strategic plan? Of course, leadership is vitally important. There is no wholly adequate substitute for it. The American people, furthermore, have shown time and again that they will respond to dynamic, vigorous, plainspoken, inspired leadership.

But we cannot afford, and should not try, to rely wholly on leadership. We must also improve our methods for developing an adequate national strategy and for winning public support for it. I believe that both Congress and the executive branch should now give intensive study to the organization of the federal government for survival in the contest with world communism, including the procedures of the National Security Council.

We should tackle this central issue of our time: How can a free society so organize its human and material resources as to outperform totalitarianism? Obviously, all study of this issue should be conducted in a nonpartisan manner. We are interested not in destructive criticism but in constructive reform.

Let me say that with the experience of your own membership in civil affairs and military government, you can be very helpful in such a review. Of all people, you know how good organization helps the performance of a vital public function, and how poor organization hurts.

Our national policy-making machinery has not been sub-

jected to careful examination since it was created by act of
Congress in 1947. It is time to study it in the light of our
experience during these twelve crisis-laden years. At times it
seems to have functioned rather well. At other times, it seems
to have functioned poorly. In any event, it has failed to produce the kind of national strategy our world position now
requires. It should be possible to find out why.

In theory, the machinery of the National Security Council
should do the job. The Planning Board plans and proposes
new policies and programs. In its preparatory work, the various departments and agencies are consulted and make known
their views. The agreed conclusions of the Planning Board are
submitted to the NSC, which serves in an advisory capacity to
the President. The President decides. The policies and programs are then carried out under the watchful eye of the
Operations Coordinating Board. The President presumably
has a clear and consistent policy to present to the Congress
and to the American people. The procedure seems as sound
as the dollar—but then the dollar is also a bit inflated these
days.

There are a few simple questions we should ask: What is the
present structure for formulating and implementing national
policy? What is it supposed to accomplish? Is it doing it? In
what areas are there grave shortcomings? Why is this the case?
What improvements should be made?

There is one operating concept that especially needs review
—that is the concept of "completed staff work." According to
this concept, the Planning Board has done its job well when
its proposals are accepted without change by the NSC and the
President.

I have serious doubts about the merit of this approach to
policy-making. It seems to me that the important decisions are
always difficult decisions, involving a choice between several
possible courses of action, each of which has advantages and
disadvantages.

I wonder to what extent the Planning Board fully analyzes
the advantages and disadvantages of alternative courses of
action and presents this analysis to the NSC. How often are

the NSC and the President confronted with sharply defined issues so that they are compelled to make, as they should, the hard choices?

For example, did the NSC ever fully consider the impact on American prestige of permitting the Russians to register scientific firsts in the intercontinental ballistic missile and in orbiting a satellite? Has the NSC debated the alternative ways this nation could support and finance an increased defense program? Has the NSC debated whether or not to make it a goal of national policy to increase the rate of growth of our gross national product from 2 or 3 percent to 5 or 6 percent a year? Has the NSC discussed whether or not we should allocate a rising proportion of our total output to public purposes, domestic and foreign?

These represent some of the tough but crucial issues which the NSC and the President must resolve. I am convinced that meaningful and firm decisions cannot evolve without vigorous discussion of alternative courses of action.

You may not find it surprising that a Senator should take this point of view. Seriously, however, one of the great merits of the Senate as a legislative body is that issues are debated —and clarified in the process. I do not suggest that the NSC should resolve its will by a vote. But I do suggest that the President is more likely to make meaningful decisions, which can be translated into purposeful, hard-hitting action, after vigorous debate rather than without it.

There is some reason to believe that the proposals prepared by the Planning Board are written in such generalities that they may mean one thing to one department and quite another thing to another department. The effort to reach agreement at too low a level—that is, at the Planning Board level—may mean that agreement is purchased at the price of clarity.

This is but one of many questions that require study. Where one will come out is, of course, not yet foreseeable. Perhaps we will be agreeably surprised. But it is my strong belief that careful, sustained study will bring forward helpful suggestions to improve our processes for the making and implementation of an integrated national policy.

One hundred seventy million Americans are committed to the ideals of democracy, individual liberty, justice, and free institutions. But devotion to principle alone will not see us through. One hundred seventy million Americans must also be dedicated to the means for preserving these ideals. We have proved that we can meet the urgent demands of a hot war. Now we must prove that we can sustain the grueling, tedious, continuing tasks of the cold war.

This type of conflict is a wholly new experience for the American people. The Soviet objective is the same as in a hot war—to defeat us. But Moscow relies on limited actions, indirect threats, and diffuse challenges, hoping not to arouse us to action. It is far more difficult for a free society to generate the effort for this kind of conflict than for the dramatic clashes of a hot war. The Soviets know this—and are counting on it. It is all the more essential, therefore, that we have an understandable plan for victory. Clearly our people cannot be dedicated to vague programs or respond enthusiastically to a host of conflicting demands. We must know where we are going and how we are going to get there. We must have a grand strategy for survival.

In closing, let me say simply this: With such a strategy I believe freedom can prevail. The earth today is an arena of clashing systems of order. But the idea of freedom is by all odds the most potent idea in history. And free men have the mental and material resources to build a world community which makes room for all peoples who wish to live in peace.

Granted, the unrelenting encounter with the Kremlin tests our ability to the limit. Surely, this is a worthy test of our national quality. A better and a stronger America can emerge from this struggle.

I believe America can and will meet the challenge.

5

Policy-making at the Presidential Level

National War College, Washington, D.C.

8 May 1961

Authorized by resolution of the Senate in July 1959, the Jackson-chaired inquiry by the Subcommittee on National Policy Machinery was the first full-scale review of the national security policy process since the discussion and debate preceding the creation of the National Security Council by act of Congress in 1947. Its public hearings extended over two years. Between January 1960 and October 1961 a series of staff reports was issued with detailed analyses and practical suggestions for improvement.

Campaigning for John F. Kennedy in 1960 as the Democratic party's national chairman, Senator Jackson drew extensively on the subcommittee's findings. He took special satisfaction that President-elect Kennedy found the subcommittee's 1960 hearings and staff reports helpful. The report entitled *The National Security Council*, issued 12 December 1960, became Kennedy's transition task force study on the NSC—"a useful starting point," as the new President said, "to strengthen and to simplify the operations of the National Security Council." [14] Shortly after his inauguration Kennedy followed a key Jackson suggestion to dispense with the overinstitutionalized, over-elaborate Operations Coordinating Board and to emphasize the authority of individual Cabinet officers to act, to monitor, and to be held responsible.

But the Senator was not through with the inquiry. It was his hope to influence not only official circles in Washington, D.C., but also potential future leaders in training at university and college centers. The Senator's speech to the National War College in May 1961 is representative of that hope.

A LITTLE OVER TWO YEARS AGO ON APRIL 16, 1959, I SPOKE to this college of the perils of the cold war—a war to determine what kind of world system is to be created on this planet, a Communist world system or a world system where free institutions can survive and flourish. The burden of my talk was that this country was poorly organized to develop and carry out a strategy for victory in the cold war. I noted the vast executive branch and the elaborate policy mechanisms, the Cabinet, the National Security Council, the Joint Chiefs of Staff, the hundreds of advisory boards, steering groups, and interdepartmental committees. Yet, I said, this modern hydra, with nine times nine heads, fails to produce the basic strategic policies and the decisive action that we need. I concluded my address by stating that I would seek the consent of the Senate to make a full dress review of our national security policy organization.

Shortly after that speech the Senate Subcommittee on National Policy Machinery was constituted. Our study has been conducted throughout on a scholarly and nonpartisan basis. We have sought to determine whether the policy-making machinery at the highest levels of our government is adequate to identify, plan, and coordinate the critical policies of national survival. The National Security Act of 1947 and the National Security Council have therefore been a central subject of our study.

We have sought the counsel and taken extensive testimony from the most eminent students and participants in the policy process—from such men as Robert A. Lovett, Christian A. Herter, W. Averell Harriman, Admiral Arthur W. Radford, General Maxwell D. Taylor, George F. Kennan, Paul H. Nitze, Robert Bowie, and Governor Nelson A. Rockefeller. Over the last months, findings of our study—in the form of staff reports —have been made available to the public, to Congress, and to the new administration. Our subcommittee is planning to complete its work in the next few months with some additional reports and such final hearings as may be appropriate. We are going to take seriously Mr. Harriman's advice that what this government needs is a "committee-killing" outfit, but in this case the lethal blow will be self-administered.

Passage of the National Security Act of 1947 was a memorable occasion; perhaps its most important section was the Declaration of Policy. In the declaration, Congress said: "In enacting this legislation, it is the intent of Congress to provide a comprehensive program for the future security of the United States." By this action Congress expressed its expectation that the Chief Executive and Commander in Chief would henceforth, to the best of his ability, use all the elements of national power and influence in a unified way to promote the nation's interests and assure its safety.

In this respect, there is an analogy between the National Security Act and the Employment Act of 1946. The Employment Act is probably less important for the machinery it created than for imposing on the President a responsibility to use his many powers to maintain high and stable levels of employment and income. Both laws have greatly influenced the President's conception of his duties and the standards by which Congress and the public judge his performance.

The National Security Council, created by the statute of 1947, is charged with advising the President "with respect to the integration of domestic, foreign, and military policies relating to the national security." The Council brings together as statutory members the President, the Vice President, the Secretaries of State and Defense, the Director of the Office of Civil and Defense Mobilization, and as statutory advisers the Director of Central Intelligence and the Chairman of the Joint Chiefs of Staff. The JCS are the principal military advisers to the Council. The President can also ask other key aides to take part in Council deliberations. The Secretary of the Treasury, for example, has attended regularly by Presidential invitation.

Despite its statutory basis, each President has great freedom in deciding how he will use the Council, in determining what policy matters will be handled within the Council framework, and how they will be handled. An important question facing a President, therefore, is how he will employ the Council to suit his own style of decision and action.

The Council has now been an ongoing institution of our government for almost a decade and a half. Much experience in its operations has been amassed; many lessons have been learned.

I would like to share with you this morning some of my own reflections on the proper use—and misuse—of the Council. Seven points impress me as particularly important:

First, the success of the National Security Council depends in the first instance on the quality of its members and the staffs which back them up. The critical national security jobs at the Cabinet and sub-Cabinet levels should be filled with absolutely first-rate people. This was true in the days of [former Secretaries of Defense Henry L.] Stimson, [James V.] Forrestal, and [Robert A.] Lovett. It is as valid today in the cold war.

Throughout our study, we have argued that appointments to these critical jobs call for special considerations. The kind of people required is in very short supply. They should not only have brains and executive ability. They should also have a feel for how business is done in the government and an understanding of the problems of national security affairs. Only a few possess this sought-for combination of talents.

We need our ablest people at work on defense and foreign policy. We need the best planners, the best administrators, and the best officers our country can provide. The "help wanted" sign is up for keeps.

Second, there are thousands or tens of thousands of decisions on which a President cannot be consulted in view of the limits of his time. The NSC process, to be of maximum assistance to the President, should help him focus his attention on basic operational and strategic issues. Sidney Souers [the first Executive Secretary of the NSC, from 1947 to 1950] summed up the correct principle in these words: "The sole touchstone for Council business, persistently relied upon, is that only those matters will be considered on which a Presidential decision is required."

Basic issues are not very numerous. For example, one is the kind of military position we need in relation to the Soviet bloc and in terms of relations with our allies. Another closely related issue is the proper balance between our national commitments and our capabilities, with all that this implies in terms of building up our capabilities or reducing our commitments. A third issue is our fundamental approach to the Soviet

Union and satellite states; another is our basic approach to underdeveloped countries; still another involves the group of "dangerous situations" such as Cuba, South Vietnam, Berlin, the Congo, nuclear test ban negotiations, and so forth, where American policy is tested in specific encounters.

If the President gives clear-cut guidance on these heart issues, it becomes easier to make delegations of responsibility. Also, a host of lesser questions can readily be solved without being forced to the President's desk for decision.

Third, whatever the particular item on the NSC agenda, the aim of a Council meeting should be to give a *full*—and I underline *full*—airing of all reasonable policy alternatives. Robert Lovett expressed this principle in his penetrating testimony to our subcommittee:

> The National Security Council process, as originally envisaged— perhaps "dreamed of" is more accurate—contemplated the devotion of whatever number of hours were necessary in order to exhaust a subject and not just exhaust the listeners.
>
> . . . The purpose was to insure that the President was in possession of all the available facts, that he got firsthand a chance to evaluate an alternative course of action disclosed by the dissenting views, and that all implications in either course of action were explored before he was asked to take the heavy responsibility of the final decision.

Of course at any particular meeting the President's decision might be to delay a finding or to request a study or a further report on a developing situation.

Obviously, to encourage frank discussion, Council meetings should be kept small, with staff attendance tightly controlled. Dean Acheson has stated this principle clearly:

> Meetings should be as small as possible. Anyone who needs or permits platoons of aides to accompany him brands himself as incompetent. All parties in interest should be present at the same time, should have their say and hear what is said by all others. They should also hear the decision, which should be in writing or recorded.

Fourth, one must guard against diminishing the effectiveness of the National Security Council through overly institutionalized procedures and complex interdepartmental committee substructures. I personally believe that the activities of the NSC Planning Board and the now defunct Operations Coordinating Board both fell victim to overinstitutionalization.

Witnesses before our subcommittee testified that the fixed Council agenda, the steady stream of "agreed" position papers, the standardized procedures, and the drafting and redrafting sessions (with Webster's dictionary the one indispensable aid of the policymaker) diminished the usefulness of the Council as an advisory body to the President. George Kennan had this to say to our subcommittee:

> The frequent experience that in moments of real urgency it becomes necessary to bypass whole great sections of the regular machinery in order to get something done is simply a proof that this machinery has achieved a degree of unwieldiness which makes it unsuitable as a vehicle for the formulation and execution of the policies of a great government in a precarious world.

Governor Rockefeller appearing before us last summer described his own experience with the Council in this fashion:

> Too much time is spent on position papers that go for a year and everything is frozen for a year. There needs to be much more flexibility with planning in depth, not just on a calendar basis. . . . The agenda is frozen months ahead.

In our staff report of December 1960 we recommended the continuation of something like the Planning Board—though far less formal. Our thought was that such a group could be used not for negotiating "agreed papers" or securing departmental concurrences but for thoroughly staffing out alternative policy lines. Composed of key departmental staff advisers, such a board would be available to criticize and comment on policy initiatives developed by the departments or stimulated by the President. But for most purposes, we felt that ad hoc task groups, built around the key people for a particular problem, would be the best vehicle for preliminary planning. In this way the flow of papers to the Council might be more flexibly adjusted to the needs of the President.

Our December staff report also stated that the case for abolishing the Operations Coordinating Board was strong. Such an interdepartmental committee has inherent limitations as an instrument for assisting and auditing policy execution. In its place, we recommended that responsibility for implementation of policy cutting across departmental lines should, wherever possible, be assigned to a particular department or to a particular action officer, assisted as necessary by an informal interdepartmental group. For his main reliance in performance auditing, however, we suggested that the President should rely heavily on his own personal assistants and on the budgetary process.

The aim must be to substitute real staff work in depth for the ritual of paperwork, clearances, concurrences, and endless committee meetings, which so often do not deserve the name of staff work at all.

Fifth, the way a President staffs himself in the White House and in the National Security Council will greatly influence what he knows, what issues will reach him, or fail to reach him, and what he can do. A President's aides, if they are the right kind, will help greatly in equipping him to ask the right questions, identify weak assumptions and faulty premises, and to take initiatives on his own.

Our staff reports have pointed out that the elimination of the Operations Coordinating Board and less reliance on an interdepartmental Planning Board make it more important than ever that the President surround himself by a number of very skilled and sensitive aides. This means not only personal assistants in the White House but a tough-minded, imaginative, and adroit NSC staff in the Executive Office. No President can afford the luxury of having only one or two channels or sources of advice on an important problem. Men are fallible —even the Council and recommendations of the most distinguished experts are, from time to time, bound to be wrong. So it is part of the job of the President's staff to keep open many channels of advice—not merely in the executive branch but by tapping sources in the Congress and outside the government.

Above all, the President needs a staff with great sales resistance—men who are as skeptical as the proverbial man from Missouri. There is probably no one in the world who is subject

day in and day out to as much superselling as the President—
and his own and the country's fate requires that he reject those
attractive propositions which prove on closer examination to
be unsound.

Sixth, the Secretary of State is crucial to the successful
operation of the Council. In our system of government the Secretary occupies a special position. By protocol he is the ranking
member of the Cabinet. But he is also "first among equals" in a
more important sense. Of the Cabinet officials, only the Secretary of State speaks and acts for the priority of national political policy over lesser considerations and goals. His orientation,
like that of the President's, is essentially political-strategic.

If the NSC is to operate effectively, some official must be
charged with continuing responsibility for presenting the initial synthesis of all the elements that go into the making of a
coherent national strategy. Some official must also be charged
with the main responsibility for raising the hard policy departures and new courses with which the Council would be
concerned. That official should clearly be the Secretary of
State.

I know of only one way the Secretary of State can take over
and keep this job of first adviser to the President. He must
be in fact the President's first helper and show that he is the
official best qualified to advise his chief on foreign policy problems. A Secretary has his own work cut out for him if he is to
earn the role of first adviser. I will mention the obvious:

Perhaps the most important problems of national security
today are joint State-Defense problems, and the Secretary of
State must therefore enter into a full and welcome partnership with his opposite number in the Pentagon—the Secretary
of Defense.

The problems of foreign policy today go far beyond those
of traditional diplomacy, and the Secretary must therefore
staff his department with first-rate people able to deal with the
issues in their full contemporary context.

And finally, a Secretary must guard against being away from
Washington so much that he is not available to advise the President, consult with the Congress, and lead his Department.

Seventh, better management of the interdepartmental and departmental committee system has long been overdue. In line with Averell Harriman's committee-killing proposal, not only the OCB but fifty-nine additional formal interdepartmental committees have recently been extinguished. In most cases the work of the committees, to the extent it is to be continued, is being assigned to specific Cabinet-level officers.

Of course many interdepartmental committees are necessary. The problem is to reap their virtues without the vices. In this connection our staff reports have recommended administrative reforms which were favorably commented upon by many witnesses before our subcommittee.

For example, we proposed that in most cases the Department of State should chair interdepartmental task groups and committees working on problems with a heavy foreign policy component. If jurisdiction is more or less evenly divided with other departments, we felt doubts should generally be resolved in favor of State.

We also proposed that committee chairmen should be given more responsibility for decision and action. Members of committees should serve in an advisory capacity to the chairman, who should take responsibility for making the final conclusions and recommendations at his level. The members ought of course to have full opportunity to present their point of view. They should be free also, if they so desire, to file dissenting comment or appeal the chairman's recommendations to higher authority.

Let me add one other point. I have become increasingly concerned about the problem of relating long-term requirements of national security to the budgetary process, and am confident that this is a matter on which certain reforms of the policy process could make an important contribution to national security.

Although the long-term nature of the contest with communism is now generally recognized, we have barely begun to face the problem of formulating strategy for the long haul, of assessing the resources required for carrying out the strategy, and of planning to meet these requirements. Intelligent planning should, of course, provide flexibility, for in many areas—notably the conduct of foreign relations—it is seldom possible to plan far ahead. At the same time, in many other areas where long lead times are involved, such as defense and foreign aid, forward planning is inescapable.

In the form in which it has long been prepared and submitted to Congress, the budget provides little insight into (a) the long-term requirements of national security and (b) the resources which will be available to meet these requirements. As a result neither Congress nor the public are helped to see present demands in the context of overall strategy and policies, and in the perspective of our steadily growing capabilities. They do not have a good basis for evaluating the wisdom of budgetary requests and related domestic policies, such as policies to promote economic growth.

What is of major importance is the development of processes within the executive branch itself which will force the departments and agencies to think ahead in strategic terms, to estimate what resources will be needed to support the strategy, and to plan to meet these requirements.

Of all the action-forcing processes, the budgetary process is surely the most important. For example, we suggested in our staff reports that a President should seek the counsel of the Secretaries of State and Defense at the target-setting stage in the annual budgetary cycle—before the initial overall budgetary ceiling is established. Assuming this consultation is more than pro forma, the two Secretaries are thereby forced to develop and staff out their best judgments about the long-run scope and nature of emerging problems and the shape and size of programs required to meet them.

Also, it may be necessary to draw the Council of Economic Advisers into a more active role in the policy process. Its projections of economic growth and policy recommendations for encouraging growth would be central to the determination of future resources availability.

The staff of the subcommittee has been at work on this subject for some time and plans to give it special attention in the next few months.

In conclusion, let me say this:

Today, the President of the United States bears the most solemn responsibilities. So much depends on one man. His is the main burden of leadership in providing for the common defense and advancing individual liberty. He must finally weigh all the factors—domestic, foreign, military—which affect our position in the world and by which we seek to influence the world environment. He cannot delegate the great decisions to any council or committee. The responsibility is his and his alone.

The new tempo and scope of the cold war make the proper exercise of this responsibility more difficult than ever before in our history. It is all the more important, therefore, that the organization and staffing at the higher levels of government give the President maximum support.

The aim must be a national policy process that brings basic issues to the level of Presidential decision—in time; that sharpens differences of view on available alternatives and reflects a weighing of all relevant factors; that exposes the President's own judgments to constructive criticism; and that facilitates rapid and thorough reexamination of past advice in light of changed circumstance.

The pursuit of excellence in policy-making is a job that never ends. The price of excellence is tenacity and vigilance—vigilance by the Chief Executive, vigilance by the Congress, and vigilance by the press and the public.

6

Organizing for National Security

Chairman's Statement Concluding Inquiry
of the United States Senate Subcommittee
on National Policy Machinery, Washington, D.C.
15 November 1961

Many congressional inquiries gain public notice without having much practical effect. Not so with this Jackson study. Among the trends in administrative philosophy that it influenced, two particularly stand out: support of the Secretary of State's right and responsibility to be the President's principal adviser on national security affairs, and recognition that the criterion for appointment to a top national security post should be ability to do the job, regardless of party.

Actual reforms in government operations sparked by the Jackson inquiry included a simplification of the operations of the National Security Council and elimination of many interdepartmental coordinating committees; devolution to individual department heads and to identified subordinates of the responsibility for overseeing the execution of decisions; improved coordination between the State and Defense Departments, including the successful State-Defense officer exchange program; the deliberate use of the Budget Bureau as a prime management tool of the President; and reduction of the rate of turnover of ranking executive officers by adopting the practice that candidates for national security posts give advance assurances that they intend to serve at the pleasure of the President and their department chiefs.

To conclude his first Jackson subcommittee inquiry in November 1961, the Senator decided to make a brief, clear statement of the principal findings to gain them further attention. Over the years he returned many times to the themes formulated in this concluding statement, most frequently perhaps to the need for excellence in government—in the executive branch and in the Congress, too.

FREE MEN ARE LOCKED IN A STRUGGLE BEING WAGED ON THE earth's continents, in the depths of its seas, and in the reaches of space. Our Communist foes acknowledge no bounds except those imposed on them by expediency. They draw twenty-year plans portraying a Communist utopia in 1981—while they build walls around their unwilling subjects in 1961. In their pursuit of power, they debase language itself. "Democracy," in their lexicon, becomes the rule of the few over the many. "Peace" becomes the surrender of free men to Communist domination.

The question is this: Can free societies outplan, outperform, outlast—and if need be, outsacrifice—totalitarian systems? Can we recognize fresh problems in a changing world —and respond in time with new plans for meeting them?

The requirements of national security press ever more strongly on our resources. Can we establish a proper scale of priorities which separates the necessary from the not really essential?

Program choice grows ever harder. Can we establish the right mix of military and economic aid? How are we to choose between competing multibillion dollar weapon systems?

Presidential control over foreign policy and defense programs becomes more difficult. How may the globe-girdling programs of the national security departments and agencies be harnessed on behalf of the Presidential purpose? How can we assure their efficient execution?

Standards of performance adequate for quieter times will no longer do. The Presidency and State and Defense and the rest of our government must now meet new tests of excellence.

First, we need a clearer understanding of where our vital national interests lie and what we must do to promote them. Faulty machinery is rarely the real culprit when our policies are inconsistent or when they lack sustained forward momentum. The underlying cause is normally found elsewhere. It consists in the absence of a clear sense of direction and coherence of policy at the top of the government.

Unless our top officials are in basic agreement about what is paramount for the national interest—what comes first and what comes second—there is bound to be drift and confusion below. This has been so under every administration. In our system, two men bear the heaviest responsibility for giving our national security policy focus and structure. One is the President. The other is his first adviser—the Secretary of State. A clear and reasoned formulation of national policy, and its effective communication downward, is the prerequisite of successful delegation and coordination. There is still much to be done in defining our vital interests and developing a basic national policy which supports them.

Second, radical additions to our existing policy machinery are unnecessary and undesirable. Our best hope lies in making our traditional policy machinery work better—not in trading it in for some new model. Plans for novel changes in the policy process include proposals for a so-called first secretary of the government who would stand between the President and his Cabinet chiefs, large planning staffs attached to the White House or the National Security Council, cold war strategy boards, and councils of wise men.

Such proposals have certain weaknesses in common: They try to do at the Presidential level things which can better be done by the departments and agencies; they violate sound administrative practice by tending to interpose officials between the President and his key Cabinet officials; they rest on the mistaken assumption that the weaknesses of one organization can be cured by creating another.

In fact, any proposals for net additions to our present national policy machinery should be greeted with a basic skepticism. This is particularly true of suggestions for new committees. Committee-killing, not creating more committees, remains the important job. Properly managed, and chaired by officials with responsibility for decision and action, committees can be useful in helping make sure that voices that should be heard are heard. But a very high percentage of committees exact a heavy toll by diluting the authority of individual executives, obscuring responsibility for getting things done, and generally slowing decision making.

Third, the heart problem of national security is not reorganization—it is getting our best people into key foreign policy and defense posts. Good national security policy requires both good policymakers and good policy machinery. But organizational changes cannot solve problems which are really not due to organizational weaknesses. More often than not, poor decisions are traceable not to machinery but to people—to their inexperience, their failure to comprehend the full significance of information crossing their desks, their indecisiveness or lack of wisdom.

Fourth, there is serious overstaffing in the national security departments and agencies. The caliber of the national service is impressively high. But like so many large private organizations, our government faces the problem of people engaged in work that does not really need doing. The size of the national security departments and agencies has swelled out of proportion even to the increased number and complexity of our problems.

The payroll costs, although formidable, are less important than the price paid in sluggishness of decision and action. Unnecessary people make for unnecessary layering, unnecessary clearances and concurrences, and unnecessary intrusions on the time of officials working on problems of real importance. Many offices have reached and passed the point where the quantity of staff reduces the quality of the product. Occasional swings of the personnel axe, accompanied by much fanfare, yield more in headlines than in lasting results. The fight against overstaffing must be waged each day anew.

Fifth, the career services should be made better training grounds for posts of national security leadership. Our career services are not producing enough officials with the large executive talents, the breadth of experience, and the width of perspective needed in top foreign policy and defense posts. A program for improvement should give officials of exceptional promise much greater flexibility and latitude in job assignments; it should stress movement of personnel between agencies; it should offer more opportunities for advanced training of the kind made available by our most efficient private corporations.

And above all, we require higher salaries at the top of the civil service and at the sub-Cabinet level. The present pay scales are dropping further and further behind those obtaining in private life—not only in business but increasingly also in the academic world. The inadequate salaries discourage too many able people from entering government service and encourage too many to leave it.

Sixth, we should reduce the needless barriers which stand in the way of private citizens called to national duty. Our system of government uniquely depends upon the contributions of distinguished citizens temporarily in high government posts, who come from and return to private life—the Stimsons, the Forrestals, and the Lovetts.

In time of hot war, we let no obstacle stand in the way of getting our ablest people to work in the government. But in this cold war, whose outcome will be equally fateful for the nation, we tolerate pointless impediments to public service.

The present conflict-of-interest laws are a prime example. We will always need regulations to deter or penalize the rare official who tries to use his public office for private gain. But the laws now on the books are archaic—most go back to the Civil War. They are more responsive to the problems of the 1860s than the 1960s and they often make it unduly hard for outstanding people to accept government posts. The job of updating these laws should be completed.

Seventh, used properly, the National Security Council can be of great value as an advisory body to the President. The true worth of the Council lies in being an accustomed place where the President can join with his chief advisers in searching examination and debate of the "great choices" of national security policy. These may be long-term strategic alternatives or crisis problems demanding immediate action. The Council provides a means of bringing the full implications of policy alternatives out on the table, and a vehicle through which the President can inform his lieutenants of his decisions and the chain of reasoning behind them.

The pitfalls to be avoided are clearly marked: At one extreme, overinstitutionalization of the NSC system—with overly elaborate procedures and the overproduction of routine papers. At the other extreme, excessive informality—with Council meetings tending in the direction of official bull sessions.

Eighth, no task is more urgent than improving the effectiveness of the Department of State. In our system, there can be no satisfactory substitute for a Secretary of State willing and able to exercise his leadership across the full range of national security matters, as they relate to foreign policy. The Secretary, assisted by his Department, must bear the chief responsibility for bringing new policy initiatives to the President's desk and for overseeing and coordinating our manifold foreign policy activities on the President's behalf.

State is not doing enough in asserting its leadership across the whole front of foreign policy. Neither is it doing enough in staffing itself for such leadership. State needs more respect for comprehensive forward planning. The Department as a whole attaches too little importance to looking ahead in foreign policy and is too wedded to a philosophy of reacting to problems as they arise. The Policy Planning Council is not now in the mainstream of policy-making.

State needs more officials who are good executive managers and who are broadly experienced in dealing with the full range of national security problems which now engage the Department. The administration of foreign policy has become "big business." This places a high premium on the ability to manage large-scale enterprises—to make decisions promptly and decisively, to delegate, and to monitor. This need for "take charge" men is particularly urgent down through the Assistant Secretary level and at our large missions abroad. Round pegs in square holes are a luxury we cannot afford.

Ninth, we need a stronger, not a weaker, Bureau of the Budget. Rich as we are, we cannot do all the things we would like to do to assure the national safety and provide for the general welfare. The job of the President is to rank the competing claims on our resources in terms of their national importance —to distinguish between what cannot wait and what can wait.

The budgetary process is the President's most helpful tool in establishing such an order of national priorities and in seeing to it that the operating programs of the departments and agencies conform to these priorities. In this task, the President needs the help of a Bureau of the Budget staffed still more strongly than it now is with officials who can interpret agency programs in terms of their contributions to the President's overall goals.

The danger is always present that Bureau members will become champions of their own, rather than the President's, program preferences. A strong Bureau requires strong Presidential control.

Tenth, the Congress should put its own house in better order. There is clearly much room for improvement on Capitol Hill. One major problem is fragmentation. The Congress is hard put to deal with national security policy as a whole. The difficulty starts with the executive branch. Except in the State of the Union and the budget messages, it presents national security information and program requests to the Congress in bits and pieces.

The present mode of operation of the congressional system compounds the problem. The authorization process treats as separable matters which are not really separable. Foreign affairs, defense matters, space policies, and atomic energy programs are handled in different committees. It is the same with money matters. Income and outgo, and the relation of each to the economy, come under different jurisdictions. There is no place in the Congress, short of the floors of the Senate and the House, where the requirements of national security and the resources needed on their behalf are considered in their totality.

The need is to give the Congress, early in each session, better opportunities to review our national security programs as a whole. For its part, the executive branch can take the initiative by presenting our national security requirements "as a package," with dollar signs attached. To put these requirements in better perspective, the Secretaries of State and Defense and other ranking officials could make themselves available for joint appearances on the Hill.

The Congress should move in parallel. At the beginning of each session, it can encourage its authorizing committees to meet jointly to take testimony on the full scope and broad thrust of our national security programs. A closer partnership can be urged upon the revenue and expenditure committees.

And parent committees can undertake to secure more comprehensive briefings on programs before dividing them up among the subcommittees for detailed analysis.

One last point: Too many people believe that the cards are stacked in favor of totalitarian systems in the cold war. Nothing could be more wrong. Democracies headline their difficulties and mistakes; dictatorships hide theirs. The archives of Nazi Germany told a story of indecision and ineptitude in policy-making on a scale never approached by our own Nation. The words spoken by Robert Lovett in 1960 are the right words:

> While the challenges of the moment are most serious in a policy-making sense, I see no reason for black despair or for defeatist doubts as to what our system of government or this country can do. We can do whatever we have to do in order to survive and to meet any form of economic or political competition we are likely to face. All this we can do with one proviso: we must be willing to do our best.

III
The Atlantic Alliance
and the United Nations

7
The U.S. in the UN:
An Independent Audit

National Press Club, Washington, D.C.
20 March 1962

Convinced that the chances for a safe future depended heavily on a strong, economically sound, and confident Atlantic community, Senator Jackson had gradually become the Senate watchdog for the Atlantic alliance. In this capacity, he was unhappy with a precedent set by President Eisenhower and continued by President Kennedy for the Ambassador to the United Nations to serve in the President's Cabinet and so have a greater part in the policy-making process than, for example, our Ambassador to NATO. Under these conditions, the effect of decisions on our relations in the UN or on so-called world opinion might receive more weight in U.S. policy-making than their effect on the strength and unity of the Atlantic community. In any case, the Senator did not want to see our Ambassador to the UN become a kind of second Secretary of State, impinging on the "first adviser" role of the Secretary of State.

These concerns led the Senator to take a hard look at U.S. relations with the UN generally and at the U.S. delegation to the UN (then headed by Ambassador Adlai Stevenson) in particular. The result was a decision to go before the National Press Club for a major speech on the UN. At the time Congress was considering whether or not to approve buying UN bonds to help finance two UN peacekeeping operations, so the subject of the UN was on the current national agenda.

The Senator's speech proved something of a sensation—headlined and commented on across the nation and in Europe, welcomed in official circles around President Kennedy, and criticized in circles around Ambassador Stevenson. The Senator was satisfied that he had encouraged a more realistic and safer U.S. approach to the United Nations.

THE PLACE OF THE UNITED NATIONS IN AMERICAN FOREIGN policy is now receiving a good deal of attention. Unfortunately, the debate seems to be polarized around extreme positions. On the one hand, there are those who say, "The UN is the only source of hope; let's leave everything to the UN." On the other hand, there are those who say, "The UN is the source of catastrophe; let's get out of the UN." Each view is like the distorted reflection in a carnival mirror—one too broad, the other too narrow. Neither view is really helpful.

No doubt the quiet, steadying majority of the American people have a more balanced view of the United Nations, and see it for what it is: an aspiration and a hope, the closest approximation we have to a code of international good conduct, and a useful forum of diplomacy for some purposes.

The United Nations is, and should continue to be, an important avenue of American foreign policy. Yet practices have developed which, I believe, lead to an undue influence of UN considerations in our national decision-making. Indeed it is necessary to ask whether the involvement of the UN in our policy-making has not at times hampered the wise definition of our national interests and the development of sound policies for their advancement.

The test of the national security policy process is this: Does it identify our vital interests and does it develop foreign and defense policies which will defend and promote these interests? In our system, two men must bear the heaviest responsibility for giving our national security policy focus and structure. One is, of course, the President. The other is his first adviser, the Secretary of State.

The United Nations is not, and was never intended to be, a substitute for our own leaders as makers and movers of American policy. The shoulders of the Secretary General were never expected to carry the burdens of the President or the Secretary of State. But do we sometimes act as though we could somehow subcontract to the UN the responsibility for national decision-making?

At the founding of the United Nations there was the hope that all its members shared a common purpose—the search for a lasting peace. This hope was dashed.

The Soviet Union was not and is not a peace-loving nation.

Khrushchev has announced his support for "wars of liberation." He has threatened to "bury" us. In their more agreeable moments the Russians promise to bury us nicely, but whatever their mood, the earth would still be six feet deep above us. We must realize that the Soviet Union sees the UN not as a forum of cooperation but as one more arena of struggle.

The maintenance of peace depends not on the United Nations as an organization but on the strength and will of its members to uphold the charter. The truth is, though we have not often spoken it in recent years, that the best hope for peace with justice does not lie in the United Nations. Indeed, the truth is almost exactly the reverse. The best hope for the United Nations lies in the maintenance of peace. In our deeply divided world, peace depends on the power and unity of the Atlantic community and on the skill of our direct diplomacy. In this light, some basic questions need to be asked:

First, are we taking an exaggerated view of the UN's role? In one way and another the conduct of UN affairs absorbs a disproportionate amount of the energy of our highest officials. The President and the Secretary of State must ration their worry time—and the hours spent on the UN cannot be spent on other matters. All too often, furthermore, the energies devoted to the UN must be spent on defensive actions—trying to defeat this or that ill-advised resolution—rather than on more constructive programs.

The Secretary of State has called the United Nations "a forum in which almost every aspect of our foreign policy comes up." The fact is correctly stated, but does it reflect a desirable state of affairs? Should we take a more restricted view of the organization's capacity for helpfulness?

I think we should. The cold war may destroy the United Nations, if that organization becomes one of its main battlegrounds, but the United Nations cannot put an end to the cold war. As a general rule, might it be more prudent, though less dramatic, not to push the UN into the fireman's suit unless we are sure the alternatives are worse and, above all, that we are not seeking to evade our own responsibilities?

I believe the United Nations can best gain stature and respect by undertaking tasks which are within its capabilities, and that its usefulness will be diminished if it is impelled into one cold war crisis after another and asked to shoulder responsibilities it cannot meet.

With these thoughts in mind, I read with some concern proposals to increase the "executive responsibilities" of the organization. Also, I have serious doubts about current suggestions to provide "more pervasive and efficient 'UN presences'" to help "halt infiltration of guerrillas across frontiers; and to help halt internal subversion instigated by a foreign power." Dag Hammarskjöld, who was a brilliant and devoted servant of the United Nations, clearly saw the dangers in overrating the peacekeeping power of the organization. In a letter to a private citizen, he once decried the tendency to force the Secretary General into a key role in great power disputes "through sheer escapism from those who should carry the responsibility."

Second, may not the most useful function of the United Nations lie in serving as a link between the West and the newly independent states? Most international business is best handled through normal bilateral contacts or through regional arrangements among the states concerned. However, the United Nations provides a useful meeting ground for many new governments with other governments. These relationships may be of mutual benefit.

The UN affords good opportunities to explain Western policies, to correct misrepresentations of the Western position, and to expose the weaknesses in the Soviet line. In fact, the Soviet singing commercials themselves offend the most hardened ear. They inspire a healthy skepticism about Russian three-way cold war pills—guaranteed to end the arms race, relieve colonial oppression, and ease poverty, if taken regularly, as directed.

The UN and its specialized agencies may be of great usefulness in supplying technical assistance for economic development, in providing financial aid, and in preparing international development programs.

The organization may sometimes be helpful in reaching peaceful settlements of certain issues and disputes of concern to the newly independent states, especially if it is used to seek out areas of agreement rather than to dramatize conflicts of interest.

In this connection there has been too great a tendency to bring every issue to a vote. Indeed, there are too many votes on too many issues in the UN, and too much of the time and energy of every delegation is spent in lobbying for votes. A vote requires a division of the house, a sharpening and even an exaggeration of points at issue, and it emphasizes the division of opinion rather than the area of agreement. Not every discussion needs to end in a vote. The purposes of the members might be better served if the UN forum becomes more often a place where diplomatic representatives quietly search for acceptable settlements of issues between their countries. Voting has a way of raising the temperature of any body, and I think that we should be doing what we can to keep the temperature of the United Nations near normal.

Third, in our approach to the UN, do we make too much of the talk and too little of the deed? New York City is the foremost communications center of the United States, if not of the world. Once the decision was made to locate the headquarters of the United Nations in New York, it was inevitable that what went on there would receive attention disproportionate to its significance. Newsmen and photographers have to produce news stories and pictures, and politicians from any land rival the celebrities of stage and screen in their hunger for free publicity.

The United States is of course host to the United Nations. Day in and day out we are conscious of the presence of the organization in our midst. And the role of host entails special obligations. Consequently, it is often difficult to keep one's sense of proportion. There is, for example, a tendency, to which the press itself is not immune, to believe the UN makes more history than it really does.

A Secretary of State—responsible for policy—must weigh his words carefully. For that reason he seldom makes good copy. One of the reasons for the extensive coverage of the United Nations is that the right to the floor of the General Assembly is not subject to the sobering influence of responsibility for action.

I have been struck, for example, by the serious disproportion in the press, radio, and television coverage of our UN delegation and the coverage of the Department of State. The space and time devoted to the former does not correctly reflect the relative importance of what is said in New York against what is said in Washington.

If the UN were used less for drumbeating on every nerve-tingling issue, and if its energies were quietly devoted to manageable problems, there might be fewer headlines from the UN but more contributions to the building of a peaceful world.

Everyone talks too much. It is a worldwide disease. Sometimes it seems that the appropriate legend to place above the portals of the UN might be: "Through these doors pass the most articulate men and women in the world."

Fourth, should our delegation to the United Nations play a larger role in the policy-making process than our representatives to NATO or to major world capitals? I think the answer is no, and the burden of proof should lie with those who advocate a unique role for our embassy in New York.

Our delegation to the United Nations is, of course, frequently and necessarily involved in promoting or opposing particular actions by the United Nations which may have an important bearing on our national security policies. If it is not to commit the United States to positions inconsistent with our national security requirements, the delegation must be kept in closest touch with and have a thorough understanding of these requirements. Furthermore, the President and Secretary of State require information and advice from our UN delegation.

This is not to say, however, that the requirements of sound national policy can be more clearly seen in New York than elsewhere, or that our embassy in New York should play a different role in policy-making from that played by other important embassies.

The precedent set by President Eisenhower in this matter and continued by this administration seems unfortunate. The Ambassador to the United Nations is not a second Secretary of

State, but the present arrangement suggests a certain imbalance in the role assigned to the UN delegation in the policy-making process. The problem is not to give the UN delegation a larger voice in policy-making but to give it the tools to help carry out the policy.

Rational, effective negotiation on complex and critical matters, like the reduction and control of armaments, requires unified guidance and instruction to those conducting the negotiations. This is a basic principle of sound administration and avoids the dangers of freewheeling. The unified source of instructions should be the Secretary of State, acting for the President, or the President himself—not others in the White House or the Executive Office, not lower levels in State, certainly not the UN delegation itself.

The UN delegation in New York should not operate as a second foreign office. Such confusion of responsibility reinforces a tendency to give undue weight in national policy formulation to considerations that seem more important in New York than they ought to seem in Washington, D.C. The effect of decisions on something called "our relations in the UN" may receive more weight than their effect on, say, the strength and unity of the Atlantic community. The result may be a weakening or dilution of policy positions in deference to what is represented in New York as world opinion.

The concept of world opinion has been, I fear, much abused. Whatever it is and whatever the importance that should be attached to it, I doubt that it can be measured by taking the temperature of the General Assembly or successfully cultivated primarily by currying favor in New York. To hide behind something called "world opinion" is all too often the device of the timid or the last resort of someone who has run out of arguments.

Fifth, is our UN delegation properly manned for the diplomatic and technical tasks we require of it? We have established the tradition of choosing for top UN posts Americans of considerable prestige—prestige acquired, furthermore, not in the practice of diplomacy but in national politics, business, the arts and sciences, and other fields of endeavor. For the most part, these people have served us well, in effective advocacy of America's concerns and in persuasive championship of progress toward a world of good neighbors.

A start has been made in staffing the UN mission more as other embassies, with experienced diplomats and experts in technical fields in which the United Nations may be able to make quiet but useful contributions. Further progress in this direction should be encouraged.

The sum of the matter is this: We need to take another look at our role in the United Nations, remembering that the UN is not a substitute for national policies wisely conceived to uphold our vital interests. We need to rethink the organization and staffing of our government for United Nations affairs. For this purpose, we should have a top-level review conducted under the authority of the President and the Secretary of State. The review should, of course, be handled in a nonpartisan manner.

Debate over the United Nations is now centered on the UN bond issue. This debate reveals some of the symptoms of the basic disturbance. Congress has been requested to approve the purchase of UN bonds up to a total of 100 million dollars to help cover the cost of two controversial peacekeeping operations. The money in question has been spent and it would be a serious mistake to prolong the financial crisis. I trust the Congress can help find a wise way to help cover the deficit.

But the fundamental questions will still remain and will plague us until they are answered: Do our present relations with the United Nations assist the wise definition of our vital interests and the establishment of sound policies? Are we sometimes deferring to the United Nations in the hope that we may somehow escape the inescapable dilemmas of leadership? Are we failing to make the most of the United Nations by encouraging it to attempt too much?

Mr. Chairman, I close as I began: The United Nations is and should continue to be an important avenue of American foreign policy. But we need to revise our attitudes in the direction of a more realistic appreciation of its limitations, more modest hopes for its accomplishments, and a more mature sense of the burdens of responsible leadership.

8
Perspective on the Atlantic Alliance

Fifth International Conference Cosponsored
by the Foundation for Foreign Affairs, Inc., of Chicago
and the Studien Gesellschaft für Fragen Mittel- und
Österreichischer Partnerschaft of Wiesbaden,
Chicago, Illinois
23 March 1968

Wanting to be sure that America continued to meet its responsibilities
in NATO, Senator Jackson gained Senate authorization for a 1965
Senate study of the alliance. (By then he was chairman of the Senate Government Operations Subcommittee on National Security and
International Operations.) This two-year inquiry was the first general review of NATO to be undertaken in the Senate since the North
Atlantic Treaty was ratified in 1949 and American troops were assigned to Europe in 1951.
The subcommittee's reports and hearings reached a wide audience
both in and outside government. Of special note, the report *Basic
Issues*, completed just before President de Gaulle withdrew French
forces from NATO and ended other key forms of French cooperation with its allies in February 1966, was welcomed by the executive
branch in Washington and by many of our embassies abroad as a
principal aid in interpreting the NATO crisis and in dealing with
it.[15] This study was a rich mine of analyses and themes for a Senator convinced of the need to preserve the cohesive stabilizing effect
of the alliance on world events. Jackson went before audience after
audience to interpret developments in the Atlantic area and to highlight the unfinished alliance tasks of mutual defense and of winning
eventual Soviet acceptance of a genuine European settlement. His
1968 address to the Fifth International Conference cosponsored by
the Foundation for Foreign Affairs, Inc., of Chicago and the Studien
Gesellschaft für Fragen Mittel- und Österreichischer Partnerschaft
of Wiesbaden, is an example.

IT IS A PECULIARITY OF TODAY'S WORLD THAT FEW ISSUES
are peculiarly national. By its very composition this conference
symbolizes the intertwined nature of European-American con-

cerns, and this meeting is but one of the countless encounters between Europeans and Americans that are taking place every twenty-four hours, year in, year out.

In Western Europe several hundred thousand young men, wearing a variety of uniforms, are rubbing shoulders daily in the joint undertaking by which the Atlantic alliance has helped assure the stability and security of its members for twenty years. Today as every day the Atlantic Ocean is filled with ships carrying the vast and growing commerce between our countries, and the sky above with planes ferrying business-men, students, scientists, government officials, tourists, and others on their travels. In conducting its economic and financial affairs each national government is keenly aware of the intricate interconnections between the welfare of its people and the welfare of its allies.

I do not need to labor the point. Over the last twenty years the Atlantic allies have created a structure of relationships and institutions, of mutual obligations, and of corresponding restrictions on freedom of action that marks a community and enables us to speak of an Atlantic community in a sense going far beyond mere sentiment.

It is no secret, however, that some doubts and uncertainties now cloud the future of the Atlantic alliance. The direction in which we should be moving is not as clear as it was when the sense of insecurity was acute and Western Europe's economy was struggling to regain its momentum. The urgency of the tasks we faced twenty years ago marvelously concentrated our attention on essentials, and it is a measure of our success in dealing with those essentials that a certain nostalgia now marks our attitudes. Once again we are enjoying the luxury of playing with ideas without running much risk—or so we think—and without giving much thought to the possibility that such playfulness might jeopardize our continued prosperity or our security.

Is a strong Atlantic alliance still desirable or useful? That is, I think, the fundamental question. It concerns all of us, and it is about this question that I wish to say a few words today.

The basic purpose of the alliance has been to achieve a military stabilization in Europe that would keep the peace and thus permit East and West to work toward adjustments of their differences by means other than the use of or threat of violence. What we have wanted, as former Secretary of State Dean Acheson recently said, is enough power outside the Soviet Union to make sure that military power would have nothing to do with the settlement of the problems arising from the division of Europe.

One member government, the French, tells us that there is no longer a Soviet threat to the Atlantic community, that the Soviet threat has disappeared, and that the danger of hegemony has been reversed, coming now not from behind the Elbe but from across the Atlantic. The Government of France declares that the danger to Europe now arises from "American hegemony" and from the presence of American forces in Europe.

This is not the place for a detailed examination of Moscow's military capacities. Have the Soviets been building impressive new missile and antimissile capabilities and making heavy investments in mobile long-range forces solely with a view to defense? It is much too large an assumption for me to make. Surely prudence requires us to recognize the possibility that their investments are aimed at something more than defense.

The Chief of the Soviet Navy recently had this to say:

> In the past our ships and naval aviation units have operated primarily near our coast, concerned mainly with operations and tactical coordination with ground troops. Now, we must be prepared for broad offensive operations against sea and ground troops of the imperialists on any point of the world's oceans and adjacent territories.

We have heard a good deal of talk about détente, but I have the uncomfortable feeling that this talk says more about the state of mind in the West than about Soviet ambition and policy toward Western Europe.

Even when the Russians have been in a condition vis-à-vis the West of admitted inferiority in strategic power and in mobile long-range forces, Moscow has periodically pressed forward policies designed to undermine the security of the West, to isolate Europe from the United States, and to open West Europe to the impact of increased Soviet pressure. One need but recall the repeated threats to the freedom of Berlin, the Cuban missile adventure, the strong encouragement given to the militant Arab forces in the dangerous Near Eastern crisis of May and June 1967, and, most recently, the bold extension of Russian naval strength and political influence into the Mediterranean and Red Sea basins.

In past Soviet probings, the strategic inferiority of Soviet power has set limits to the extent of the risks that Moscow was willing to run. It is disquieting to contemplate the risks which the Kremlin might consider taking in the future if it was confident of being closer to an equality or a superiority of overall deterrent strength and also possessed a local superiority of forces.

It is of course difficult for an American to suppose that anyone in Western Europe really believes that a danger of hegemony now comes from the United States. The word connotes for us a preponderant or dominating influence or authority. No one in the American Government, I think, has felt that he possessed such influence or authority or is likely to in the future, least of all, perhaps with reference to the President of the French Republic. It may be that the word appropriately described the kind of authority exercised by Roosevelt and Churchill in the crisis of war and liberation, but one trusts that the hold of the past on the present does not extend to a revival of ancient and anachronistic grievances.

It should not be necessary to say that the United States has no desire to dominate Europe. We want an independent Europe, which means we see no necessary conflict between European independence and Atlantic community and cooperation.

The original American conception, in the time of General Marshall and Robert Lovett, was of one Europe—"the European world," "Europe as a whole." That is still the American objective. As in the past, the United States looks forward to a genuine European settlement which would make possible, among other things, a safe end to Europe's unhappy division and the reciprocal withdrawal of American and Soviet forces from Central Europe.

Meanwhile, we have supported the efforts of Europeans to develop the Coal and Steel Community, Euratom [European Atomic Energy Community], and the Common Market. Indeed Americans well disposed to France ask why the French nation is not seizing the opportunity to act in the grand style of her tradition and to work for the development of the strength and unity of Western Europe, including Great Britain. It is with a deep sense of regret that many American friends of France observe that France is not providing a positive, broad, enlightened leadership of this kind. What a sad waste of talents and energies!

We hear the celebrated formulas: "nation with free hands," "never to accept any kind of dependence," "to drink from one's glass while clinking glasses all around," "France does not deny herself any possibility." We can all sympathize with the desire for national independence, although I doubt that any of us was ever quite as independent as we thought or that any of us can be truly independent in the modern world. To the extent that independence is possible, it is a function of strength, and strength in the modern world is related to size, as well as to will and to the support of allies—to area, population, economic output, scientific and technological resources, and so forth. Western Europe surely has the potential to play an independent role in the world—within the limits applicable to any nation, even to a great power—but it must be doubted whether any West European country by itself can realistically aspire to grandeur and greatness by "going it alone." It has been an understanding of this fact that has inspired the movement toward unity in Western Europe, and it is this fact that imparts an archaic and feckless quality to present French policy.

The United States is not looking for a pretext to keep its forces in Western Europe, nor is it insisting upon the retention without modification of the North Atlantic Treaty.

We gave our support to the Western European union arrangement at the end of the forties. We supported the European defense community in the early fifties, and were disappointed when France was unable to obtain parliamentary approval of her own proposal. Had the defense community been created, it is not likely that there would be talk today about an imbalance in the alliance. We are still prepared to take this route. A few months ago, Secretary of State Rusk said that the United States "would welcome now, as before, a European caucus, if they want to call it that, in NATO, something like a European defense community, as a full partner in a reconstituted alliance."

I myself could go even further. If a day comes when the Atlantic alliance is not wanted by the majority of Europeans, the alliance will of course cease to exist and we would not try to prolong its life. We have the power and will, if need be, to manage without it. But we believe the alliance is still needed and useful, and, if the Europeans want to continue it, use it, and modify it, we will contribute our fair proportion of the effort.

Let me repeat so that there will be no misunderstanding. If it is really true that the presence of American troops in West Europe is not wanted by the Europeans, so be it. If, in light of the call to action last April from Communist Party Secretary Leonid Brezhnev to dismantle NATO by 1969, to remove all American forces from Europe, and to eliminate the American Sixth Fleet from the Mediterranean, a majority of West European opinion is prepared to see an end to the American military presence in Europe, then they have only to say so. If West Europe feels it has enough strength to go it alone, if it has looked to the end of that road, sees where it would lead, and wants to go down it, then tell us just that. The United States has enormous responsibilities for defense of other areas of importance to world stability. It would be convenient for a number of reasons, not least our balance of payments difficulties, to reduce our forces in Europe. If the message from the majority in West Europe really is "Yankee go home," if that is honestly what most Europeans want, then that is that, and it will be done.

The United States has no desire to keep its forces in Europe unless Western Europe believes they are still needed there for the security of the Atlantic community.

On the contrary, the problem that I and others face in the Senate is to maintain American forces in Western Europe at or near their present strength. There are many influential Senators who think that the United States could and should reduce its forces in Europe. Indeed, the pressures to reduce them are mounting, given what seems to many Americans a not entirely reciprocated effort on the part of a prosperous Western Europe and given now, in addition, the attitude of the French Government.

Contrary to the notion of some critics, the American people have not expected gratitude for past American help to Europe; but they have expected a fair deal.

In all frankness, I think our European allies should recognize that there is inevitably a relation between their willingness to draw on their own resources for their own defense and the willingness of the American people and the American Congress to give solid support to the principle of mutual aid.

The French Government is a special case. Americans friendly to France ask why the French nation, with all its wealth and talent, is not making a larger contribution to the defense of Europe. If it is really true, as we are told by the French leadership, that France is the most important power in Europe, why does she not give more practical help?

France withdrew her forces from NATO, denied to NATO the air bases that were also designed to safeguard France, stripped NATO of its support and communication facilities, and unceremoniously evicted allied headquarters from French soil. The allies whose presence she once earnestly solicited have been treated in a manner usually reserved for a disagreeable tenant. At the same time, of course, France desires to participate in certain NATO activities of immediate advantage to herself. For example, she is sharing in the development of NADGE [NATO Air Defense Ground Environment], without which the French air force would be seriously handicapped. And she continues to claim the right to be treated as an ally, having first unilaterally redefined her obligations, as these are jointly defined in the North Atlantic Treaty.

The French President advocates what he calls "European Europe" existing "by itself for itself." But a Europe effectively protecting itself "by itself" is far from de Gaulle's thoughts. He is assuming the constant protection of the American nuclear umbrella, no matter how he insults us and no matter to what lengths he goes in trying to make the American presence in Europe uncomfortable.

In the aftermath of the June war in the Middle East, the French President suddenly reversed direction—as we have learned to expect—from support of Israel to support of the Arab states. Apparently he felt that France had little to gain from support of Israel, while the vast Arab world, disgruntled with Great Britain and the United States, presented opportunities to France.

Our friends in France may understand that this has the appearance of attempting to feather one's nest at the expense of others.

I believe most impartial observers would say that the United States, as a nation, has shown great restraint in the face of the whimsical obstructionism and bitter anti-Americanism of the present French leadership. One reason for this restraint is the desire not to complicate the problems of West Germany. We recognize that it would be very difficult for the West Germans to have to make a fundamental choice between France and the United States. If the French Government pulls out of the alliance altogether, that will be its decision. We do not intend to force the issue.

The American people have tried to be patient. For example, we have tried not to remind others that when they were experiencing temporary economic difficulties we did not use our gold as a weapon against them but as a means of coming to their support. Questions of psychology are important, as any politician knows, in international as in national affairs, and it is not, or should not be, surprising that Gaullist acrobatics have diminished the respect, confidence, and admiration of the American people for the French nation, their oldest ally.

As you well know, the basic objective of allied policy in Europe is not strength for strength's sake, or to freeze the status quo, but to create an environment for a genuine European settlement serving the legitimate security interests of all concerned. The hope is that one day security can be achieved on terms which will end the grim and dangerous injustice of a divided Germany.

President Johnson's major policy speech on Europe in October 1966 proposed a greater effort in building bridges to East Europe as a basis for Germany's peaceful reunification. The West German leadership is obviously thinking and working along the same lines and has begun a long and delicate effort to recast its relations with East Europe. Through expanded trade relations, closer diplomatic ties, and increased cultural and tourist contacts, the Bonn Government is doing its part to foster a climate of mutual trust and understanding as a foundation of German reunification. There will undoubtedly be many dead-end streets, detours, and disappointments along the way, but we believe the West Germans are on the right track.

We are also glad to see that all fifteen NATO foreign ministers, at their meeting in December last year, agreed on the importance of using the alliance and the North Atlantic Council "constructively in the interests of détente."

Nevertheless, a possibility that certain East European countries and the Soviet Union may prove willing to make some East-West adjustments does not provide a reason to pay less attention to the defense of Europe. The Harmel report of December 1967 on the *Future Tasks of the Alliance* contains the appropriate comment:

> Military security and a policy of détente are not contradictory but complementary. Collective defense is a stabilizing factor in world politics. It is the necessary condition for effective policies directed towards a greater relaxation of tensions.

Is a strong Atlantic alliance still desirable and useful? Most of us think so. In the years that lie ahead the alliance will undergo many changes. It must if it is to serve the purposes and interests of the members. But I personally cannot imagine a time when, or circumstances in which, the alliance will be obsolete, because the future, as I see it, will be filled with tasks we can best meet not in isolation but in intimate and friendly association.

Let me conclude, therefore, with the profound hope that all of us—men and women of good will on both sides of the Atlantic—will keep up our dialogue, taking advantage of every opportunity to play our part in creating a world in which individual liberty can survive and flourish.

9

U.S. Forces in Europe and the Mansfield Amendment

United States Senate
13 and 18 May 1971

In September 1966 Senator Jackson went to the Senate floor to help in what proved a successful effort to prevent passage of a version of the so-called Mansfield amendment, which called, in effect, for a substantial reduction of U.S. forces stationed in Europe. Senator Mike Mansfield, the Democratic majority leader, was Jackson's very good friend, but on this issue they were on different sides. Jackson had emerged as the Senate's chief defender of a strong American presence in Europe.

In May 1971 Senator Mansfield revived his earlier amendment in a version proposing the withdrawal, by the end of 1971, of what amounted to half of the U.S. forces stationed in Europe. The Vietnam War was still going on and there was danger of another conflict in the Middle East. Surely, according to Jackson, this was hardly the time to leave the world with the impression that we were retreating from our responsibilities as a world power. Beyond that, Jackson had long been persuaded that the crucial element in the West's deterrent capability in Europe was the American presence.

Senate consideration of the Mansfield amendment was high drama, the kind of decisive legislative battle in which the Senator excelled. He and his like-minded colleagues found the Senate vote on the amendment reassuring: 36 in favor and 63 against.

13 May 1971

MR. PRESIDENT, THE ATLANTIC ALLIANCE HAS NEVER BEEN an end in itself. But it has unfinished business as an agency of the common defense, a foundation for a genuine European settlement, and as a source of stability in Europe as a pillar of a peaceful international society.

The need for the forces and firmness of the alliance is as

111

compelling as ever. Today's political leaders—executive and legislative—have solemn duties. A principal task is to maintain those forces and to enhance the will to collaborate in the unfinished work of the alliance. This is no time to disintegrate the NATO shield and to demoralize the Western will. Therefore, Mr. President, I oppose the amendment proposed by the Senator from Montana, Senator Mansfield, requiring that we cut in half the number of American troops stationed in Europe.

I understand and share the feeling of many Americans that, overall, Western Europe is still *not* making a reasonably proportionate contribution to the common defense effort. I have spoken frankly and bluntly to our allies on this point. Last November I told the North Atlantic Assembly in The Hague that more concrete and substantial progress in "burden-sharing" is essential.

There has recently been some movement in Europe toward sharing more of the burden—no great advance, but progress in the right direction. We should press in particular for greater European offsetting payments on military account. Some NATO countries can clearly increase their force contributions to NATO and further improve the quality of present forces. But, above all, this is a time for steadiness on the part of the United States, not for demoralizing our friends and allies.

These wide-ranging issues require patient, thorough consideration. They cannot be settled in haste here on the Senate floor and still be settled wisely—without even an opportunity for hearings. If changes in NATO force posture and "burden-sharing" are to be made, they should flow from give-and-take discussions and decisions by the North Atlantic Council and should be executed with a view to minimizing the danger that their significance will be misinterpreted by the Soviet Union— or by allied governments and publics. This obviously applies with special emphasis to any cutbacks in American combat forces on the Continent.

Since 1966 resolutions have been introduced which in effect call for a substantial reduction of U.S. forces stationed in Europe. Some proponents talked confidently of Senate passage of such a resolution in 1968—at the very moment when Soviet forces invaded Czechoslovakia. There was some sudden backpedaling and a change in tune and talk that "the time is obviously not propitious for a substantial reduction of U.S. forces in Europe."

The time is no more propitious today. The United States is deeply engaged in crucial East-West negotiations on arms control at SALT. The situation in the Middle East is highly explosive, as the Soviets exploit the tragic conflict between Arabs and Jews in pursuit of their priority interest—to multiply their influence in the Mediterranean-African area on the southern flank of NATO.

To those who say we must take risks for peace by smashing up the Western deterrent, I say: you are not proposing risks *for* peace, you are proposing a policy that would heighten the risk of confrontation or war. You are risking loss of security or freedom for Americans and our friends throughout the world.

I for one do not want any part in this precipitate and irresponsible move and I shall vote against this amendment.

Mr. President, the American military presence in Europe is the hard nub of the Western deterrent. The chief purpose of the American troop commitment is political: to leave no doubt in the Kremlin that the United States would be involved, deeply involved, from the outset of a Soviet-inspired crisis or a Soviet move against the NATO area. It needs to be perfectly clear to the Russians that their forces would meet enough American forces to make the crisis a Soviet-American crisis, not just a European one. This means that a token American force is not adequate. It should be an effective American combat force, not just something to be tripped over, but a force capable of putting up a serious fight.

The primary function of NATO's conventional forces, with their vital American component, is to meet an emergency as effectively as they can, posing the continual threat that if the emergency continues and enlarges, the risks of escalation continue and enlarge with it. To perform this function NATO forces capable of containing a sizable, though limited, attack are required. Anything less would be a standing temptation to Soviet probes of allied mettle, and such probes would force the allies to retreat or to engage in brinkmanship, with all the risks either course would involve.

The mishandling by the West of a single emergency could profoundly alter the prospects for stability in Europe. And in an emergency we must be able, without any delay, to put military forces into small confrontations to hold ground, not give it, and thus to improve our diplomatic position. The need is for forces on the ready which can act without unnecessarily difficult political preparations. The ability of NATO to move conventional forces, with a strong American component, in several crises in Berlin was of critical importance in the management of those crises.

Indeed, NATO's conventional power is needed not only to respond to emergencies that Moscow would deliberately contrive, but also to deal with the unforeseeable contingencies that history sometimes contrives—border incidents, upheavals in satellite nations that splash over the line, and so forth.

The sizable cutback of American troops proposed in this amendment would imply a greater reliance on nuclear weapons and their incorporation in military operations at a very early phase of hostilities. Is this what sponsors of the amendment really want? Are they in favor of a one-option policy of massive retaliation? Would this serve the best interests of the United States and its allies? Hardly! We must not leave the American President with only the nuclear button in his hand in the event of crises.

The drastic cutback of American troops proposed in this amendment would also lead to a preponderantly large German army on the Central European front. Is this what sponsors of the amendment really want? I would have thought they understood that a disproportionately large West German contribution can revive old fears and animosities among smaller West European countries. It can help the Russians to nourish East European fears of Germany, prejudice West Germany's chances of improving its relations with Eastern Europe, and thus delay the working out of a genuine settlement in Europe which advances the legitimate security interests of all nations concerned.

NATO force requirements are designed, of course, not only to contribute to deterrence and defense but also to fortify the diplomatic bargaining position of the West vis-à-vis the East. A major and as yet unachieved purpose of the Atlantic alliance is to reach a genuine, stable European settlement with the Soviet Union. Among other things, such a settlement will involve the return of Soviet forces to the Soviet Union. How can the Soviet Government be encouraged to move in this direction? Certainly not by following the line of this amendment and demolishing *unilaterally* the bargaining position we have worked so long and hard to construct. Clearly, we should sustain our bargaining position and actively pursue acceptance of *gradual and balanced reductions* in forces on both sides of the Iron Curtain.

Thank you, Mr. President. I will have more to say on this critical matter during the course of this debate.

18 May 1971

MR. PRESIDENT, AS THE DEBATE ON THE AMENDMENT IN-troduced by Senator Mansfield continues it is important that we consider the repercussions of its adoption not only in Europe but throughout the world. Passage of this amendment would, in my view, suggest to our friends and our enemies around the world that this country, having failed to learn the lesson of the 1930s, is retreating into isolationism. So severe and precipitate a reduction in our presence in Europe will not be understood as a mere economy measure or as a positive effort to encourage détente with the Soviet Union.

We are in Europe today not as a favor to the Europeans, but because we have learned that the security of the United States is inextricably tied to the security of Europe. In 1914 and again in 1939 we learned that the failure to maintain a balance of power on the European continent could lead to world war. The North Atlantic alliance was born as a response to that twice-learned and terribly costly lesson, and it has succeeded in maintaining the balance that is vital to the maintenance of peace. Some people argue that we can safely bring our NATO troops home because twenty-six years have passed peacefully since the end of World War II. But this overlooks the fact that the peace we have enjoyed in Europe these last twenty-six years is largely a product of the success of the Atlantic alliance in deterring a general war and in containing recurring explosive incidents within the Soviet bloc. I find the view that after twenty-six years we can pack up and go home a little like the view that because the town has not burned to the ground for twenty-six years we can cut in half the size of the fire department.

The immediate result of a withdrawal from Europe on anything approaching the magnitude of the proposed amendment would be a collapse of confidence in American assurances and in the orderly formulation of American foreign policy. The United States cannot expect collaboration with friends and allies in the common defense if our own defense and foreign policies are subjected to sudden and capricious reversals with far-reaching consequences.

In the case of NATO, we and our European allies have over the years developed agreed-upon consultative machinery for the formulation of common policies. It is difficult to imagine a more disruptive monkey wrench in that machinery than to present our allies with a fait accompli of the magnitude we are discussing here.

What is here at issue is nothing less than a reversal of America's postwar European policy and a rejection of the creative Atlantic alliance that has, since World War II, kept the peace and maintained Western security.

We must not lose sight of the fact that all over the world there are men and women whose lives and freedoms depend, in the last analysis, on the capacity of the United States to lead the common defense effort of the free world. Our leadership cannot survive a policy process in which our relations with a whole continent are changed overnight. And our leadership —our ability to bring together those independent states who value their independence and freedom—is the best guarantee of security for the American people.

I am concerned, Mr. President, not only at the reaction in Europe that would follow adoption of this amendment. I am concerned at the reaction in the Soviet Union. Cutting our strength in Europe in half would encourage the Soviets in the belief that the United States has begun a process of disengagement from the world that would call into question the many partnerships that have acted to deter Soviet adventurism. Such a drastic move will signal a failure of our will and invite the conclusion that we will not stand firm in a crisis.

In my view the most immediate victims of the precipitate withdrawal of American forces from Europe would not be our Western European allies but those countries in more exposed and more precarious forward positions. The Middle East, perhaps more than anywhere else, would feel the effects of such an American withdrawal of forces from Europe.

The American presence in Europe and especially our naval deployments in Italy and on board the Sixth Fleet serve both to protect Europe and help maintain the stability of the Middle East. A test of our resolve in one place will have immediate repercussions in the other. A lessening of American interest in the defense of Europe will inevitably be seen as foreshadowing a decline of our determination to help preserve stability in the Middle East and to protect our interests and our friends and allies there.

Our friends in Israel would view with the most urgent alarm an indication that the United States was no longer prepared to maintain an adequate defensive capability in Europe. If America, in response to a fluctuation in the market for Eurodollars, is prepared to revise its relations with a whole continent, how would America respond to a crisis in the Middle East?

In the Middle East, moreover, some of us have been concerned about the relative strength and effectiveness of those forces that the United States maintains in order to protect the security of the Eastern Mediterranean. The drastic cutback proposed by this amendment would necessitate a reduction in our forces in the Eastern Mediterranean, which are already threatened by the increasing penetration of the Soviet Union in the Middle East.

A few days ago President Johnson told of the events of early June 1967 and of how he moved the U.S. Sixth Fleet forward in response to an explicit threat of Soviet intervention in the war against Israel. In 1967—and again in the Jordanian crisis last year—our Mediterranean fleet spoke louder than words. In 1971 we are not going to be very persuasive with the Russians if they see us bringing home the instruments of persuasion.

It is striking, Mr. President, that in the several days of debate on the proposed amendment there has been virtually no indication of support for it by those statesmen, past and present, who have been responsible for the conduct of American foreign policy. There has been little or no indication of support from those academic political scientists and historians whose area of expertise is concerned with defense and foreign policy and European affairs. There has been very little editorial support for the drastic cutbacks that are proposed in this amendment.

On the contrary, we have seen, in the last few days, an unprecedented outpouring of opposition to the amendment. Presidents Truman and Johnson, joined by their Secretaries of State, have added their voices to those of us who take pride in the steadiness of the policies of the Atlantic alliance since World War II.

I am not surprised by this. I have great confidence in the sound judgment of the American people. In particular, I am confident that the American people would not wish to see this country act in a way that, turning our back on history, would turn us inward. Americans have come to expect that our security and that of the free world depend on our courage and determination—and on our leadership. The American people understand that we cannot afford to retreat into isolation, that we can and must work together with those nations who love freedom and independence in order to provide for the common defense.

IV
Arms Control Negotiations

10

The Limited Nuclear Test Ban Treaty

United States Senate
13 September 1963

Jackson's approach to the Limited Test Ban Treaty in 1963 exemplifies his role in the development of arms control policy and in the handling of arms control treaties and agreements that came before the Senate. It was, in brief, to try to improve them.

President Kennedy was relying on Senator Jackson to support the Atmospheric Nuclear Test Ban, which he submitted to the Senate in August 1963. But Senator Jackson had some hard questions to ask the administration, particularly whether the United States would maintain a vigorous test program when only underground testing was permitted. In hearings of the Senate Armed Services Committee and its Preparedness Investigating Subcommittee the Senator pounded away with his questions, gaining the support of a group of Senators whose votes President Kennedy needed for ratification. He then negotiated with the administration. The result was a series of four "safeguards," agreed to by the President, that would accompany the treaty if it was ratified by the Senate. With agreement on the safeguards, Jackson and the several Senators who had followed his lead voted to ratify the treaty.

During the hearings and the ratification debate, the Senator was widely considered to be an opponent of the treaty. In fact, his efforts resulted in a safer and more balanced outcome, which made ratification of the treaty certain.

On September 13, as the Senate moved toward final action on the treaty, Jackson went to the Senate floor to place on record the agreement on safeguards and to help counter unwarranted euphoria by putting the treaty in a broad geopolitical perspective.

THE LIMITED NUCLEAR TEST BAN TREATY WE ARE CONSIDering has been described by some as a step toward peace and by others as a step toward war. If it were plainly the former, the Senate would of course promptly and enthusiastically give its advice and consent to ratification. If it were plainly the latter, we would of course refuse to approve it. We have held extensive hearings and are now engaged in debate because the issue is not plain.

The fact of the matter is that although the treaty is indeed a step in some direction, we do not know, and moreover we cannot know, in what direction it leads. For the treaty does not determine the direction. What we do from now on, and what the rest of the world does from now on—these are the determining factors.

Even those who most seriously doubt the wisdom of this treaty have not argued that it seals our fate. And most of those who strongly support the treaty have taken pains to underline the risks inherent in it. The consequences hinge, at least in large part, on the wisdom of our future policies and the will and determination with which we pursue them. Obviously, this is no routine agreement: it has major foreign and defense policy implications, and its provisions relate directly to the present and future credibility of the military deterrent which has been the free world's mainstay in stopping aggression and keeping the peace since World War II.

It has seemed clear to me from the outset that this treaty would not serve the interests of peace and security unless we entered upon its undertakings with a firm understanding of the lines of policy required of us in the new circumstances created by the treaty. We must understand what is required to protect and maintain the free world's ability to deter or survive a nuclear attack and to respond effectively against any aggressor. We must be ready to pursue the necessary policies without reservations of mind or heart.

It was for this reason that, prior to Senate consideration of the treaty, I propounded on this floor a number of national security issues on which, in my judgment, frank and adequate assurances from responsible officials of the executive branch were needed before the Senate could prudently determine whether to give its advice and consent to ratification.

It is for this same reason that the Joint Chiefs of Staff attach great importance to what they call safeguards. In their testimony before the Preparedness Investigating Subcommittee of the Armed Services Committee and before the Foreign Relations Committee, the Joint Chiefs defined certain safeguards which they believe can reduce the disadvantages and risks of the treaty. These safeguards include:

a. The conduct of comprehensive, aggressive, and continuing underground nuclear test programs designed to add to our knowledge and improve our weapons in all areas of significance to our military posture for the future.

b. The maintenance of modern nuclear laboratory facilities and programs in theoretical and exploratory nuclear technology which will attract, retain, and ensure the continued application of our human scientific resources to these programs, on which continued progress in nuclear technology depends.

c. The maintenance of the facilities and resources necessary to institute promptly nuclear tests in the atmosphere should they be deemed essential to our national security or should the treaty or any of its terms be abrogated by the Soviet Union.

d. The improvement of our capability, within feasible and practical limits, to monitor the terms of the treaty, to detect violations, and to maintain our knowledge of Sino-Soviet nuclear activity, capabilities, and achievements.

On August 14 the Preparedness Investigating Subcommittee unanimously adopted a motion which I made and which was subsequently unanimously adopted by the Armed Services Committee, a motion calling on the Joint Chiefs to supplement their testimony by providing to the Armed Services Committee a statement of the specific requirements to implement the necessary safeguards they had defined.

Senator [Richard B.] Russell [Chairman, Senate Armed Services Committee] forwarded this motion to the Secretary of Defense. The part of the response made public and included in the Interim Report of the Preparedness Investigating Subcommittee consists of two items: One, a letter from the Deputy Secretary of Defense setting forth in some detail both the assurances that the safeguards stated by the Joint Chiefs are recognized and accepted at the highest levels of the government and also the standards that will be observed and a preliminary outline of the measures that will be taken to implement these safeguards; and, Two, a letter from the Chairman of the Joint Chiefs enclosing a memorandum defining "Criteria to Ensure Fulfillment of the Safeguards Proposed by the Joint Chiefs of Staff."

It should be emphasized that there has been no disagreement on the part of anyone in a responsible position in the executive branch about the importance of action to implement the safeguards. On the contrary, there has been endorsement of the position that the United States will take determined, willing, and vigorous action to honor the safeguards, and the Senate is entitled to assume that no reservations attach to this resolve.

This commitment should be recognized by every official of the executive branch having anything to do with the actions needed to fulfill these safeguards. It is something which should be recognized by Congress, for it may well be that Congress, contrary to the expectations of many people, will have to vote additional appropriations in order to translate the commitment into effective programs of action.

Secretary McNamara's testimony to the Foreign Relations Committee already indicates, for example, that in order to compensate for uncertainties which could only be removed or reduced by tests forbidden by the treaty, we may have to produce and deploy greater numbers of delivery systems and radars and to disperse them more widely than would have been necessary without a treaty. Thus the Secretary acknowledges that if we are going to design around uncertainties, we shall have to have additional military hardware. It is apparent that this may well mean among other things greater numbers of present delivery systems and new mobile systems to reduce vulnerability. All of this costs money. I believe it would be unwarranted to assume that under the new environment of the treaty our security requirements can be maintained by less expenditures for national defense, or even by the same level of expenditure.

The commitment to an effective safeguards program needs

emphasis now because voices are already being heard outside government to the effect that the safeguards should not be implemented and are indeed inconsistent with the spirit of the treaty. For example, the well-known physicist Dr. Leo Szilard, in a statement submitted to the Foreign Relations Committee, argues that if the United States were to proceed

with an extensive program of underground bomb testing, then, rather than furthering the cause of peace, the test-ban agreement would be likely to do just the opposite.

Lest there be a misunderstanding inside or outside government on this critical issue—a misunderstanding that might seriously interfere with the full execution of the safeguards program—the legislative history being written here should make it clear that the executive branch has given responsible assurances of effective action to carry out the safeguards and that the Senate, through its appropriate committees, will monitor the actions taken for this purpose. In this connection I wish to cite the following passage from the Interim Report of the Preparedness Investigating Subcommittee:

If the treaty is ratified it is the intention of the Preparedness Investigating Subcommittee to monitor the implementation of the safeguards and it would also be our hope that other committees of the Congress having jurisdiction in these areas would cooperate in this important program.

I believe that the Senate has played a constructive role in this critical matter. The understanding that has been reached between the executive branch and the legislative branch will be helpful in the months ahead. It may be of even more importance when responsibility for national security passes to men who have not been engaged in the consideration of this treaty and its implications.

I have become persuaded in the course of studies of the national security process over the past few years by subcommittees of the Government Operations Committee that a key problem faced by every President is to make his views and intentions prevail throughout the vast organization he heads.

His statements have to be interpreted in the course of policy execution, and even subordinates acting in good faith sometimes read their own views into their interpretations of the President's will. I hope and believe that the discussion of safeguards has helped to bring about the kind of understanding throughout the executive branch that is the key to effective action in harmony with the intentions of the President.

As we approach a decision, I believe that my colleagues may find helpful the opinion of a great American, the distinguished former Secretary of Defense, Robert A. Lovett. Since his retirement as Secretary of Defense, Mr. Lovett has continued to serve the nation in a number of sensitive assignments and is eminently qualified to advise us and the country on the matter before us. In a letter addressed to the Senator from Arkansas, the chairman of the Foreign Relations Committee, in response to a request for his views, Mr. Lovett states the case for ratification in an admirably balanced way:

On the basis of the testimony so far presented, particularly by the Secretary of State and the Secretary of Defense, there would seem to be positive assurances that this administration has, first, the necessary will and determination to continue our research and developmental laboratories at the level of activity necessary to permit us to retain any nuclear superiority we may currently have and to improve, if possible, our relative position in this field so that our deterrent capability is not lessened by deterioration of either effort or facilities; and, secondly, that our policy, after signing the treaty, will be to continue actively those tests permitted under it and to maintain as insurance a program for atmospheric tests in a status permitting prompt use in the event of abrogation or other emergent events.

Under these conditions—which represent my understanding of definite assurances given by these officials—I believe that consent to ratification can properly be given.

This is also the conclusion I have reached. In light of the testimony that has been given and the understandings that have been reached with respect to the policy of the administration in safeguarding the national interest and in light of considerations I shall state in a few moments, I believe that the Senate may prudently give its advice and consent to ratification.

I now wish to indicate the other considerations that have led me to this conclusion. They emerge from the testimony presented to the Preparedness Investigating Subcommittee and to the Foreign Relations Committee and from my own long concern with national security affairs.

One. No responsible official has based his recommendations on the view that basic Soviet purposes have changed. Their purposes remain incompatible with ours. In response to a question of Senator Russell's, Secretary of State Rusk said:

> Mr. Khrushchev has made it very clear that there is no such thing as ideological coexistence. His purposes remain to work toward a Communist world. And that is deeply obnoxious as an idea to us, and the practices which would be used to pursue that idea would be hostile to our own interests.

Two. No responsible official has disputed the view that in the future, as in the past, our national security will depend on, among other things, a favorable military position. In response to a question of mine addressed to Secretary Rusk, the following exchange took place:

> SECRETARY RUSK. Senator, I believe that the United States must maintain in its own security interests a very large overall nuclear superiority with respect to the Soviet Union. This involves primarily the capacity to demonstrate that regardless of who strikes first, the United States will be in a position effectively to destroy an aggressor. . . .
> SENATOR JACKSON. . . . I am glad to hear you say we should maintain not a balanced but a superior position in order to maintain peace. Is this essentially your view?
> SECRETARY RUSK. That is correct, sir.

Three. No responsible official has rested the case for the treaty on a belief that the Soviet Government can be trusted. Senator [John] Sparkman raised this issue, which troubles many senators as well as many citizens who have written to us about the treaty, and was assured by Secretary Rusk that the treaty did not rest upon the element of faith and trust. The Secretary added:

We will know if there are significant violations of this treaty, we will be free to do whatever is necessary in our own security, and I would think that this is not a matter of trust.

Four. Secretary of Defense McNamara and the Joint Chiefs have testified that the balance of military power is in our favor at the present moment.

Five. With respect to the effects of the treaty on the future balance of military power, we enter of course a more controversial area. Although the views are not necessarily inconsistent, there are notable differences of emphasis. Secretary McNamara believes that there is nothing in the treaty which will shift the balance. The Joint Chiefs, according to testimony to the Foreign Relations Committee by General LeMay, examined the military and technical aspects of the treaty and came up with a net disadvantage in that field, but as General Taylor stated:

. . . the Joint Chiefs have reached the determination that while there are military disadvantages to the treaty, they are not so serious as to render it unacceptable.

General Power and General Schriever, however, attached greater importance to the military and technical disadvantages in their testimony to the Preparedness Investigating Subcommittee. And I think it is correct to say that scientists holding responsible posts recognize that the treaty definitely imposes limitations on research and development, though they differ greatly in their views about the desirability of the treaty.

From the evidence presented to the Senate I am compelled to conclude, as indicated in the Interim Report of the Preparedness Subcommittee, that the treaty involves serious—perhaps even formidable—military and technical disadvantages. It should also be added, in the words of that report, that:

No safeguards can provide the benefits of testing where testing is not permitted, nor can they assure that this nation will acquire the highest quality weapons systems of which it is capable when the means for achieving that objective are denied.

I have followed military, scientific, and technological developments with interest and care during my service in the House and in the Senate. I have great respect for the views of those men who, like General Power and General Schriever and like Dr. Foster and Dr. Teller, have serious doubts about the wisdom of this treaty or who actually oppose its ratification. But I am also convinced that these men, and the many others who work with them, are men of dedication, imagination, and ingenuity and that they will employ these qualities to offset insofar as it is possible the undoubted military and technical disadvantages. It is indeed in large part because men of their talents will be devoting their energies to ways to overcome these disadvantages that I believe we can accept the risks we necessarily will run.

Six. The administration in effect recommends acceptance of certain military and technical disadvantages and their attendant risks in the hope that certain gains may be made in other fields. Upon examination these hoped-for gains are either rather precise but insubstantial or they are quite difficult to specify but hopefully significant. Secretary Rusk testified as follows:

> This is a limited treaty. The President listed the things it does not do, and we must keep them in mind in judging its significance. At the same time, if—as seems likely—most of the nations of the world adhere to the treaty, and if they observe its obligations, this will in itself bring concrete gains.
>
> First, the United States and the Soviet Union already have enough nuclear power to inflict enormous destruction on each other. Still, the search for bigger, more destructive weapons goes on. Each generation of major weapons has been more expensive than the last. Each has involved an increasing burden, an increasing diversion of resources from the great unfinished business of mankind. Yet greater armament has not demonstrably brought greater security. The treaty, if observed, should slow this spiral, without damage to our relative strength.

I do not know, however, how to reconcile this alleged gain with Secretary McNamara's testimony, already cited, where the possible need for additional appropriations for greater numbers of delivery systems and radars and wider dispersal is brought out. It is my conclusion that it would be a mistake to count on any reduction of the armament burden as a result of this treaty. On the contrary, the evidence points to an increase in the burden.

Secretary Rusk's testimony continues:

> Second, the treaty will help contain the spread of nuclear weapons. We cannot guarantee it. Most of the countries with the capacity and the incentive to develop nuclear weapons over the next decade or so have already announced that they will accept the self-denying ordinance of the treaty. These countries do not include, by the way, mainland China or France.
>
> While this does not guarantee that they will never become nuclear powers, their renunciation of atmospheric testing will act as a deterrent by making it much more difficult and expensive for them to develop nuclear weapons.

Efforts to limit the spread of nuclear weapons deserve our serious attention. But I believe the role of the treaty in inhibiting proliferation has been generally overestimated. Most of the countries that have signed the test ban, or will sign it, do not have the capacity or desire to develop nuclear weapons. France, it should be noted, is already regarded by the administration as a nuclear power and is proceeding with an independent nuclear program. The major concern we have is with the development of nuclear capabilities by Communist China, which has rejected the treaty. I doubt that anyone wishes to argue that something called "world opinion" is likely to have an inhibiting effect on the determination of Peking to become a nuclear power.

Secretary Rusk's testimony continues:

> Third, the treaty will reduce the radioactive pollution of the planet. The increased radioactivity from nuclear testing has thus far stayed within tolerable limits, in a statistical sense. But as the President said: "This is not a natural hazard, and it is not a statistical issue."
>
> Moreover, if testing were not restricted, more and more countries would conduct tests. Many of them would lack either the incentive or

the means to minimize the fallout. We have a high obligation to safeguard life and health and the genetic integrity of the human race. Today no one can say for certain how much fallout is too much. But if this treaty is observed it will go a long way to assure that we do not transgress those limits.

There is little doubt, I believe, that this argument weighs heavily in the public mind. But unpopular though it may be to say so, there is also little doubt that the fears that have been aroused are out of all proportion to the hazards. Other things being equal, we should of course minimize fallout. But if other things are not equal, and they may not be, we may be compelled at some future date to accept the small hazards of fallout to protect ourselves against larger hazards to peace and security. Nevertheless, I believe that it is proper to conclude that the reduction of fallout is a positive advantage of the treaty.

Secretary Rusk comes next to his last and most important point:

For 18 years we have held the Communist drive in check largely by the deterrent force of our massive military strength. We shall maintain that overwhelming strength until we are certain that freedom can be assured by other means.

But throughout we have known that a lasting peace could not be founded upon armed might alone. It can be secured only by durable international institutions, and by a respect for law and its procedures.

The problem has been to convince the Communist world that its interest also lay in that direction.

The most important thing about the treaty is, therefore, what it may symbolize and what new paths it may open. That, no one can now foretell.

Almost at once, however, in response to a question of Senator Russell's, Secretary Rusk put this, his fourth and, in his eyes, his most important point, in perspective in these words:

We have pressing issues with the Communist world in one form or another right around the globe, with almost a million men in uniform outside the continental limits of the United States because of these issues, in Laos, South Vietnam, Cuba, Berlin, and other places. There are other practices, some of them bilateral in character, which do cause friction. I do not anticipate, to come specifically to your question, sir, I do not anticipate that there is much chance or much wisdom in an attempted comprehensive negotiation. It would not be for Washington and Moscow to try to sit down in some way and resolve all of these problems or even try to resolve them because the interests of many, many nations are involved and, quite frankly, the total question is probably too big to take hold of all at once.

And so despite the fact that there are some highly inflammable questions we still think we ought to keep open the possibility of finding particular points of agreement in the hope that if those can be achieved, it might reduce the fever somewhat and throw some different atmosphere and light on some of the more dangerous problems so we would be prepared to consider other questions.

At the moment I cannot report that there is another question which is as highly promising as this—as of today.

I repeat that we are being asked to accept certain military and technological disadvantages in the hope of making certain small gains and of opening up new paths, though the Secretary cannot see, as of today, any issues which may be negotiable. The Secretary is to be commended for his frank statement. He has not encouraged great expectations.

But hope is not to be dismissed as a basis for action, even the slender hope held out by Secretary Rusk. It is largely because we are deeply committed as a nation to do what we can to keep alive the hopes of men everywhere for a decent future —including, I trust, the peoples of Russia and China—that we shall ratify this treaty.

In doing so, what are the risks we run? Let me emphasize five among the many that might be mentioned.

First, there is the risk that we will relax and fall back into a state which the Senate has learned to call euphoria—which is, if I may play the same game, a state in which one believes that he has serendipity and is therefore likely to display velleity for vigorous action. In this regard, our previous record as a nation is not too reassuring. On occasions when we should have stayed awake, we went to sleep. Through halfhearted support and the pinching effect of the budget, critical programs have been degraded and vital policies stifled.

My good friend, the distinguished Senator from Minnesota, has said we need hopers, not doubters. I wonder whether he would accept a change of emphasis. We need men of hope *and* skepticism *and* action. Skepticism, not cynicism.

Our task, as I see it, is, while remaining skeptical, to act with hope and pursue those policies which may safeguard the opportunities to move the world along a path toward peace.

Second, there may be a serious misjudgment of the basis for the change in Soviet policy. It is to be hoped that it is in fact our strength and not a major Soviet military-technological advance that has persuaded Moscow that this agreement is advantageous. But the pessimistic possibility cannot be dismissed. It could be, as some witnesses suggested, that the Soviet Union has learned something important that, in its judgment, we do not know but might learn were we free to continue testing in any and all environments. The Soviet Government may believe that what it has learned can be the basis, as its development work proceeds, for upsetting the military balance.

If we come to the conclusion at any time that this is the case, we must be prepared to exercise our right of withdrawal from the treaty.

Third, we run the risk of planned abrogation of the treaty by the Soviet Union. The safeguards program is designed among other things to enable us to take necessary measures promptly in the event of Soviet bad faith.

Fourth, it is generally conceded that the Communist Chinese are now engaged in a substantial nuclear weapons program and that in the very near future they will be testing in the atmosphere. The advent of this new unchecked nuclear power may well require us to withdraw from the agreement.

Fifth, it is altogether possible and indeed, in my opinion, probable that a group of nations, with Soviet encouragement, will seek to amend the treaty in the not distant future so as to ban underground tests without inspection or with wholly inadequate arrangements for inspection. In this connection

I noted with interest the statement of Ambassador Arthur Dean [former chief of the U.S. delegation to the 1961 Geneva nuclear test ban negotiations] to the Foreign Relations Committee:

> We will undoubtedly be urged, in the spirit of amity and good will, to halt underground testing. But in my judgment without an adequate and effective treaty banning underground tests this would be a tragic mistake.

We may find ourselves under strong pressure in the months ahead to accept an amendment to the treaty banning underground tests without satisfactory inspection. We must be prepared to take our knocks, if necessary, and remain firm in our resolve that a ban on underground tests must be conditioned on fully satisfactory arrangements for inspection. I trust that the Department of State will be alert to this danger and will do what it can to forestall an effort to isolate the United States on this matter.

It is my belief that these and other risks that we will inevitably run under this agreement are tolerable: *Provided,* that it is firm national policy to keep alert and to protect the present and future credibility of our military deterrent; and *Provided,* furthermore, that it is firm national policy to use the protections provided in the treaty when, as, and if needed to guard vital national interests, including the right of withdrawal and the right to exercise the veto by withholding our consent under article 2 to any attempt to change the treaty by amendment in a form imperiling our vital interests. These protections constitute our explicit rights under the agreement, they form a basic part of the document, we deliberately had them included, and we should be ready to exercise them if emergent events so require.

The essence of my view on this treaty, which has been referred to as a limited treaty, is that it is indeed limited. Actually it is not a treaty, but a loose commitment, a statement of present intentions of the parties not to engage in nuclear weapon test explosions in the atmosphere, in outer space, or under water. This nation's commitment will rest on the assumption that certain conditions are met—including the condition that the supreme interests of this nation are not jeopardized. Should those interests be jeopardized we shall be released from our commitment.

In conclusion, the national security interests of this country are of course deeply involved in a number of other situations quite apart from this treaty. For example, the development of NATO and the obvious efforts of France to reduce its importance; the question of economic and political relations between the European Common Market and other Western European countries, especially the United Kingdom; the strengthening of the international position of the dollar; the security of West Berlin; the removal of Soviet forces from Cuba, and the neutralization of Cuba as a base for Communist subversion and penetration in the Western Hemisphere; the question of American policy in Southeast Asia, particularly Vietnam; and the question of appropriate American policy toward the developing nations of Asia, Africa, and Latin America. This series of problems certainly gives us no excuse to relax.

If this debate helps the people of the United States really understand what they have to do to provide for the safety of the nation and the preservation of their freedoms, then any time and attention given to this test ban agreement is well spent. The Senate will have done what it can to put the treaty in the proper perspective.

11
The Senate
and the Interim SALT I Agreement

United States Senate
11 August 1972

During 1969 Senator Jackson had marshaled Senate support for the Nixon administration's deployment of the Safeguard Anti–Ballistic Missile System, finally shepherding it through the Senate by a one-vote margin. Only advances on ballistic missile defense, he believed, would bring Moscow to serious negotiations in SALT.

In May 1972 President Nixon returned from Moscow with a treaty on the Limitation of Anti–Ballistic Missile Systems and an Interim Agreement on Strategic Offensive Arms. Jackson found that key Safeguard anti–ballistic missile deployments had been bargained away to "halt the momentum of Soviet offensive forces." Yet, rather than halting Soviet programs, the SALT I Interim Agreement permitted them to grow and to reach a level of offensive weapons higher than that of the United States—a 50 percent Soviet advantage in land-based missiles and a 30 percent advantage in sea-based missiles.

The Senator voted for the ABM treaty. But he was determined to improve the Interim Agreement or, in any case, to do what he could to ensure that the inequalities that favored Moscow would not be repeated in any permanent SALT treaty. Undertaking a series of Armed Services Committee hearings, he authored what became known as the Jackson amendment on equality, which would put the Senate on record that any future agreement on offensive arms must "not limit the United States to levels of intercontinental strategic forces inferior to the limits provided for the Soviet Union." (In 1956, on the floor of the Senate, Jackson had said that "American superiority in advanced weapons systems is the minimum prerequisite of peace." He saw that the nuclear deterrent preserved the peace and gave our allies the incentive to maintain at least the minimum conventional force structure. Over time, as it became clear that the Kremlin could and would field many more nuclear weapons than the United States might, he recognized that adding more and more such weapons to our stockpile was of diminishing usefulness. Therefore, he argued for equality in nuclear capabilities and especially for the maintenance of a U.S. triad of strategic nuclear forces—land, sea, and air.)

After weeks of Senate debate on the Jackson equality amendment, it was adopted on 14 September by a vote of 56 to 35 (and later signed into law by the President). The Senator then voted for the Interim Agreement. Henceforth no present or future administration could be confident of the ratification of a treaty with Moscow that provided for a less-than-equal ceiling on strategic forces.

In an essay published in 1987, Richard Perle comments that the Senator

could not have known that fourteen years later, in a negotiating session that lasted all night in Reykjavik, Iceland, Ambassador Paul Nitze would say to Soviet Marshal Akhromeyev that the United States could not agree to a less-than-equal ceiling on strategic forces because the Congress of the United States had spoken to this issue and had insisted on equality in any future agreement. And he could surely not have known that, after conferring with the Soviet leadership at three in the morning, Marshal Akhromeyev would concede the point and agree to equal ceilings on Soviet and American strategic forces at sharply reduced levels. As I listened to the Soviet Marshal, Chief of the Soviet Armed Forces, I could feel Scoop smiling over the proceedings.[16]

MR. PRESIDENT, THE SENATE FULLY APPRECIATES THAT IT has before it an arms limitation measure of very great importance. Equally important, in my view, is how we in the Congress come to judge that agreement and how we convey our judgment to the Soviet Union, to our allies, to the executive branch, and to the American people.

International agreements, this one included, have always had a dimension deeper than their words—a dimension that embodies hopes and expectations and reservations, all unwritten, and all of which reflect the blend of risks, doubts, and assurances of which treaties are made. The present agreement, which rests to so remarkable a degree on statements with which the other party did not concur, has all of these in full measure.

SOME AMBIGUITIES RESOLVED

In an agreement that goes to the heart of America's security—our capacity to deter nuclear war—nothing is more important than a precise understanding of what the parties have agreed to. Precision can never weaken an arms control agreement; ambiguity can be a source of future tension.

From the moment the agreements were signed in Moscow, there were vague and conflicting reports about the contents of the accords. The press relied on confusing background briefings held in Moscow. Various statements and attachments, integral parts of the agreements, were not made public for weeks. Public figures issued statements of support before the terms of the accords were revealed or analyzed. High administration spokesmen offered contradictory interpretations.

Thus, when the President finally submitted these agreements to the Congress, I was concerned that the Senate and the American people understand what we and the Russians could and could not do within their terms. The Senate Armed Services Committee, under the distinguished chairmanship of my able friend the Senator from Mississippi, held extensive hearings on the military implications of the SALT accords during which we tried very hard to bring before the American people the terms, and the meaning of the terms, of the Interim Agreement and the ABM Treaty. We endeavored to obtain a clear and consistent administration position on key provisions—which was not always easy.

Let me illustrate the kinds of problems the committee hearings had to address. Article 1 of the Interim Agreement obligates the parties not to build ICBM launchers after July 1, 1972. But nowhere in the agreement does there appear the number of ICBMs the Soviets are thereby permitted to have. Article 2 contains a prohibition against substituting "heavy" ICBM launchers for "light" ICBM launchers. But nowhere is there an agreed-upon bilateral definition of what a "heavy" ICBM is. Terms like "modernization" and "significant increase" were used in the agreement, but precise definitions of these terms are not provided.

Mr. President, although the texts of the treaty and the executive agreement contain few numbers, many more numbers have been discussed in connection with the SALT accords. In the last several weeks we have heard these: 1,054; 1,618; 313; 41; 44; 62; 84; 710; 740; 656; 950; and zero. The crucial question for the nation and for the cause of world peace is whether these numbers add up to stable parity or unstable inferiority. It may clear the air to discuss some of them.

a. 1,054—this is the maximum number of land-based ICBMs that the United States is permitted to retain under the agreement.

b. 1,618—this is the maximum number of land-based ICBMs that the Soviet Union is permitted to retain given *our understanding* of the agreement. I emphasize "our understanding" because the figure 1,618 is a U.S. intelligence estimate and not a Soviet-supplied number. This vagueness on the Soviet part is most unfortunate and can only lead to uncertainty and possible tensions. The agreement would be much improved by the use of specific numbers on both sides.

c. 710—this is the maximum number of submarine-launched ballistic missiles that the United States is permitted to deploy under the agreement. It is arrived at by adding our present 656 Polaris/Poseidon missiles to our potential, under the agreement, to replace 54 of our Titan missiles with new submarine-launched ballistic missiles.

d. 950—this is the maximum number of submarine-launched ballistic missiles that the Soviet Union is permitted to deploy under the agreement. To achieve this total the Soviets would retire their obsolete SS-7 and SS-8 ICBMs and replace them with new submarine-based missiles. This would give the Soviets a total of 62 modern nuclear (Y-Class) submarines.

e. 84—the total permissible number of Soviet missile-firing submarines that can be deployed under the agreement. This is derived by adding 22 Soviet G-Class submarines to the 62 Y-Class submarines that they are permitted to construct.

f. 44—the total permissible number of American missile-firing submarines that can be deployed under the agreement. However, only 41 in actual fact are part of the U.S. deterrent in this period.

g. 313—this is the maximum number of "heavy" ICBMs that the Soviet Union is permitted to deploy under the agreement. This again is a U.S. intelligence estimate; not a confirmed Soviet figure. Each of these missiles can carry at least a 25-megaton warhead and perhaps, eventually, as much as 50 megatons. Of course the Soviets are free to replace single large warheads with many MIRV [multiple independently targetable reentry vehicle] warheads per missile when they are able to do so.

h. 0—this is the maximum number of "heavy" ICBMs that the United States is permitted to deploy under the agreement.

These numbers, Mr. President, are merely representative of the thrust of the agreements—which is to confer on the Soviet Union the authority to retain or deploy a number of weapons based on land and at sea that exceeds our own in every category, and by a 50 percent margin.

Now there will be some who argue that "numbers don't matter"—that both sides have "sufficiency" and that therefore the strategic balance is stable. How curious it is that the people who hold to the "numbers don't matter" doctrine are the same ones who believe that without an immediate arms control agreement the world is in danger of a great nuclear war. Either numbers matter or agreements don't—you can't have it both ways.

I have never seen an international agreement that depends so greatly on the attachment of unilateral statements. Clearly each of these unilateral statements reflects not U.S.-Soviet agreement but, on the contrary, a failure to reach agreement. In my view the Interim Agreement is substantially weakened as a result of the failures indicated by the resort to unilateral assertions with no legal standing. No long-term treaty covering these vital matters would be acceptable to me and, I suspect, to a majority of my colleagues if it depended to the extent of the present agreement on unilateral statements. The fact that the present agreement runs for only five years mitigates a situation that would be intolerable in a future treaty. I believe that in expressing this view I am joined by Ambassador

[Gerard C.] Smith [Director, Arms Control and Disarmament Agency, 1969–73], who informed the Armed Services Committee that he expected provisions that could not be agreed upon in SALT I to be resolved on a bilateral basis in SALT II.

In seeking to establish clearly what the parties were permitted to do over the next five years and what they would be prohibited from doing—not all of which was self-evident—two points were of particular interest and illustrate the complications that arise from vague language in the agreement and from negotiating not only against one's adversary but against self-imposed deadlines as well:

(1) Under the terms of the agreement, the Soviets are permitted to have *operational*, by July 1, 1972, 62 Polaris-type Y-Class submarines. The agreement is very explicit on this. Owing to a provision that could have constituted a serious loophole, the issue arose as to whether the Soviets might have additional such submarines *under construction*, but not yet operational, on July 1, 1977. Some witnesses, including Ambassador Smith and Chief of Naval Operations, Admiral Zumwalt, indicated that, technically, this was permissible. Were that the case, the Soviets could continue to turn out Y-Class submarines like sausages, eight per year, with absolutely no perturbation of their deployment momentum.

Therefore, on July 24, I raised this problem with Secretary Laird in order to get the administration position as understood at the highest levels. Secretary Laird said: "The protocol to the Interim Agreement specifies that the Soviet Union may have 950 SLBM [submarine-launched ballistic missile] launchers and not more than 62 modern ballistic missile submarines." Then Secretary Laird, speaking for the administration, said: "In the event that during the period of the Interim Agreement they were to initiate construction of additional modern ballistic missile submarines beyond the number necessary to reach the total of 62, this could be done only as replacements [for older Y-Class submarines] and this would be under the procedures as specified under article 3 of the Interim Agreement. We would consider any new construction starts which were merely for the purpose of maintaining the momentum of the Soviet Union construction program to be contrary to the intent of the agreement."

This point is made equally clear in a colloquy between the Secretary and me. In order to understand the administration view, I asked: "I take it that it is your judgment and the view of the President and the administration that any attempt to use this ambiguity to build up—especially toward the end of this five-year period—a pipeline of advanced Y-Class boats under construction, as a technical means of getting around the limit of 62 operational submarines, would be in clear violation of what we understand to be the agreement." Secretary Laird answered: "I would, and that would also apply to the United States."

(2) Another area of potential misunderstanding relates to the modernization of missile silos under the agreement. The agreement allows for the modernization of existing silo-launchers, but stipulates that, in the process of modernization, the dimensions of those silos cannot be significantly increased. In a further attachment to the agreement, a significant increase is defined as not greater than 15 percent.

Testimony from administration witnesses on the meaning of these provisions was conflicting. Therefore, on July 24, I asked Secretary Laird for the definitive administration position. He replied: "I would not go along with the interpretation that some Members of the Senate and House have given to that provision in which they read that the 10 to 15 percent increase in dimensions could allow an increase in both dimensions." I then asked: "Diameter and length?" Mr. Laird said: "Yes." He went on to say: "The major increase that would be possible under the agreement would be in any one silo dimension."

In order that there be no misunderstanding on this point, I want to cite the colloquy which followed this official policy declaration by Mr. Laird:

SENATOR JACKSON. Do you reject the interpretation that an increase in both dimensions is allowable?

SECRETARY LAIRD. I have always rejected that from the first day that the treaty and the agreement became public—the idea that both diameter and depth could be increased by as much as 15 percent.

SENATOR JACKSON. It is the administration's position that only one dimension of a silo can be increased?

SECRETARY LAIRD. That is correct. That is the administration's position.

SENATOR JACKSON. It cannot be both dimensions?

SECRETARY LAIRD. It cannot be both diameter and depth.

THE MOMENTUM ARGUMENT; OR, HOW TO GO FORWARD WHILE STANDING IN PLACE

Mr. President, the present agreement is intended to slow the momentum of the buildup of Soviet offensive forces, a buildup that has taken the Soviets far beyond the force levels required for implementing a deterrent posture based on a simple notion of "assured destruction." My own examination and assessment of the appropriate intelligence data coupled with an analysis of the latitude granted under the terms of the agreement has brought me to the conclusion that, as a means of halting the Soviet momentum it is a failure and as a means of slowing Soviet momentum it accomplishes far less than has been claimed.

Mr. President, it is instructive to examine the comments made by the President and by his national security adviser, Dr. Kissinger, on the effect of the Interim Agreement. They add up to what I would call the "headache theory of treaty-making," according to which one signs an agreement not because it is good but because nonagreement is worse. That's about as close as public policy can come to beating your head against the wall because it feels so good when you stop. Listen to Dr. Kissinger:

> I do not deny that the initial reaction of some people will be to look at the gap in numbers. But once they understand . . . what the gap would be without this agreement . . . I believe that many of those who express some hesitation will come around.

Now, what I understand Dr. Kissinger to be saying is that those of us who are concerned at the gap in numbers in the Interim Agreement will be persuaded that a balance even more adverse to the United States would have resulted from a failure to reach the Interim Agreement. The President himself made this argument in his press conference of June 29, 1972, when he said:

> Had there been no arms control agreement, the Soviet Union had a program under way in the field of submarines which would have brought them up to over 90. The agreement limits them to 62.
>
> Had there been no arms control agreement—and this is the most important point—in the terms of offensive strategic weapons, the Soviet Union that has now passed us in offensive strategic weapons— they have 1,600; we have roughly 1,000—they would have built 1,000 more over the next five years. Now, under those circumstances, any President of the United States could see that in five years the United States would be hopelessly behind; our security would be threatened, our allies would be terrified, particularly in those areas, and our friends in the Mideast, where the possibility of Soviet adventurism is considered to be rather great.
>
> Therefore, the arms control agreement at least put a brake on new weapons.

So we have before us an agreement designed to see us through the next few years, the chief virtue of which is that life under it will be less dangerous, hopefully, than life without it. This may be a sufficient argument for the Senate giving approval to the Interim Agreement. It is not, in my view, a sufficient argument for allowing our approval to go unqualified, either by our recognition of the risks or the assertion of our own view of the future.

Understanding what the agreement does is of such importance that I raised the question of the extent to which it slows Soviet momentum on a number of occasions. For example, on July 19 I had the following exchange with General Ryan, Chief of Staff of the Air Force:

SENATOR JACKSON. One method of assessing the impact of the SALT accords on Soviet programs would be to compare what they are free to do under the agreement with what we have projected that they might have done in the absence of the agreement. Speaking generally, and without getting into precise estimates, how does the lower end of the spectrum of official estimates of the Soviet strategic offensive force for mid-1977 compare with the permitted Soviet force under the SALT accords?

GENERAL RYAN. Roughly equivalent, Senator, lower end of the spectrum.

Again, on July 21, I put the same question to the Chief of Naval Operations, Admiral Zumwalt, who, like General Ryan, is fully apprised of our intelligence projections. The admiral answered:

The lower end of the spectrum of the official estimates is lower than the force permitted under the SALT accords.

Mr. President, I ought to make clear for the record that I put the same question to both Ambassador Smith and General Allison of the SALT delegation when they appeared before the Armed Services Committee on June 28. Both gentlemen declined to answer, stating that security considerations precluded comment. Now, the figures in question are readily available to any Senator who wishes to judge for himself the extent to which the forward momentum of the Soviet buildup has been slowed by the Interim Agreement.

The Director of Defense Research and Engineering commented on this question of the impact of the Interim Agreement on Soviet deployment programs when he appeared before the Armed Services Committee in executive session on June 22, 1972. At that time Dr. Foster engaged in an important exchange with my good friend the Senator from Nevada:

SENATOR CANNON. I want to turn for a moment to the discussion of momentum that Senator Jackson was talking about that both sides have in building strategic weapons and how that will change our relative strategic posture as a result of SALT. I think this is a subject which is relevant to a meaningful discussion of the role of the ABM in the NCA [National Command Authority] defense.

The Interim Offensive Agreement limits both the United States and the Soviets to their present ICBM force, with allowances made for the Soviets to complete 90-odd silos now under construction. Therefore, the Soviets have slightly more than a 1.5 to 1 ratio of ICBM launchers and their numerical advantage is about 600.

The Interim Agreement also allows the Soviets to build up to a 62-

submarine force, an increase of about 40 or so from their present level of about 22 Yankee class.

On the other hand, we are essentially frozen at a maximum of 44 submarines, only three more than our present level, and therefore, the agreement grants the Soviets the advantage of completing their current momentum in submarine building.

Is that not basically correct?

DR. FOSTER. Yes, that is correct.

SENATOR CANNON. Concerning the quid pro quo of the treaty and agreement, is it not true that the Soviets will not have to exercise restraint in their momentum; that is, they will not have to curtail their current building rate of production on submarines for at least three years and perhaps more?

DR. FOSTER. Yes, sir, that is correct.

SENATOR CANNON. In other words, they will not be giving up anything in terms of momentum until at least three years from now and possibly four to five.

On the other hand, the United States has agreed to give up something this year, and that is work on three ABM sites at the Minuteman missile installations. In fact, we will actually be dismantling work already started at Malmstrom Air Force Base. Thus we are giving up something now whereas they might give up something three years from now, or then again they might not.

Is that a correct assessment?

DR. FOSTER. Yes, that is correct.

Mr. President, I have tried to put in perspective the claim that the Interim Agreement halts the momentum of the Soviet buildup not to reflect adversely on the Interim Agreement, but to help the Senate form a judgment that bears directly on our policy with respect to SALT II. It is essential, in my view, that we enter the second phase of the SALT deliberations with a clear view of the emerging strategic relationship between the United States and the Soviet Union and with the conviction that SALT II, whatever else it does, must assure equality between the parties on offensive intercontinental strategic arms. To insist on such equality with respect to offensive weapons is to require no more than was done, at Soviet insistence, with defensive weapons in the ABM Treaty.

THE CASE FOR THE AMENDMENT

Mr. President, my amendment, which is broadly cosponsored by a bipartisan group of Senators, deals with three issues: (1) the threat to the survivability of the U.S. strategic deterrent under the Interim Agreement; (2) the need for equality in any follow-on agreement on offensive intercontinental strategic weapons; and (3) the need for research, development, and force modernization. These are issues that I have thoroughly discussed with the administration, with the witnesses before the Armed Services Committee, and, in many cases, with my colleagues in the Senate. It is my firm conviction that we ought to state our views with respect to these issues and I believe my amendment is a medium for the expression of views that I am confident are shared by a majority of my colleagues.

(1) The Threat to the Survivability of the U.S. Strategic Deterrent

Clearly any treaty that authorizes the latitude retained by the parties under this Interim Agreement contains certain risks. How severe those risks prove out to be depends less on the letter of the Interim Agreement than on the spirit of it. The simple fact is that the Soviets could, by pursuing an aggressive program of qualitative improvement to their offense, acquire the capability to destroy virtually the entire U.S. land-based deterrent force, missiles and bombers. This could be accomplished within the agreed number of launchers by such means as increasing the throw weight of the Soviet offensive force (already four times that of the United States), extensive MIRVing coupled with improved missile accuracy, etc. Since we would be prohibited by the agreement and treaty from a number of stabilizing responses, the strategic balance could deteriorate under the terms of the Interim Agreement.

The situation we face in this regard was developed, in part, in testimony by the Director of Defense Research and Engineering, Dr. John Foster, before the Committee on Armed Services on June 22. In response to a question put by my friend, the Senator from Ohio, Dr. Foster identified some potential sources of instability that are wholly within the terms of the Interim Agreement:

SENATOR SAXBE. . . . you state that Soviet exploitation of their numbers and throw-weight capabilities could adversely affect the strategic balance. Will you elaborate on that statement and indicate specifically how and when?

DR. FOSTER. I was referring simply to the fact that the Soviet strategic missile capability exceeds our own capability in both numbers and payload-carrying ability. In numbers of ICBMs alone, they exceed us by approximately 50 percent, and in payload capability by greater than 50 percent.

If they were to exploit these numerically greater capabilities, such as by improving accuracy, resorting to MIRV, use of warheads having higher yield-to-weight ratios, upgrading their SAMs, or some combination of these and others, the strategic balance would be affected adversely. For example, with MIRV and accuracy improvements, the SS-9 force alone could be a severe threat to prelaunch survivability of our own land-based force. Or, other Soviet land-based missiles exist in sufficient numbers so that, with accuracy improvement, they could threaten our land-based force, leaving the SS-9 for other things— such as threatening our cities.

You asked when this could occur. I am not able to answer when it will or if it will. Should they wish such a capability, it could be achieved in perhaps three to five years.

It is my great hope, Mr. President, that these developments will not occur, that the Soviet Union will recognize that the overriding intent of the Interim Agreement is to contain the threat to the survivability of our deterrent forces and that, consistent with this intent, they will refrain from programs that would undermine it.

What we have sought in our negotiations with the Soviets is a stable strategic relationship based on survivable strategic forces. Therefore, any action by the Soviets that threatens the survivability of our deterrent forces must be a source of great concern.

I pursued this problem with Secretary Laird on July 24, and I believe our colloquy on this subject is highly instructive:

SENATOR JACKSON. The intent of the agreements is to enhance our security by enhancing the survivability of our deterrent. So you would view Soviet behavior that threatens the survivability of our deterrent as a violation of the intent of the agreements?

SECRETARY LAIRD. I would agree.

SENATOR JACKSON. If there is a pattern which threatens the survivability of our deterrent, you would treat that as a violation of the intent of the parties in making this agreement, would you not?

SECRETARY LAIRD. I certainly would.

SENATOR JACKSON. For example, the replacement provision on submarines, which we have discussed, as a subterfuge for sustaining momentum—

SECRETARY LAIRD. That is correct. We would interpret it the same way and it applies to us, too.

SENATOR JACKSON. That is, on a bilateral basis?

SECRETARY LAIRD. That's right.

SENATOR JACKSON. An aggressive program, beyond modernization, to deploy silo-killing warheads, which threatens the survivability of our Minuteman force—you would treat that in the same way?

SECRETARY LAIRD. Yes, sir, and would recommend action if such a program were developed and tested.

Mr. President, Senators who share my view that the Senate ought to go on record in support of the policy of the United States to seek a follow-on agreement that limits the threat to the survivability of our deterrent forces will welcome my amendment. The first part does precisely that. It urges restraint on the part of the Soviet Union by indicating that a failure to achieve a threat-limiting agreement could jeopardize the supreme national interests of the United States. In so doing, the amendment takes account of the fact that while the Interim Agreement may have some slight effect on the rate of growth of the Soviet threat to the survivability of our deterrent, it does not halt it. Therefore, should the threat overtake the negotiation of a follow-on agreement at any time within the next five years, our supreme national interests could be jeopardized. I will be surprised, Mr. President, to learn that there is any substantial opposition to this view within the Senate.

(2) Equality in SALT II

Mr. President, I have elsewhere described the present agreement as providing the United States with "interim subparity." The agreement confers on the Soviets a 50 percent advantage in numbers of land- and sea-based launchers and a 400 percent advantage in throw weight. Now, the argument is made that this enormous disparity in numbers of launchers and throw weight is offset by superior technology and numbers of warheads on our side. There is a certain limited truth to this claim. It is not an enduring truth; for while numbers are limited under the agreement, technology is not. It stands to reason, therefore, that in the long run "superior" technology cannot be relied upon to offset inferior numbers.

The inability of technology to compensate for numbers is not only true in general but is, in the present case, true for specific reasons as well. The greatest part of our presumed technological advantage lies in our lead over the Soviets in the development and deployment of MIRV warheads on our missile forces. This lead is not one that can be maintained at anything approaching our current margin. On the contrary, when the Soviets develop a MIRV capability—and they are expected to do so at "any moment"—the combination of that capability and their vastly superior throw weight will give them, given time and effort on their part, superiority in numbers of warheads.

There is an enormous volume of misinformation on the subject of alleged U.S. advantages arising from technology and geography. There is no doubt that in the long run technology will tend toward equalization. How well I remember those who argued that the Soviets would require a decade or more to catch up with the United States in developing hydrogen weapons. The same sort of scientists who today argue that we can rest comfortably with inferior numbers of launchers because of an unbridgeable advantage in technology miscalculated by about nine and a half out of ten years back in 1947. The Russians, of course, were only months behind us, and our scientists were behind the eight ball.

As to geography I have heard it argued—the Chairman of the Foreign Relations Committee made the case himself last week—that owing to our possession of forward bases for our submarine fleet we need fewer submarines than the Soviets in order to maintain on-station times equal to theirs. Now, sea-based strategic forces are assuming increasing importance so it is essential that we be correct on this point. Despite some statements to the contrary, the geographical asymmetries favor the Soviet submarine fleet and not our own. With the increased range such as that of the Soviet SSNX-8 submarine-launched missile, the importance of forward bases is greatly diminished. Russian submarines will be on station with respect to a large number of U.S. targets within one day's travel time from Murmansk or Petropavlovsk. This is not substantially different from the situation of our submarines operating out of their forward bases. What is more important, however, is that the Russians have a very large landmass between our submarines and their vulnerable points, while we do not—most of the U.S. points that are targets for Soviet submarine-launched missiles are coastal or near-coastal.

So there is little substance to the claim that we are in a favorable geographical situation.

The point I wish to make, Mr. President, is that, over the long run, there is no substitute for equal numbers of launchers taking account of throw weight differentials. I believe that the Senate should join with our negotiators and administration spokesmen in rejecting, for the future, the sort of disparities that we have agreed to, on an interim basis, in the present agreement. And in so doing I believe that we ought to insist that the principle that was applied in the case of the ABM Treaty—the principle of equality on which the Russians insisted—ought to be applied to a treaty on offensive weapons.

I was concerned, Mr. President, that our consent to the Interim Agreement, containing, as it does, the wide disparities to which I have referred, might be misunderstood as reflecting on the acceptability of such disparities in a follow-on treaty. In order to make the record clear I asked a number of witnesses before the Armed Services Committee to comment on this issue.

On July 18, I asked Ambassador Gerard Smith, the Director of the Arms Control and Disarmament Agency and head of our SALT delegation: "Would the present Interim Agreement be acceptable as a permanent agreement?" Ambassador Smith replied: "Not to me." I then directed the same question to other members of the SALT delegation. Former Deputy Secretary of Defense and now Assistant to the Secretary of Defense for SALT, Mr. Paul Nitze, said: "No." General Royal Allison, a member of the delegation and Assistant to the Chairman of the Joint Chiefs of Staff for Strategic Arms Negotiations, also said: "No."

On July 24, I directed a similar question to Secretary Laird, with respect to whether a SALT II agreement should continue the numerical relationships established in the Interim Agreement. Secretary Laird, speaking for the administration, said:

> I would hope that in these negotiations we could move in the direction of equality as far as numbers and also as far as some of the other important areas dealing with offensive strategic weapon systems. I feel that this should be a very important thrust of our negotiations because this is very basic to the continued support of the obligations that we have undertaken with our friends and allies throughout the world in order to prevent the possibility of a nuclear exchange in the future.

Chief of Naval Operations, Admiral Zumwalt, testified:

> It is my view that in SALT II, we must achieve an equality of numbers. Just as the Soviets insisted on symmetry with regard to the ABM Treaty, if we are going to go into a permanent treaty on the strategic side, I think we absolutely must insist on symmetry.

I know of no one in a responsible position in the administration who is in disagreement with this widely expressed view.

My amendment provides the Senate with an opportunity to declare itself in favor of equality in a follow-on agreement and I am certain that in view of the basic good sense of that position and the overwhelming testimony before us we will act to affirm it.

Mr. President, the question of what is to be included in the computation of equal forces in a follow-on agreement is related to the difficult issue of our forward deployments in Europe which are dedicated to the defense of our European allies and which are at sea.

The intent of my amendment as it bears on this matter

is, I believe, perfectly clear and straightforward. In stating that "the Congress recognizes the principle of United States–Soviet Union equality reflected in the Anti–Ballistic Missile Treaty" and that accordingly "the Congress requests the President to seek a future treaty that, *inter alia,* would not limit the United States to levels of intercontinental strategic forces inferior to the limits provided for the Soviet Union" it is unmistakably clear that so-called forward-based systems, which are not intercontinental, should not be included in that calculation of equality. It is my view, and the intent of the pending amendment, that any eventual treaty must recognize the necessity that the intercontinental strategic forces of the U.S. and the U.S.S.R., by which I mean to include ICBMs, submarine-launched nuclear missiles, and intercontinental range bombers of the two powers, should bear an equal relationship to one another. This says nothing about the eventual role of or disposition of the issue of forward-based systems.

With regard to the question of forward-based systems it has been my understanding, as clearly set forth by representatives of the administration in testimony before the Senate, that the U.S. has refused to negotiate the issue of forward-based systems in a bilateral U.S.-U.S.S.R. negotiation. I understand that this position was based on the entirely justifiable view that such systems are part and parcel of our alliance defense commitment and could not appropriately be considered without satisfactory alliance participation. I fully support the administration's views on this matter and there is nothing in my amendment which in any way contradicts that position.

(3) Research, Development, Modernization

My amendment, in its final sentences, simply points to the need for a vigorous program of research, development, and modernization leading to a prudent strategic posture. I wish to emphasize that adoption of this language is not intended to bear upon the wisdom of any particular procurement item. Decisions on procurement ought to be taken on a case-by-case basis. So while it is useful for the Senate to go on record to the effect that we must continue our efforts in the research, development, and modernization area, Senators can rest assured that this does not constitute an endorsement of any particular weapons system or any particular research and development effort. I emphasize this, Mr. President, because I would not wish Senators to gain the impression that in voting for my amendment they are committing themselves to any future action on procurement items.

Mr. President, I began my remarks by observing that international agreements always involve unwritten hopes and expectations and reservations. Sometimes it helps to set them down. In the present case I hope, and I am sure my colleagues share this hope, that a follow-on agreement will limit the threat to the survivability of our strategic deterrent forces. It is, in my view, well to underline this hope by language that lets the Soviets know that a failure to achieve this result would jeopardize our supreme national interests. My amendment does that.

I fully expect that our negotiators at SALT II will insist upon equality just as the Soviets insisted upon equality in the ABM Treaty. The issue of whether the present agreement adds up to equality is beside the point; and there will be differences of opinion on that. But what I am certain we can agree on is the necessity that we *not* accept in SALT II levels of intercontinental strategic weapons that are inferior to the levels of intercontinental forces permitted for the Soviet Union. My amendment does that.

Finally, I am confident that the Senate would wish to reaffirm its confidence in the importance of our research and development efforts.

Mr. President, the overriding hope and expectation of all of us is that the SALT deliberations will eventually produce a treaty that will assure the survivability, and therefore the credibility, of our deterrent posture. Such a treaty would be an enormous step toward world peace.

Mr. President, I want to see the Senate of the United States play a full and equal role in the effort to bring about such a treaty. The place to start is by giving our advice as well as our consent to the present agreement. We have an obligation to give direction to the future efforts of the government on SALT policy. I believe that direction must be toward survivable forces and toward equality. I am confident the Senate shares this view and that it will act to support my amendment.

12
Détente and SALT

Overseas Press Club, New York, New York
22 April 1974

Having led the effort to provide that any permanent SALT treaty would respect the principle of U.S.-Soviet equality, Senator Jackson set about monitoring the SALT II negotiations in an extended series of hearings as chairman of the Subcommittee on Arms Control of the Senate Armed Services Committee. In these hearings, in White House meetings, in press conferences, and in speeches, Jackson pressed for substantially reducing strategic forces down to equal levels. His themes were equality and reductions.

President Nixon and later President Ford—with Henry Kissinger as their adviser—were noticeably cool to the Senator's advice. But Jackson was persistent. He had a responsibility to identify and clarify the issues and prepare for the time when a SALT II treaty would come before the Senate for ratification. He also anticipated that his hearings and public statements might be highly important in the long-term process of developing American arms control policy. As it turned out, he anticipated correctly.

Jackson understood that the phrase *arms reductions* sounds good no matter what the numbers, but that reductions *do* good only if the numbers are right. For the numbers to be right they must enhance the stability of deterrence. That means focusing not only on the specific forces to be reduced or eliminated but also on the levels of the forces that would remain, and on whether or not they would promote stability.

On occasion the Senator would explain in detail what he meant by "a stabilizing arms reduction." A good example is his 22 April 1974 address to the Overseas Press Club.

IN RECENT YEARS, AND ESPECIALLY IN RECENT MONTHS, the foreign policy of the Nixon administration has been centered on the development of a relationship between East and West which they have called détente. No matter how hard or in which direction it has been punched—in the Middle East, in the SALT negotiations, on matters of human rights—the foreign policy of the administration has revolved, like a tether ball, around the pole of that détente.

The détente has gone from a dream to an incantation without acquiring a definition along the way. And we have been left without a clear sense of where we are going or, for that matter, a common understanding of where we have been.

In its most fundamental sense détente must mean a relaxation of tensions accompanied by an effort to achieve mutual accommodation through the negotiating process. Defined in this manner, as a process of negotiation, it has the broad support of the American people. But like any process, the process of détente must be judged by the substantive results of the negotiations themselves and by the actual behavior that follows after agreements are negotiated.

Thus the issue facing us is not whether we want a détente but how to achieve a real détente that will produce results favorable to a more peaceful world.

The centerpiece of the 1972 Moscow summit and the first test of the product of détente was the treaty on anti–ballistic missiles and the Interim Agreement on strategic offensive weapons—SALT I. I had considerable misgivings about the SALT I outcome, especially the Interim Agreement. The military advantage that the Interim Agreement conferred on the Soviets was, in my judgment, an inauspicious beginning.

Now we are engaged in SALT II, and it is this set of negotiations, perhaps more than any other, that will determine what real meaning détente will have. I welcome this opportunity to share with you a proposal that could stabilize the strategic balance through substantial reductions in the strategic forces of both the United States and the Soviet Union. In the course of my remarks tonight, which are directed to the SALT II negotiations, I have tried to develop a new direction in the effort to bring strategic arms under control—a direction based on the search for the sort of wide-ranging disarmament that would do much to bring us closer to a genuine détente and a more peaceful world.

In recent months we have seen the development by the Soviet Union of a significant number of new weapon systems incorporating an impressive range of new and costly technology. Not only have the Soviets achieved a genuine MIRV capability, but they have done so by developing two quite distinct MIRV technologies. They have tested a whole new generation of intercontinental ballistic missiles, land- and sea-based, incorporating new technologies as well as new launch techniques. They have developed a mobile, land-based ICBM. They have moved to increase by a very substantial factor the throw weight of their missile forces despite the fact that they already enjoy a threefold advantage in this area. These developments, all of which have come to light since the SALT Interim Agreement, which was supposed to limit offensive weapons, have, individually and in combination, added significantly to the offensive potential of the Soviet missile forces.

In assessing the significance of these developments, all of which are consistent with the often ambiguous terms of the SALT Interim Agreement, it is necessary to digress for a moment to consider the rationale by which the Interim Agreement was defended.

The numerical disadvantage into which the United States was frozen by the SALT I Interim Agreement was held by some to be effectively offset by our technological superiority. The most obvious American technological advantage—obvious in part because of the frequency with which Dr. Kissinger reiterated it—lay in the fact that we had achieved a MIRV capability and the Soviet Union had not. Today our monopoly in MIRV technology has vanished like last year's snow and the lead in this area that we still possess by virtue of our earlier development of MIRVs can be expected to diminish rapidly as time goes on. This is neither novel nor surprising. In the long run—made longer if we find ourselves forced into a technological arms race and shorter if we do not—technology tends to even out. That is the history of technology; and it is, in particular, the history of military technology. Given the numbers and throw weights agreed to in the SALT I Interim Agreement, under which the Soviets enjoy a protected advantage, technological equality will mean Soviet superiority in strategic weapons.

In the final analysis, an arms control agreement will not be stable if it freezes for one side an advantage in quantity while the other has to rely on an edge in quality that it cannot maintain. In the Interim Agreement we agreed to inferior numbers but the Soviets did not agree to inferior technology. We should never have presumed—I, for one, did not—that they would fail to seek the combination of superior numbers and comparable technology that add up to overall superiority; and this is precisely the direction that they have chosen.

In the current SALT II negotiations the Soviets are seeking to consolidate the advantage they obtained in the Interim Agreement while pressing for equality in technology. Again and again when the Interim Agreement was before the Senate I warned that this would be the Soviet strategy at SALT II. My amendment to the authorization for the Interim Agreement placed the Congress and the administration on record on this issue by insisting that the Interim Agreement was not an acceptable basis for a SALT II treaty.

Now, with negotiations under way, we find that just as expected, the Soviets have actually hardened their position. Far from viewing SALT II as an occasion to search for the sort of stable strategic balance that can result only from equality, they are insisting on a SALT II arrangement that would widen and deepen their strategic margin still further.

The response of the administration to this situation has been disappointing in the extreme. For rather than concentrating on the design and presentation of an arms control proposal that could form the basis for a long-term stabilization of the strategic balance, the administration has concentrated on quick-fix, short-term proposals that can be readied in time for the forthcoming June summit meeting in Moscow.

In their desire to preserve the impression of momentum in the SALT negotiations, the administration has abandoned its previous conviction that the essential purpose of a follow-on agreement should be to rectify the imbalance of SALT I.

In their haste to meet an arbitrary and politically expedient self-imposed June deadline, the administration has now begun to entertain Soviet proposals which are inimical to the national security of the United States and to the prospects for a SALT II treaty based on U.S.-Soviet equality.

Kept on such a course, SALT II is doomed to fail in the supreme mission of reducing the risk of mutual destruction. Indeed, instead of putting a damper on the arms race, such a failure would add fuel to the fire. Given this situation, I am persuaded the time is ripe for the United States to put forward a bold and imaginative proposal for serious disarmament—a proposal that will test uncertain Soviet intentions by inviting them to join with us in concluding a far-reaching agreement to bring about a measure of stability in the nuclear balance at sharply reduced levels of strategic forces.

Instead of arms limitation agreements that do not limit, it is time for serious arms reductions by both sides—a stabilizing disarmament. In outlining my proposal it is useful to begin by recalling the numbers agreed to under the terms of the SALT I Interim Agreement, according to which the United States may have no more than 1,054 intercontinental ballistic missiles. This force consists principally of Minuteman missiles that are termed "light" (in contrast to "heavy") under the definitions worked out in conjunction with the Interim Agreement. For their part, the Soviets are permitted 1,618 intercontinental ballistic missiles, of which approximately 1,300 are of the "light" variety. The other 300 Soviet ICBMs are "heavy" —so heavy, in fact, that these 300 alone carry as much throw weight as the entire permitted U.S. force of 1,000 Minuteman missiles. With respect to the Soviet missile force the terms "light" and "heavy" are misleading because the missile that the Soviets apparently intend to deploy as a substitute in the "light" category for the missiles in that category at the time of the Interim Agreement are several times more powerful, several times "heavier" than our comparable systems.

At sea the Interim Agreement provides that the United States may have up to 44 missile-firing nuclear submarines containing 710 launch tubes. The Soviets are permitted up to

62 comparable submarines, with 950 launch tubes, in addition to a number of older type submarines. The Soviets are now engaged in building up to these levels.

I believe that strategic forces on both sides are larger than they need to be, *provided* that we can negotiate with the Soviets toward a common ceiling at a sharply lower level. Therefore I propose that we invite the Soviets to consider a SALT II agreement in which each side would be limited to 800 ICBMs and to no more than 560 submarine-launched missiles, equivalent to 35 missile-firing submarines of the Poseidon type. Long-range strategic bombers, which were not included under the Interim Agreement, would also be limited to 400 on each side. Because the throw weight of the Soviet missile force is so much greater than that of our own, the two SALT delegations would be instructed to negotiate a formula for varying these basic numbers so as to bring the throw weight of the two intercontinental strategic forces into approximate equality.

The numbers resulting from the negotiating process need not be precisely the numbers outlined here, although I believe that significant variation from these numbers, if essential to successful negotiation, ought to move in the direction of further reductions rather than upward adjustments. Because the strategic forces of the countries are structured differently at present and because we are always searching for ways in which to reduce the potential vulnerability of our deterrent, the treaty need not follow the precise numbers for each type of weapon system I have suggested—so long as the aggregate total of intercontinental strategic launchers was 1,760 or less. Reductions to a level of equality would be carried out, in phases, over a period of time to be negotiated.

A treaty reflecting the essential features that I have outlined here would represent a real and significant step in the direction of stabilizing disarmament. It would put to rest many of the misgivings that we now have that the Soviets are seeking to attain strategic superiority by consolidating their advantage in SALT I. It would permit both sides to shift their resources from the building up of nuclear arsenals to the building up of their economies.

The Soviet Union has turned to the United States for economic assistance, for our capital, our agricultural produce, and our advanced technology. So long as the Soviets support the greatly exaggerated military sector of their economy at anything approaching current levels, an American program of subsidized economic transactions and the transfer of sophisticated technology, whatever its intended purpose, will inevitably amount to aid to the Russian army, naval, and air forces.

At a time when the Soviet economy is in great difficulty we ought to be able to persuade them that a reordering of their priorities away from the military sector is the best way to achieve economic well-being. Adoption of my proposal could be an important step along a path that could lead eventually to billions of dollars in savings on strategic weapons systems.

It would enable us *both* to reorder our priorities.

If agreed to, it would mark a turning point in U.S.-Soviet relations of historic proportions. It would carry us to the brink of peace.

Such an accord could transform the atmosphere of mistrust and apprehension that has clouded the horizon of East-West relations since the end of World War II. It would add immeasurably to the confidence of both our peoples, indeed, of all mankind, that the grim prospect of thermonuclear war can be set aside and our energies devoted to purposes more constructive and more enduring than the amassing of the weapons of war. It would be, if ever there was one, a genuine conceptual breakthrough.

In the new and more hopeful world that would result, we could look forward to a broadening of the foundation of mutual accommodation, a deepening of the spirit of cooperation in trade and commerce, science and technology and the arts, and in the freer movement of people and ideas.

This is a program for the beginning of a more peaceful world. It is worthy of our best efforts. And I am committed to do whatever I can to bring it about. I am under no illusion about the difficulty of negotiating an arms reduction agreement along the lines outlined here. It will take time and hard bargaining. The view of some in the administration that force reductions are not negotiable is premature; and there are many who do not share this judgment. After all, it was Henry Kissinger himself who warned—in his book *The Necessity for Choice*—that to reject sound proposals because they appeared to be nonnegotiable was to acquiesce in negotiating on Soviet terms.

Some weeks ago I urged the President to consider the program that I have outlined here tonight. The response has not been encouraging. The refusal of the administration to consider seriously a program for Soviet-American force reductions is as disappointing as the tendency to seek a quick cosmetic agreement in June is dangerous.

There is no critical point for negotiations that will be passed if June comes and goes without a follow-on SALT arrangement. There is nothing unique about the month of June that would justify an extension of the SALT I Interim Agreement and thereby legitimize its terms beyond 1977 and prejudice the prospects for a meaningful and stabilizing SALT II treaty.

I am not content to let the matter rest upon the complex and multipurpose judgments of an embattled White House, or with a Department of State whose passion for momentum is sometimes indifferent to the direction in which it is headed. I have today requested, as chairman of the Arms Control Subcommittee of the Senate Committee on Armed Services, that the Secretary of Defense undertake an immediate and thorough assessment of my arms reduction proposal for transmission to the subcommittee.

Adoption of this proposal would mark a radical departure from the tentative and often marginal approach to arms control that we have followed in SALT. Reductions on the scale I am proposing will encounter opposition, not least of all from those in the military services whose training, experience, and orientation are likely to militate against strategic force reductions in general, and extensive reductions in particular. While it would be imprudent to discard the professional judgment of the military and irresponsible to ignore their advice, I believe that we must not allow their skepticism to stand in the way of a proposal which will enhance our security.

I am confident that American military planners can be persuaded of the advantages of bilateral cutbacks in strategic weapons and that they too, in the final analysis, reflect the hopes we all share for a more stable strategic balance and a more peaceful world. I would hope that the Soviet military, which has been unreceptive to proposals such as this in the past, would give careful consideration to the promise of a better life for the Soviet people, who could be freed from part of the enormous burden of the arms they now bear. Here the job of persuasion must fall to the Politburo, and to them I am simply saying: Let us break with the troubled past and seek a more fruitful and secure future for both our peoples.

13
SALT and the Future of Freedom

North Atlantic Assembly, Ottawa, Canada
26 October 1979

The SALT II treaty, signed by President Carter and Leonid Brezhnev at a Vienna summit in June 1979, included a number of provisions that Senator Jackson had advised against during the course of the negotiations. Most disappointing was that it violated the principle of equality by protection of a large Soviet advantage in heavy missiles and ballistic throw weight, its verification provisions were seriously deficient, and it did not provide for mutual reductions.

Jurisdiction over the treaty belonged to the Foreign Relations Committee. But the Armed Services Committee was entitled to hold hearings on the treaty's military implications and to issue a report. Working with the chairman of the committee, Senator John Stennis, Jackson helped organize a set of hearings in which the treaty was examined in detail and its impact on the national interest evaluated. Over the years, many of the Senator's colleagues had participated with him in monitoring SALT discussions; the issues were familiar, the ground was well prepared, and Jackson was out front. The Armed Services Committee report, when agreed upon, advised that "as it now stands," the SALT II treaty "is not in the national security interests of the United States of America."[17] The report identified major changes in the treaty considered essential if the treaty was to serve U.S. national security. The vote for the report was 10-0, with 7 abstentions.

Given only a narrow favorable vote in the Foreign Relations Committee, the SALT II treaty was certain to lack the required two-thirds majority, even before the December 1979 Soviet invasion of Afghanistan and President Carter's abrupt recall of the unratified treaty from the Senate's calendar.

Believing our NATO allies should hear about SALT not only from administration officials but also from informed Senators, Jackson went before an October 1979 plenary session of the North Atlantic Assembly in Ottawa, Canada.

LIKE SO MANY OTHERS, I AM DISAPPOINTED AT THE OUT-
come of the SALT II negotiations. What is required for the
peace of the world is serious East-West arms reduction—a
genuine stabilizing arms limitation. Tragically, the SALT II
treaty submitted to the Senate turns out to be an unbalanced
charter sanctioning the massive buildup of Soviet strategic
power, advantaging the Soviets in critical respects, and containing provisions of great importance that we are unable to
verify.

My friends, it is time for all men and women who cherish
freedom to face reality. A decade of the "SALT process" has
been accompanied by an unparalleled Soviet strategic buildup.

In 1969, the United States led the Soviet Union in every
single indicator of strategic military strength: the number
of land-based and sea-based missiles, the number of warheads, the megatonnage of its missile force, the accuracy of its
weapons, the potential of its missiles to strike protected military targets, and so forth. Now, the Soviet Union leads the
United States in every one of these same indicators with only
one exception, the number of warheads. And the American
lead in warheads is rapidly evaporating.

For the first time, after a decade of arms control negotiations, the Soviets have acquired the capability to destroy a significant portion of the American strategic retaliatory forces—
something they were never able to do before, and something
that we cannot do to their forces even now.

It is now generally recognized that the SALT agreement of
1972 did not, as its proponents hoped, moderate the growth
of Soviet strategic forces. In fact, the Soviet devotion of resources to strategic forces actually increased after the 1972
agreement. Today they devote more than three times as much
resources as the United States to strategic offensive and defensive forces, as measured in constant-dollar terms. Indeed, the
Soviets have invested in the last decade over 104 billion dollars
more than the United States in strategic nuclear forces alone.

In conventional weapons, the situation is also serious: the
Soviets lead us in tanks by 5 to 1, in artillery pieces by 2.3 to 1,
in attack submarines by 3.5 to 1, in ground forces divisions by

10 to 1, in medium bombers by 11 to 1, and in air defense missile systems by 278 to 1. And in this last decade we have begun to see the development of a sophisticated, ocean-going Soviet navy, including nuclear-powered surface combatants.

The adverse shift in the strategic and conventional equation is bound to have far-reaching effects upon world politics. As the Kremlin becomes confident of possessing strategic superiority—combined with Soviet conventional superiority in local situations—the willingness of the Soviet leaders to confront and intimidate the NATO nations and their vital interests will grow correspondingly. We are all aware that during this same period we in the West increasingly will be dependent on various countries in the Third World for raw materials, especially energy resources.

The great danger ahead is the Kremlin's political use of strategic superiority as an umbrella under which to pursue a series of probes—on their own or through the foreign legions of their surrogates—to expand Soviet power and weaken the position of the Western nations. The fateful question for us is whether the NATO countries can conduct effective foreign policies, which will ensure their national security, from a position of strategic and conventional inferiority. Can our leaders bargain confidently and stubbornly, can they stand up to Soviet blackmail, can they hold their ground in crisis situations —from a position of relative military weakness?

On October 6, 1938, following the Munich summit, as the policy of appeasement lay in ruins, Neville Chamberlain said in the House of Commons, "Our past experience has shown us only too clearly that weakness in armed strength means weakness in diplomacy." This year—four decades after Munich— what the world needed from SALT II was a treaty that would substantially reduce strategic forces—a move toward genuine arms control.

In 1974 and 1975 I outlined and urged just that sort of treaty. In March 1977 President Carter proposed significant mutual force reductions and a ban on the deployment of new ICBMs. Many of us in Congress warmly supported that proposal. But the administration's initial position collapsed at the very first Soviet objection: it did not have the conviction to hold its ground with the Russians.

However, the SALT II agreement, which the Soviets did not object to, will permit them to continue unabated their huge increase in strategic forces, just as did SALT I. During the seven years of this treaty, Moscow is expected to add more than 5,000 strategic nuclear warheads to its already formidable arsenal. Far from limiting the Soviets to just one "new type" ICBM as has been claimed, a close reading of the treaty makes it clear that loopholes in the definition of the term "new" will enable the Soviets to continue to develop and deploy their very new ICBMs in the guise of modernization.

The new treaty allows the Soviets some 300 heavy missiles, each with 10 warheads. The United States is not allowed any heavy missiles nor are we compensated for the imbalance in throw weight. SALT II thus violates the congressional mandate to provide for equal levels of strategic forces, taking into account missile throw weight. That mandate is contained in the Jackson amendment, which has been part of American statute law since 1972.

And even our light missiles, which have a third the throw weight of the Soviet light missiles, are permitted to carry only half as many warheads—six on each missile for them and three on each missile for us. More important, we can no longer rely on our earlier advantage in accuracy to compensate for this quantitative imbalance.

The Soviets have a new supersonic bomber, the Backfire, currently in production. It doesn't count in the treaty. We have an old subsonic bomber, built 20 years ago, called the B-52. Each B-52 counts under the treaty—even those that have been cannibalized for spare parts.

There are more inequalities in this treaty. For instance, why is it "equal" for the Soviet Union to be allowed to deploy yet more SS-20s targeted against Europe during the same period that we are prohibited from deploying intermediate range cruise missiles? What is equal about a protocol that codifies the notion that we must hold back on our most promising new theater systems, while the Soviets proceed to build up their theater nuclear capabilities? Both in public and in private the Soviets have made clear they regard the protocol limitations as not temporary in nature. And the current Soviet campaign of public pressure against NATO's theater modernization is only the beginning.

Already Dutch Parliamentarians and some others in Europe are telling us that ratification of SALT II is a prerequisite for adoption of the theater force modernization program. As Senator [Sam] Nunn [of Georgia] has responded:

This reminds me of a Marx brothers movie where Chico, whose life is being threatened by armed thugs, points a gun at his own head and shouts, "If you come any closer, I'll pull the trigger."

To accept this threat as a serious argument for SALT II ratification, one would have to conclude that our allies are not dedicated to their own defense. If this is the case, the future of the alliance is not bright, whether SALT II is ratified or rejected.

If the United States settles for an unequal SALT II agreement, what is going to persuade Moscow to accept an "equal" agreement in a SALT III or a SALT IV? Once SALT II sets the precedent for inequality, do you believe Moscow will give it up when dealing with us collectively in some MBFR [mutual and balanced force reductions] agreement, or in a SALT III which incorporates theater systems? The free nations will be far better off if the United States Senate insists on equality now, in SALT II, rather than hope that the "next time around" equality will be achieved. It won't be if we fail to demand it now. Just remember that SALT II was to have been the "next time" as a follow-on to SALT I.

Moreover, there are significant aspects of SALT II which cannot be verified sufficiently. The protocol to the treaty, which deals with cruise missiles and mobile missiles, effectively cannot be verified—it's as simple as that. There are other areas where the treaty causes serious verification problems, including Brezhnev's Backfire statement, the number of reentry vehicles deployed on the SS-18s, and the encryption of telemetry allowed the Soviets. Thus, many Senators believe that this treaty as submitted is not adequately verifiable.

As Lord Chalfont* recently said:

Those who support the treaty seem to suggest that it is in itself a Good Thing, like cricket or brotherly love, and that anybody who does not support it is either a cad or some kind of irredeemable right-wing reactionary.

My friends, the treaty is not like cricket or brotherly love. It is not a measure of disarmament. It is not a breakthrough of any kind. It is an unequal charter for the massive Soviet strategic buildup—an altogether ironic outcome for a so-called arms control agreement.

As Lord Chalfont went on to say:

It is argued by people both in this country and in the United States that, if the Senate were to fail to ratify this treaty or outrage the Russians by demanding any form of amendment, the prestige of President Carter and of the whole American Presidency would be undermined; and that this would have effects upon the world balance of power altogether disproportionate to the importance of the SALT agreement. I find this argument difficult to follow. If the treaty itself is bad and ineffective, then it seems to me that it would be far more dangerous to accept it uncritically than to say so now while the Senate is in the process of debating the ratification. It will be no good saying it afterwards.

As you well know, the Senate of the United States has a constitutional responsibility not only to give or withhold its consent to the administration's proposed treaty but to give its advice as well. That is just what we are doing. And we are also taking a hard look at our overall defense posture.

Many of us in the Senate believe that the treaty as submitted is dangerously defective. And in our political system the means of bringing about change in a proposed treaty are numerous. They include Senate amendments and motions to recommit a treaty to the President with instructions to reopen the negotiations and with guidelines as to the outcome we should seek. Many of us believe that no SALT II treaty would be preferable

*British politician, statesman, and author; Minister of State for Foreign Affairs, 1964–70; Minister for Disarmament, 1965–67, 1969–70.

to an unsafe one and that the current treaty will not be safe unless its most serious deficiencies are corrected.

In short, a major undertaking is under way in the Senate to help fashion a balanced SALT II treaty that provides for equality and greater verifiability and protects the bargaining position of the NATO alliance for genuine, mutual arms reduction.

14
Does America Have a Peace Strategy?

Plymouth Congregational Church, Seattle, Washington
4 June 1982

At the invitation of President-elect Reagan, Senator Jackson served as a member of Reagan's 1980 Presidential transition team. In that capacity, as well as in private talks and in a personal 24 March 1981 letter, Senator Jackson advised the new President to seize the initiative in a dramatic peace offensive by fashioning a plan and strategy that would provide for a mutual reduction of U.S.-Soviet strategic nuclear forces in a stabilizing manner. He wrote that if such an initiative proved successful, "it would be a turning point in East-West relations of historic proportions."[18]

President Reagan was a good listener, and Jackson had allies within the councils of the administration. The Senator's tenacity began to pay off in the moves by Washington and then Moscow to focus the ongoing arms control negotiations on reducing nuclear weapons rather than setting ceilings for their future growth. In December 1987 (four years and a few months after Senator Jackson died) President Reagan and Mikhail Gorbachev signed the Intermediate-Range Nuclear Forces (INF) Treaty to eliminate an entire category of nuclear weapons. This was a distinct achievement, though a modest one, since the weapons to be eliminated constitute but a small fraction of the superpowers' arsenals. However, for the first time on-site inspections of sensitive missile bases, training facilities, and industrial plants are allowed. This treaty may prove to be the beginning of a wholly new stage in arms control—the start of mutual, verifiable reductions. And the treaty respects the principle of U.S.-Soviet equality—so long championed by the Senator—by eliminating substantially more Soviet weapons than American ones to alleviate the inequality in forces.

Also of note, a proposal presented in the spring of 1982 by Jackson (with Democratic Senator Sam Nunn of Georgia and Republican Senator John Warner of Virginia) emerged in modified form in a September 1987 U.S.-Soviet agreement to set up "risk-reduction centers" in Washington and Moscow to encourage the systematic exchange of information, including giving advance notice of nuclear and missile tests and major military exercises.

In the spring of 1982, Senator Jackson welcomed an invitation from the Seattle-based World Without War Council to explore a peace strategy for America. His remarks keynoted the conference, which included representatives of a full range of opinion on the "peace issue."

I AM DELIGHTED TO BE HERE THIS MORNING TO SHARE IN this pathbreaking event with representatives of so many of the key sectors of the Seattle community. We are all deeply grateful to the World Without War Council—especially to Stephen Boyd [executive director] and George Weigel [scholar-in-residence]—for organizing this exploration of America's peace strategy that goes beyond the easy stereotypes and the common polarizations.

No one in a position of public authority—least of all one who has faced the problem of national security and world security for many years—takes the problem of war and its threat lightly. We know, from hard experience, just how fragile the peace of the world is. At one moment, the invasion of Afghanistan, at another moment the crushing of freedom in Poland, and now a dispute over two small islands in the South Atlantic: these events remind us that, for all that we have accomplished in preventing a general war for thirty-seven years, the structure of peace in the world rests on shaky foundations.

No one in this room can claim to have all the answers. All of us who have worked for peace are, in a sense, still students. But we should now think of ourselves as *experienced* students, who have at least learned what approaches don't work. Listening to each other, and reflecting on our various points of view —in short, learning from our experiences—is one of the aims of this conference, and I applaud it.

Now, let me get right down to the task assigned me: to indicate assumptions and judgments that lie behind my approach to a productive peace strategy.

First of all, America needs nothing so much as a genuine peace effort. I wrote a private letter to President Reagan two months after he took office (March 24, 1981) urging him to launch a great American peace offensive at a very early opportunity. In that letter, I said: "Strategic forces on both sides are larger than they need to be, provided that we can negotiate with the Soviets toward a common ceiling at sharply reduced levels."

As I see it, a sound peace strategy has three requirements.

One. It should set the right goal, that is, arms reductions, leading toward verifiable disarmament.

Two. It should soberly face the obstacles that now block the way to the goal, particularly the problems of dealing with the Soviets.

Three. It should hold both these realities together—the need for substantial, mutual, verifiable arms reductions and the harsh facts of Soviet power and performance.

I recall the words of the distinguished theologian Reinhold Niebuhr:

> There has never been a scheme of justice in history which did not have a balance of power at its foundation. If the democratic nations fail, their failure must be partly attributed to the faulty strategy of idealists who have too many illusions when they face realists who have too little conscience.

Those in public office are grateful when they encounter a peace effort that strengthens the nation's capacity to champion *mutual* arms restraint, *balanced* arms reductions, and *verifiable* disarmament. This provides the needed civic base on which to conduct a responsible American peace strategy.

Now a second point: Peace in this world of conflicting values and interests is not a process of conversion: it is a *political* accomplishment. Promoting a peace with justice and individual liberty requires an *instrument.* Among available instruments, the best is our own nation; partly because of its power but also because the best in our religious, ethical, and political-philosophical traditions requires us to put work for peace at the top of our public agenda.

If America is to be the instrument for peace that it can be, we need to create a mature patriotism—one that is not overwhelmed with guilt at our national shortcomings and seeks to withdraw from the world and, on the other hand, one that is not stridently jingoistic in its sense of an American "messianic" role in the world. As I see it, helping create that kind of mature patriotism ought to be one function of the public effort for peace.

A third point: There is no magic formula that will achieve a just and durable peace overnight. History teaches that to achieve that goal we must be prepared for prolonged negotiations.

There is no other way. Unfortunately, no amount of wishing and hoping—no amount of orating or marching—will produce a stable peace. That achievement is in sight only when we sit down at the table with the Soviets—and others—and negotiate agreement to limitations, reductions, and dismantlements of the world's arsenals.

Do we have the patience to engage in this kind of tough, protracted negotiations? Do we have the will to stay the course? That is the fundamental question.

Fourthly, a sound peace strategy should not ignore political-diplomatic steps that we can take, almost immediately, to deal with the most nerve-wracking dimension of the nuclear threat —the danger of nuclear war by accident or miscalculation or through terrorism. That is why I have been urging that our government now put a high priority on establishing with the Soviets a permanent joint U.S.-U.S.S.R. consultation center that would represent and assure continuing superpower dialogue. Such a center would be staffed by very senior Soviet and American civilian professionals. It would build on the present hot line and have communications links that gave it sure and instant access to the White House and the Kremlin. Such a center would provide what could be a literally life-saving arrangement for instant information exchange and consultation when incidents occurred that could be misinterpreted as harbingers of an imminent nuclear assault by one power against the other.

As I have said, arms reduction negotiations are bound to be lengthy and complicated. However, it could well be possible to reach almost immediate agreement on a consultation center, whose establishment would be so clearly in the interests of both sides and would help build world confidence in the possibilities for stability and peace.

Finally, we can take pride that the Seattle community, led by the World Without War Council and others, has become one of the places where what the country most needs can take place: an exploration of the range of opinion on what ought to be America's peace strategy—but an exploration under the discipline of taking seriously the threat that adversary power poses to us and to the future of individual liberty.

I applaud this conference's effort to move beyond present polarizations to a perspective on the problem of peace that allows those with diverse experience to work together. This kind of conference should be emulated throughout the nation. Whether you succeed in building agreement on America's peace strategy here at home will have much to do with America's success as a peacemaker in the world.

V
Human Rights
and Fundamental Freedoms

15

The Jackson Amendment
on Freedom of Emigration

United States Senate
27 September 1972

Senator Jackson had long held that the United States had an obligation to safeguard and foster basic human rights. This obligation arose, he believed, from profound ethical and political considerations, and also from concerns for world stability and a durable peace. A government, especially the government of a powerful nation, that denies its citizens the basic liberties deprives itself of an effective public opinion that can influence and check its conduct in international affairs.

Of all the individual liberties affirmed in the UN Universal Declaration of Human Rights, none was more fundamental to Senator Jackson than the right to emigrate. He called it the "touchstone of human rights" because not only is it the life-saving liberty of last resort, but also, when this right is respected, governments must pay some honor to other basic freedoms or risk losing too many of their citizens. (As George Will commented in the aftermath of the 1989 breaching of the Berlin Wall, the right to emigrate is a sharp chisel for cracking the concrete of tyranny.)

Following Israel's victory in the 1967 Six-Day War, the resurgent self-regard among Soviet Jews led to internal pressures for emigration to Israel. The Kremlin began to allow more Jews and others to leave. As the number of applicants increased, however, the Soviets had second thoughts. In 1972, they imposed a so-called education tax purporting to compensate the state for the costs of higher education but actually designed to curtail and frustrate emigration efforts. Meanwhile, in the name of détente, President Nixon and Henry Kissinger were seeking authority in the East-West Trade Relations Act of 1971 to make the Soviet Union eligible for most-favored-nation tariff treatment and increased official lending subsidies.

The moment was opportune. In June 1972 Jackson advanced an amendment to the East-West Trade Relations Act to link the granting of MFN and official credits to the Soviet Union and other non-market-economy countries with clear evidence of their respect for the right to emigrate. The Jackson amendment applied to the emigration of Jews, Christians, and others, without discrimination on the basis of religion, race, or national origin. It did not affect U.S.-Soviet trade on a pay-as-you-go basis. In his remarks to the Senate on 27 September 1972, Jackson began a historic legislative struggle that lasted over two years.

MR. PRESIDENT, I WILL BE OFFERING ON BEHALF OF A BIPARtisan group of my colleagues an amendment to the East-West Trade Relations Act of 1971, S. 2620.* It is a simple amendment. It arises out of and is rooted in our traditional commitment to the cause of individual liberty. It is a simple plea for simple justice. But unlike other such pleadings, it has some teeth in it.

Our amendment would add a new section 10 to the bill, consisting of nine parts, that would extend most-favored-nation treatment to Communist countries. It would establish a direct legislative link between that status and other trade and credit concessions, on the one hand, and the freedom to emigrate without the payment of prohibitive taxes amounting to ransom, on the other. Under this amendment no country would be eligible to receive most-favored-nation treatment or to participate in U.S. credit and credit and investment guarantee programs unless that country permits its citizens the opportunity to emigrate to the country of their choice. Moreover, the amendment would require the President to judge and report in detail upon the compliance with this condition of any country wishing to obtain most-favored-nation status or U.S. credits. Such a report, updated at regular intervals, would make

*The East-West Trade Relations Act of 1971, the Jackson amendment to it, and a similar amendment introduced in the House of Representatives by Congressman Charles Vanik failed to become law by the close of the 92d Congress. Jackson therefore reintroduced the amendment in the first session of the 93d Congress, attaching it to the Trade Reform Act of 1973. Vanik did likewise in the House. By the time the Jackson-Vanik amendment was adopted in the second session of the 93d Congress and signed into law by President Nixon, it had become a section in the Trade Reform Act of 1974.

available our best information as to the nature, content, application, implementation, and effects of the emigration laws and conditions in the countries concerned.

Mr. President, the Nobel lecture of the great Russian writer Alexander Solzhenitsyn was recently published in the West. It is more than an eloquent defense of truth and justice. It is more than a sharp condemnation of tyranny. It contains the profound message that "mankind's sole salvation lies in everyone making everything his business, in the people in the East being vitally concerned with what is thought in the West, the people of the West vitally concerned with what goes on in the East." Mr. President, the "thought in the West" is contained in our amendment. I propose that this great Senate concern itself with what goes on in the East.

We have received numerous reports of late about the intensification of state repression in the Soviet Union. Intellectuals and other dissidents have been arrested and sent to labor camps, hospitals, and mental institutions. In Lithuania demonstrations by Roman Catholics demanding religious and cultural freedom have been brutally put down. And the Soviet regime has stepped up its campaign against Jews seeking to emigrate to Israel.

The most dramatic violation of basic human rights is the recent decision of the Politburo to demand a ransom from Jews wishing to leave the Soviet Union. The reaction to this decision in the West has been one of outrage and revulsion. It violates our most deeply held convictions about human freedom and dignity. It recalls to us a dark age when human beings were enslaved and traded as chattel. In our own land it took a civil war to blot out that disgrace and vindicate the principles of our Constitution.

Mr. President, those of us who lived during the time of the Third Reich remember when Himmler sold exit permits for Jews. As the great British historian Robert Conquest has pointed out, the Soviet leaders may be unaware of this unflattering parallel since none of the Western literature on the Holocaust has been published in Russia. But we are aware of the Holocaust. We see the parallel. And that is why we must do whatever we can to prevent a repetition of that horrible catastrophe.

I will not here catalog the continuing record of oppression suffered by the Soviet Jews and by other minorities and dissidents in the Soviet Union. But I must express my fear that the current ransom program, wicked in itself, carries with it the potential to exacerbate anti-Semitism in the Soviet Union to an extent and a depth that we hoped had perished for all time with the collapse of the Third Reich. For in the effort to justify this barbaric trade in human beings the Soviets have appealed to the basest instincts. The reports reaching us affirming the popularity of the ransom policy are the most painful of all. They portend the unleashing of bitter forces that even a totalitarian regime as adept at regimenting its people as the Soviet state cannot always control. Nor is it certain that control is what the leaders in the Kremlin desire.

Now, the Soviet leaders have explained that the exorbitant emigration taxes, amounting to thousands of dollars, are in reality a tax on education incurred by the student as a consequence of his state-supported studies. The more audacious Soviet spokesmen have gone so far as to compare these taxes to the obligation incurred by the graduates of our military academies who undertake to spend a specified period of time following graduation in the armed services. In principle there is nothing wrong with the making of an agreement between student and institution of learning—or, for that matter, between the student and the state—in which the student undertakes certain obligations in return for his tuition. But that is not what is involved in the Soviet case and it is a lie to suggest otherwise. For one thing the emigration taxes have been retroactively imposed on all citizens. They do not arise out of any agreement or understanding or voluntary obligation. For another, the Soviet student is denied recourse to private educational institutions so that even if the obligations were placed on a voluntary basis, which they are not, there would be no way to avoid them. One would be forced either to accept the state's terms or go without any education. Moreover, the taxes imposed on emigration, unlike agreements sometimes made in Western countries to serve after graduation in a prearranged capacity, are prohibitive and intended to be so. Soviet citizens are simply not permitted to earn or amass the sums necessary to purchase their freedom. To attempt to borrow the huge amounts involved opens one to persecution for economic crimes, and no one earns the sort of income that would enable him to pay the visa tax for an advanced education without borrowing. So the funds cannot be generated internally.

The fact is, Mr. President, that a decision to pay the ransom demand would be to submit to blackmail of the most ominous sort. Where would it stop? Would it spread to other countries as aerial hijacking did when first attempted and then emulated? Would the remnant of scattered minorities, Jews and others, become the new medium of international exchange? Would we organize the agencies, arrange for the planes and ships, transfer the foreign exchange, negotiate the prices—in short, would we institutionalize the sale of a whole people? I say no—and I ask the Senate to join with me in saying no.

There will be those who will say, even as Mr. Brezhnev must surely have said to the President in Moscow, that the action we are proposing is an intrusion in the internal affairs of the Soviet Union. To this I would quote Solzhenitsyn: "There are no internal affairs left on our crowded Earth."

The fact is, of course, that the ransom—were it to be paid—would be paid out of funds raised primarily in the United States. That surely gives us the right as a government, quite apart from the dedication to our own high principles, to be "vitally concerned with what goes on in the East."

Mr. President, we Americans are fortunate to have at our service the greatest economy the world has ever known. It can do more than enrich our lives. It can be pressed into service as an instrument of our commitment to individual liberty. We can deny our vast markets to the Soviet Union. We can reserve participation in our credit and investment programs—our "internal" matters—to those countries who accord their citizens the fundamental human right to emigrate. We can, and we must, keep the faith of our own highest traditions.

We must not now, as we did once, acquiesce to tyranny while there are those, at greater risk than ourselves, who dare to resist.

16
Détente and Human Rights

Pacem in Terris Conference, Washington, D.C.
11 October 1973

By the spring of 1973, the Jackson amendment (reintroduced in the Senate as an amendment to the Trade Reform Act of 1973) had 75 Senate cosponsors. Similar legislation introduced in the House of Representatives by Congressman Charles Vanik gained 272 cosponsors.

The impact of the amendment when first advanced in 1972 had been immediate. To try to placate the Congress, the Soviets had suspended their so-called education tax only six months after its enactment. This was a hopeful sign, but only a start. Where was the assurance that Moscow would end harassment and maintain high levels of emigration?

Also in hopes of placating the Congress, Moscow allowed an increase in Jewish emigration. (The number actually reached an annual high of nearly 35,000 by the end of 1973.) Here was another victory for the amendment. But what about the future if the Jackson amendment was not approved by the Congress and so would no longer be part of the bargaining process?

Meanwhile, President Nixon and Secretary of State Kissinger— with powerful allies in the American business community—were doing what they could to frustrate passage of the amendment, charging in particular that this was a Jackson ploy to wreck détente. (As for this accusation, it should now be abundantly evident that the breakdown of the so-called détente of the 1970s had more deep-rooted causes, including the Kremlin's geopolitical ambitions and expansionist activities. The Senator clearly believed that any genuine détente must be grounded in a greater Soviet respect for fundamental freedoms. The Jackson-Vanik amendment was modest legislation focused on the single right to emigrate, and it proved of considerable influence. But one can scarcely attribute to it the Middle East war of 1973, the violation of the 1973 Indochina peace accords, the Soviet-Cuban invasion of Angola, North Vietnam's invasion of Cambodia, or the Soviet invasion of Afghanistan, not to mention various Kremlin violations of strategic arms control agreements.)

With the lines drawn for and against the amendment, the Senator went about explaining his case to a wide audience. A good example is his address to the Pacem in Terris Conference on 11 October 1973.

AT NO TIME SINCE THE END OF WORLD WAR II HAS THE WEST-ern democratic world been more hopeful, or the struggling democrats in the East more apprehensive, at the prospects of the developing international détente. And nowhere should the fears and apprehensions of those whose love of freedom has survived behind the Iron Curtain find a more receptive and thoughtful consideration than at a gathering devoted to pacem in terris. So my remarks this morning are devoted to the question of détente and human rights.

On Monday night the Secretary of State and the chairman of the Senate Foreign Relations Committee—who agree on little else—came before you to share their belief that it is wrong for the United States to condition trade concessions to the Soviet Union on adherence to the free emigration provision of the Universal Declaration of Human Rights.

Senator Fulbright, who is beguiled by the Soviets, and Dr. Kissinger, who believes that he is beguiling them, manage to find common ground in rejecting Dr. Andrei Sakharov's wise counsel against promoting a "détente" unaccompanied by in-creased openness and trust.

I believe in the Universal Declaration of Human Rights and I believe that now, twenty-five years after its adoption by the United Nations, it is not too late or too early to begin to im-plement it. And I am sustained in the belief that the best way to do this is through pressing my amendment to the trade bill by these brave words from the great Soviet physicist Andrei Sakharov:

> The abandonment of a policy of principle would be a betrayal of the thousands of Jews and non-Jews who want to emigrate, of the hundreds in camps and mental hospitals, of the victims of the Berlin Wall.
>
> Such a denial would lead to stronger repressions on ideological grounds. It would be tantamount to total capitulation of democratic

principles in face of blackmail, deceit and violence. The consequences of such a capitulation for international confidence, détente and the entire future of mankind are difficult to predict.

I express the hope that the Congress of the United States, reflecting the will and the traditional love of freedom of the American people, will realize its historical responsibility before mankind and will find the strength to rise above temporary partisan considerations of commercialism and prestige.

I hope that the Congress will support the Jackson amendment.

In an age of nuclear weapons, Senator Fulbright suggests, the Soviet Union is "the one country whose cooperation is absolutely essential." Dr. Kissinger, who recognizes that our traditional commitment to individual liberty poses moral dilemmas, implies that this commitment must be weighed against "the profound moral concern . . . of the attainment of peace." Senator Fulbright hints darkly that our very survival may depend on the pursuit of a détente without human rights.

But is the risk of nuclear war really going to increase if the Congress conditions most-favored-nation treatment to the Soviet Union on free emigration? Does Senator Fulbright believe that the Soviet Union will be any less cautious about the risks of a suicidal nuclear war if we choose not to subsidize their foreign borrowing? I concur in Dr. Sakharov's belief that "the danger of nuclear war continues to be the foremost concern for all of humanity," and with him I support "all measures to avert this danger including proposed measures of armament reduction." The process of reducing the risks of nuclear war can and will continue because it is in the mutual interest of both the United States and the Soviet Union to do so. But the development of more extensive mutual interest, of a closer and more cordial relationship between the two countries, must be based on something more solid and more enduring and more comprehensive than bargain-basement credits and one-sided commercial transactions.

A true peace, an enduring peace, can only be built on a moral consensus. What better place to begin building this consensus than on the principles embodied in the Universal Declaration of Human Rights, among which the right to choose the country one lives in—the right to emigrate freely—is perhaps the most basic.

We are asked to believe that the prospects for peace are enhanced by the flow of Pepsi-Cola to the Soviet Union and the flow of vodka to the United States. I say that we will move much further along the road to a stable peace when we see the free flow of people and ideas across the barriers that divide East from West—a flow unchecked by arbitrary and capricious power.

Now, at this time in history, we have been presented with an unparalleled opportunity. The growth of the Soviet economy—the means by which the Soviet Union has so long been hoping to "overtake and surpass" the United States—has begun to falter badly. The Soviet economy, despite enormous inefficiencies, had managed to sustain significant economic growth only by resort to a staggering rate of capital investments, twice that of the United States. In recent years, the productivity of that capital has declined drastically. The inflexible Soviet economy has found it increasingly difficult to assimilate modern technology. Even massive infusion of their own capital no longer promises to sustain economic growth.

If the Soviet Union were a minor country with no external ambitions, it might stagger along indefinitely with a no-growth or slow-growth economy. But she is not such a country—and therein lies our opportunity and our challenge. The task that the Soviet leaders wish to impose on their rigid economic system is nothing less than to make the Soviet Union the dominant world power—economically, militarily, and politically. They hope to achieve a high rate of economic growth and hold their economy up as a model for the less-developed world. They want to continue to divert a disproportionate share of their resources to military spending—more than twice the percentage of GNP as in our case—to sustain their buildup of strategic arms and conventional forces in Eastern Europe and on the Chinese border and to underwrite the military forces of their Arab allies. The Soviet Government needs desperately to improve the quality and quantity of goods available to the Soviet consumer, because it is only too aware of the political threat posed by the continued frustration of consumer demands. Yet the Soviet leaders are also afraid—or perhaps they do not know how—to relax their rigidly controlled economy, and so they have come to us for help. We would be ill-advised to treat this request as just another business proposition, or even as a routine request for foreign aid.

In my judgment, the most abundant and positive source of much needed help for the Soviet economy should come, not from the United States, but through a reordering of Soviet priorities away from the military into the civilian sector. And in this connection, it is high time that we propose serious disarmament at the SALT negotiations—not the sort of fiddling at the margins that has characterized the approach to arms control thus far, but serious reductions of strategic weapons on both sides. I see no reason, for example, why we cannot, in concert with the Soviet Union, agree that 900 ICBMs and 35 nuclear submarines are adequate for both sides. Would this not be better than the present situation in which they have 1,600 ICBMs and are building toward 62 submarines and we have 1,000 ICBMs and 41 submarines?

The Soviets are seeking billions of dollars in U.S. Government subsidized credits—long-term loans at 6 percent interest. Neither Dr. Kissinger nor Senator Fulbright chose to dwell on this aspect of what the Secretary of State euphemistically termed "a carefully shaped, overall mosaic." What is involved here are credit transfers that will dwarf last year's grain deal —or, as I prefer to call it, the great grain robbery.

There are, in my judgment, countries and purposes more deserving of our assistance, whose needs are greater—in some cases dire—and whose use of our aid for humanitarian purposes is more readily assured. The drought-stricken nations of the African Sahel come immediately to mind.

Let us not lose this opportunity to bargain hard for human rights. Let us not be misled by arguments that the time is not yet ripe or that we will be able to accomplish more later, after we have enmeshed the Soviets in some entangling web of investments and business deals. As Dr. Kissinger so eloquently stated here a few nights ago, opportunities once lost may never recur again. What are now clearly recognized by the Russians as concessions on our part will eventually be demanded as the normal way of doing things. Already we see Dr. Kissinger insisting that the discretion of the Congress to grant or deny or condition most-favored-nation status no longer exists because he has bargained it away, never minding that he had no authority to do so. Does anyone believe that American corporations will be more willing, when they have massive investments to protect, to insist on the rights of Soviet dissenters than they are now? At this moment we have an opportunity —which may not again be repeated—when the Soviet people are graced with men with the stature and prestige of Sakharov and Solzhenitsyn who have courageously spoken out on behalf of human rights. Their plea must not fall on deaf ears.

As Sakharov said in his open letter to the Congress:

> The Jackson amendment is made even more significant by the fact that the world is only just entering on a new course of détente and it is therefore essential that the proper direction be followed from the outset. This is a fundamental issue, extending far beyond the question of emigration.

I believe that we ought to press our traditional commitment to human rights in the emerging détente not only because this commitment is a most solemn pledge, not only because these values are right in themselves, but because it must be a purpose of the détente to bring the Soviet Union into the community of civilized nations, to hasten the end of what Sakharov has called "an intolerable isolation, bringing with it the ugliest consequences." The isolation of the Soviet Union, which, in Sakharov's words, "is highly perilous for all mankind, for international confidence and détente," is as dangerous as and comparable to the isolation of Germany in 1937. In that year the great German writer Thomas Mann wrote these words:

> Why isolation, world hostility, lawlessness, intellectual interdict, cultural darkness, and every other evil? Why not rather Germany's voluntary return to the European system, her reconciliation with Europe, with all the inward accompaniments of freedom, justice, well-

being, and human decency, and a jubilant welcome from the rest of the world? Why not? Only because a regime which, in word and deed, denies the rights of man, which wants above all else to remain in power, would stultify itself and be abolished if, since it cannot make war, it actually made peace.

Too often, those who insist that the pace and development of détente should reflect progress in the area of human rights are accused of opposition to détente itself. Nothing could be further from the truth. The argument is not between the proponents and detractors of détente, but between those who wish a genuine era of international accommodation based on progress toward individual liberty and those who, in the final analysis, are indifferent to such progress.

We will have moved from the appearance to the reality of détente when East Europeans can freely visit the West, when Soviet students in significant numbers can come to American universities, and when American students in significant numbers can study in Russia. When reading the Western press and listening to Western broadcasts is no longer an act of treason, when families can be reunited across national borders, when emigration is free—then we shall have a genuine détente between peoples and not a formula between governments for capitulation on the issue of human rights.

Without bringing about an increasing measure of individual liberty in the Communist world there can be no genuine détente, there can be no real movement toward a more peaceful world. If we permit form to substitute for substance, if we are content with what in Washington is referred to as "atmospherics," we will not only fail to keep our own most solemn promises, we will, in the long run, fail to keep the peace.

17
Freer Emigration from the Soviet Union

National Conference on Soviet Jewry, Washington, D.C.
17 May 1976

Finally, in the fall of 1974 the Congress and the Nixon administration reached a compromise on the Jackson-Vanik amendment. Painstakingly negotiated by Secretary of State Kissinger with the Soviets and with Jackson, the compromise was set forth in a Kissinger-Jackson exchange of letters that amounted to an agreement between the United States and Moscow. In response to explicit Soviet assurances for freer emigration reported to Congress in the exchange of letters and in formal testimony before Congress by Kissinger, and confirmed by President Ford, the amendment was modified to include a waiver provision. A President was authorized to grant a waiver—annually subject to congressional approval—if he reports to Congress that he has determined that such waiver will substantially promote the objective of free emigration and that he has received assurances that the emigration practices of that country will henceforth lead substantially to the achievement of free emigration.

The entire Trade Reform Act of 1974, including the modified amendment, was then promptly adopted by overwhelming votes. In January 1975 the Soviets denounced the trade agreement with the United States of which the provision for most-favored-nation (MFN) status was to be a part and publicly withdrew from the compromise expressed in the Kissinger-Jackson letters.

The two-year struggle to make the amendment the law of the land is a story of considerable complexity. President Nixon and Secretary Kissinger fashioned their own versions of what took place. In May 1976 the Senator was moved to help set the record straight in a speech to the National Conference on Soviet Jewry.

What the Senator emphasized in this 1976 speech is still the case at this writing. The amendment remains the law of the land and is at the heart of ongoing bargaining with Moscow for freer emigration. No President is able to confer MFN status or certain other trade benefits on the Soviet Union unless he is able to certify to the Congress that the Soviets are prepared to honor assurances for freer emigration comparable in significance to the 1974 assurances that were the precondition for congressional agreement to the waiver provision in the first place.

FOUR YEARS AGO I APPEARED BEFORE YOU TO ASK FOR YOUR support in preventing this country from walking yet another one-way street in the name of détente. I urged you to join me in turning the cul-de-sac of unilateral trade concessions into a highway to freedom for the thousands of brave Soviet Jews and non-Jews who demanded the right to emigrate. I called upon Americans of all faiths to support our national commitment to human rights by requiring respect for those rights, on a nondiscriminatory basis, as a condition of most-favored-nation status and access to subsidized credits.

The fight for free emigration from the Soviet Union is part of the larger struggle for human rights in all lands and for all people. We see it taking place today in Rhodesia, in Chile, in the Far East, and in Latin America. We see it in the Soviet Union, among Jews and Gentiles, in the Baltic States, in the assertion of new demands for local autonomy. The struggle is being waged by Catholics, by Baptists, by ethnic Germans, and Tartars. It has acquired a universal character to which Americans have proved themselves generous in responding.

The Jackson amendment has been a part of this great movement. Contrary to the general impression created by the media, the Jackson amendment applies to many countries and to all the people in those countries—whether they be Jew or Gentile, without discrimination on the basis of race, religion, or national origin. It is as universal as the movement of which it is a part, limited only by its application to those countries that did not enjoy the benefits of most-favored-nation status on the date that it was enacted.

The response of the American people has been overwhelming, a reaffirmation of our deepest national values. By staggering majorities in the House and Senate the Congress adopted the Jackson amendment. And despite a massive campaign by the Soviet Union, the White House, and powerful businessmen, all efforts to abandon the commitment to freedom embodied in that historic legislation have been turned aside.

I don't need to tell those of you who have been in from the beginning that we made every effort to achieve a reasonable compromise with an administration that opposed us every step of the way. But because the history of our effort to achieve a reasonable arrangement is so widely misunderstood, I wish to take a moment to recall the flow of events.

Following the passage of the Jackson amendment in the House in December 1973 and with its passage in the Senate, where it had 77 cosponsors, virtually assured, the Soviets and the administration began to show interest in a compromise. There followed a long negotiation extending over many months that culminated in an agreement on the texts of two letters—one from Secretary Kissinger to me and one from me to him. The exchange of letters embodying the compromise we had achieved took place at the White House on October 18, 1974. In essence the compromise was this: The administration would convey assurances to the Congress that the rate of emigration from the Soviet Union would increase and punitive action against persons wishing to emigrate would cease. In exchange I agreed to introduce an amendment to the trade bill that would authorize the President to waive the credit and most-favored-nation restrictions of the Jackson amendment for 18 months with subsequent one-year waivers subject to congressional approval.

The compromise of October 18 had been negotiated with Secretary Kissinger and approved by President Ford. Indeed, it was President Ford who invited the White House photographers into his office to record what we all regarded as a constructive compromise.

The October 18 compromise thus revolved around the assurances conveyed to Congress. As a result, the Soviet renunciation of the [U.S.-U.S.S.R.] Trade Agreement cannot be understood unless the substance of those assurances and the attitude of the participants toward the compromise to which they led are clear. On these issues Secretary Kissinger's testimony before the Senate Finance Committee on December 3 is especially instructive. Asked about the nature of the assurances in his October 18 letter, Secretary Kissinger went beyond what had already been made public:

I have had many conferences on this subject with Ambassador Dobrynin and conferences with Foreign Minister Gromyko. . . . In addition, when President Ford took office he had some conferences in which the statements that I have made here were reconfirmed by the same individuals. Finally, General Secretary Brezhnev has made analogous statements to President Nixon, to myself and recently to President Ford. This is the structure of the assurances that we have.

SENATOR HARTKE. Are the assurances then made from Mr. Brezhnev, Mr. Gromyko and Mr. Dobrynin?

SECRETARY KISSINGER. That is correct.

At the same hearing, urging support for the new proposed waiver amendment, Secretary Kissinger stated:

I believe a satisfactory compromise was achieved on an unprecedented and extraordinarily sensitive set of issues. . . . I believe it is now essential to let the provisions and understandings of the compromise proceed in practice.

Clearly, an arrangement such as the October 18 compromise could only be negotiated on the basis of good faith on the part of all the participants, and continuing good faith was a prerequisite for a successful implementation. Secretary Kissinger and President Ford understood this well. As the Secretary put it on December 3:

This understanding which is reflected in these letters can operate only on the basis of good faith by all the parties concerned and good will among the Senators and ourselves. . . . This is a specific assurance which has been extended on a number of occasions, the violation of which would certainly be one that the administration would take very seriously. The President, on a number of occasions, has told the three Senators that with respect to what is contained in our letter he believes that he can stand behind it.

It is significant that when the trade bill containing the modified Jackson amendment was finally signed by President Ford at the White House on January 3, 1975, Stanley Lowell [Chairman, National Conference on Soviet Jewry] and Israel Miller [Chairman, Conference of Presidents of Major Jewish Organizations] were among the invited guests. Clearly the President regarded the October 18 compromise as a milestone in the struggle to obtain freedom for Russian Jewry.

Between the agreement of October 18 and the December 3 testimony by Secretary Kissinger that I cited, an important event took place in Moscow. On October 26, eight days after the compromise, Foreign Secretary Gromyko handed Secretary of State Kissinger a letter that had the effect of repudiating the assurances conveyed to the Congress on October 18. The Secretary of State never informed me even of the existence of such a letter, much less its contents. Nor, so far as I have been able to determine, was anyone else outside the administration apprised of that startling development. The letter only came to light when the Soviets chose to release it on the eve of passage of the trade bill.

The withholding of that crucial document must surely rank among the shabbiest deceits ever perpetrated by a Secretary of State on the Congress of the United States. As it is, I suspect that we shall have to wait for Dr. Kissinger's memoir to discover how he intends to answer for this deplorable breach of good faith.*

What is most disturbing in all of this is the Ford administra-

*As far as I have been able to discover, what the Senator calls "this deplorable breach of good faith" is not answered for in either Kissinger's published memoirs or in his other writings as of this date. One incident in this connection not widely known is worth recounting here.

In late 1976, at the point Henry Kissinger was about to depart his post as Secretary of State and return to private life, he turned up on Capitol Hill and called Senator Jackson out of a committee meeting under way in the Senate Caucus Room of the Russell Senate Office Building. Kissinger referred to his testimony before the Senate Finance Committee on 3 December 1974, in which he had repeatedly assured the Senators that the Soviet leaders were in agreement with the undertakings he had ascribed to them in his 18 October exchange of letters with Jackson, when, in fact, at the time he testified, he had in his pocket the Gromyko letter of 26 October disassociating Moscow from those very undertakings. Secretary Kissinger apologized to the Senator for lying to him and to the Congress. Jackson reported this apology to his staff, but Kissinger has never, to my knowledge, put it on the public record.

tion's refusal to stand by its pledge to support the compromise of which it was a part. The facts are simple: on January 14, a mere eleven days after the President signed the trade bill into law, the Secretary of State announced the intention of the administration to seek its repeal. The ink was hardly dry when the Secretary of State sent the Kremlin an astounding message: despite the assurances, despite the negotiations, despite the Presidential pledges, the administration would work to wreck the law of the land by contriving to give the Soviets what they wanted. President Ford echoed this dismal message in his State of the Union speech.

We always knew that even a negotiated agreement with the Soviets could, if they so chose, be violated. We did not believe that the man who put in writing the Soviet pledge to permit freer emigration, the Secretary of State, would violate his solemn undertaking. And to this very day I remain disappointed beyond my capacity to express it at the ease with which the President of the United States callously betrayed the confidence we had placed in him in agreeing to a compromise version of the Jackson amendment.

From the time we met four years ago, at the beginning of a long and hard and still uncompleted journey, much has been accomplished. Under the threat of the Jackson amendment the odious education tax, that threatened to bring to a halt the emigration of educated Russians, was rescinded. In 1972, 1973, and 1974, unprecedented numbers of Soviet Jews were permitted to seek freedom in the West. We have succeeded in placing the issue of human rights on the agenda of successive summit meetings, in bringing it to the center stage of world attention, in forcing the question of freedom on the conscience of a world that has too often looked the other way when individual liberty was threatened. I believe that our efforts that began in the circumstances in which we meet again today had much to do with the inclusion of human rights provisions in the Helsinki accords.

Of the course upon which we set four years ago there has been much criticism. I have heard it all. I have heard it from Moscow. I have heard it from the board rooms of corporations. I have heard it from the Department of State and from the White House. I have listened to the criticism.

And I remain proud of what we have accomplished. I remain firm in my conviction. I will not retreat. I will not turn my back on those who are struggling to obtain their freedom. They have the will to fight and I am proud to fight alongside them. Let those who believe that the Soviets will reward weakness and retreat with a generous emigration policy take their case to Moscow—to Levich and Lerner, to Vitaly Rubin and Georgi Vins, to Edward Kuznetsov and Sender Levin. And let them visit the camps as well as the Kremlin.

I urge those who wish to see the Jackson amendment modified to begin by reading the Jackson amendment. Do they know that the President can extend most-favored-nation status and Exim [Export-Import Bank] credits if he certifies that doing so will lead to a significant improvement in Soviet emigration policy? Do they know—those who argue that a gesture now will free those who languish in the camps—that the Jackson amendment gives the President all the legal authority he needs to make the gesture they are urging? The logic of the Jackson amendment is simple: the Soviet rulers must choose between their emigration practices and trade concessions from the United States. They cannot have both. Freer emigration will bring the trade relationship they desire, and it will do so under the Jackson amendment. Those who wish to modify the amendment must understand that they will relieve the Soviets of the necessity to choose; for their approach would enable the Soviets to receive the trade benefits they desire without changing their brutal and capricious emigration policy.

I am not prepared to let the Soviets escape the choice they now face. We have seen the results of giving the Soviets what they desire first and waiting for the promise of progress on human rights later. That is the formula to which we succumbed at Helsinki. It didn't work there and it will not work here.

What will work is patience, steadfastness, and unity within the government of the United States. Nothing has been so damaging to the cause of free emigration as the administration's ill-conceived pledge to reward the Soviets with a reversal of the Jackson amendment in return for Moscow's refusal to honor its pledge to freer emigration. The day that the President of the United States makes it plain to the Soviet leaders that he will uphold the law of the land, that there will be no trade concessions without movement toward free emigration, we will see the beginning of the change for which we have fought so long.

Let us look for that day—together.

18
Internationally Recognized Human Rights

United States Senate
11 February 1977

Controversy had surrounded the Jackson-Vanik amendment from its inception. Through it all the Senator kept his eye on what was being accomplished: tens of thousands of Soviet and Romanian Jews and others gaining their freedom in the West; successive summit meetings impelled to place the issue of human rights on the agenda; moving human rights issues to the forefront of international attention; setting the stage for the inclusion of human rights provisions in the Helsinki Final Act.

In the midst of all the controversy, the Senator remained unusually sensitive to the situation of individual human rights victims: Aleksandr Solzhenitsyn, hounded and exiled for writing the truth about the totalitarian state; longtime refuseniks Alexander Lerner, Vladimir Slepak, and Professor Naum Meiman; poet and songwriter Alexander Galich, denied the right to have his work published or produced; cellist Mstislav Rostropovich and soprano Galina Vishnevskaya, forbidden to perform in large Soviet cities or in the West; and so on. Knowing that the Jackson amendment as the law of the land gave him some continuing leverage with the Kremlin, the Senator believed his attention to particular cases could be helpful—at the least, it might protect those individuals from the very worst that might be done.

The Senator's February 1977 address to the Senate was prompted by the Kremlin's systematic harassment of the unofficial U.S.S.R. group monitoring compliance with the human rights provisions of the Helsinki accords signed by thirty-five nations in 1975. Jackson used the occasion to combine a major statement on American human rights policy with a special appeal on three individual cases. This was a pattern the Senator followed in hundreds of his speeches, press conferences, and radio and television appearances during the 1970s and 1980s.

In this case, he speaks for Alexander Ginzburg, Yuri Orlov, and Mykola Rudenko. All three, in time, were released from prison; Ginzburg and later Orlov made it to freedom in the West. There was great rejoicing when Ginzburg came to the U.S. Capitol—one of the many

moving occasions when the Senator finally met the individuals he and
the Jackson-Vanik amendment had helped bring to freedom.

MR. PRESIDENT, IN THE PAST WEEK WORLD ATTENTION HAS
been focused on the renewed efforts of the Soviet Government to silence—and to imprison—an extraordinary group
of human rights activists. The human rights movement in the
U.S.S.R. is not only the conscience of that unhappy country, it is
also one of the best hopes that the Soviet Union can be brought
to respect internationally recognized standards of conduct. It
is for these reasons that the Senate of the United States should
address the recent developments in the Soviet Union and recognize their great importance. For the issue of human rights
is fundamental—and certainly central to our foreign policy.

When I first entered the Congress in 1941 the world was
already in the midst of World War II—a conflict to determine
whether Western civilization and its values would survive. The
real horror of modern totalitarianism became fully apparent only after the conclusion of the war, when we learned
the whole and terrible history of the Nazi regime. I visited
Buchenwald just after its liberation, and was profoundly
moved. I believe the world inherited an obligation to insure
that such barbarous crimes are never again repeated.

Americans learned more slowly perhaps but no less surely of
Soviet totalitarianism, of mass executions and deportation, of
the "Gulag Archipelago." In 1968 I talked to Robert Conquest,
the British author, and read his classic book *The Great Terror*. That monumental work definitively describes the dread-
ful authoritarian excesses in the Soviet Union that still haunt
the world. The bloody massacres, the suppression of whole
peoples, the persecution of racial and religious minorities, the
mass imprisonment of individuals for their political views—
all these are sources of international instability and turmoil.
Indeed, we have learned that governments that engage in
wholesale violations of human rights are, more often than not,
threats to the peace.

The fact that modern society can be a mask for ancient

brutalities explains, I think, the strong interest of the American people in human rights on a worldwide basis. In 1948, with the spirited leadership of Eleanor Roosevelt, the United States pressed for the adoption of the Universal Declaration of Human Rights. We did so precisely because we had learned that those deprived of their basic rights in any one country needed the protection of international law even against their own governments. The Declaration, unanimously adopted by the UN General Assembly, sets forth standards of individual liberty in a splendid, pioneering "Bill of Rights" for the world.

The Declaration affirms the right to freedom from torture and freedom from arbitrary arrest, detention, or exile; it affirms the right to leave any country, including one's own; it affirms the right to freedom of peaceful assembly and association; it affirms the right to freedom of opinion and expression; and it emphasizes freedom of thought, conscience, and religion and freedom—either alone or in community with others and in public or private—to manifest one's religion or belief in teaching, practice, worship, and observance.

Subsequently, this UN Declaration was reaffirmed in the International Convention on the Elimination of All Forms of Racial Discrimination of 1965 and the International Covenant on Civil and Political Rights of 1966, each of which was ratified by the Soviet Union.

Most recently, in the final act of the Helsinki Conference, thirty-three European countries, including the Soviet Union, together with Canada and the United States have agreed to act in conformity with the Universal Declaration of Human Rights. While the Helsinki accords dealing with specific rights are often imprecise and hedged, they nevertheless constitute an official commitment by the governments that—

> In the field of human rights and fundamental freedoms, the participating States will act in conformity with the purposes and principles of the Charter of the United Nations and with the Universal Declaration of Human Rights. They will also fulfill their obligations as set forth in the international declarations and agreements in this field, including *inter alia* the International Covenants on Human Rights, by which they may be bound.

So, in the struggle for human rights and fundamental free-doms the peoples of the world have international law on their side. Their governments have made individual rights and free contacts matters of legitimate international concern—indeed of international responsibility.

Mr. President, the bright promise of these international ac-cords has not been realized. Abuses of human rights constitute a continuing chronicle of suffering and injustice.

Ours is not only a humanitarian concern for our fellow men and women, although I personally believe that alone would justify efforts on their behalf. There is also the matter of con-tributing to the achievement of a more civilized world, the only kind of world where peace can flourish. For real peace must be based on international trust and openness, measured in part by increased respect for the standards which the Uni-versal Declaration of Human Rights enshrined in the body of international law.

We must be willing to use our human rights concerns in the bargaining process with other nations. Nations seek our grain, our arms, our technology. Why should we not seek greater protection for internationally recognized human rights? That is the essence of our effort in Congress to place America's economic power behind the basic right to emigrate.

Of all the individual liberties contained in the UN Declara-tion of Human Rights, none is more fundamental than that in article 13—the right to free emigration. The Congress has particularly emphasized that right, because it is the touch-stone of all human rights. The right to emigrate is critical for oppressed minorities, dissident intellectuals, and divided families. It has been the traditional, vital lifeline for victims of religious and racial persecution throughout the world, many of whom found relief in the United States and helped to estab-lish the freedoms we take for granted in our own country.

Virtually all of us owe our American citizenship to the right to emigrate. There is a famous story about Franklin D. Roose-velt once causing a great stir by addressing an audience of the DAR [Daughters of the American Revolution] as "My fellow immigrants. . . ." But the fact is, as I often remind American audiences, we are a nation of immigrants—and that gives us a special responsibility for the right to emigrate.

The Jackson-Vanik amendment on East-West trade and freedom of emigration is supported by an impressive coalition of groups representing diverse religious and ethnic backgrounds. It became part of the law of the land in the Trade Act of 1974. It states, in essence, that if the Soviets and other Eastern bloc countries want U.S. trade concessions and special subsidies, they will have to moderate their restrictive policies on the emigration of their citizens. The amendment applies to Jews and Gentiles, without discrimination on the basis of race, religion, or national origin.

Also, the amendment does not affect normal trade on a pay-as-you-go basis. It simply withholds special trade concessions and unlimited U.S. credit until the trading partner moves substantially to respect the obligations on freer emigration which it has already subscribed to in solemn international agreements. The Jackson amendment, far from being an intrusion into anyone's internal affairs, is one small step along the road to an international community based on law.

Tens of thousands of people—Jews and non-Jews alike—have escaped from captivity because of the Jackson-Vanik amendment on freer emigration. It was only after Henry Kissinger pledged that the Ford administration would try to destroy the amendment that the Kremlin tightened the screws once again. If the Soviets want some of the trade benefits from the United States that other countries enjoy, let them at least honor the right to emigrate.

Mr. President, it is of profound importance that our country—as the leader of the free nations and the most influential voice in Western public opinion—use the opportunities we have to promote greater respect for internationally recognized human rights. While the United States can and must deal with nations whose systems of government may be anathema to us, there should be no doubt that the United States stands opposed to flagrant violations of human rights and fundamental freedoms.

So I applauded the State Department's move this week in

standing up for the Russian poet Alexander I. Ginzburg in the name of internationally accepted human rights.

It has often been the case that senior officials in the Department of State—who tend, naturally perhaps, to value a superficial cordiality—shy away from speaking out on behalf of human rights where doing so may be regarded as an irritant in our relations with authoritarian governments.

But is not the best path to our silence on these issues a change in Soviet practice on human rights? So I commended President Carter for saying at his first press conference this week that he intends to speak out strongly and forcefully on behalf of human rights, expressing at the same time his deep regret at the incarceration of Alexander I. Ginzburg.

Today, in the presence of my Senate colleagues, I want to protest the arbitrary arrest in the last few days of Alexander I. Ginzburg, Yuri Orlov, and Mykola Rudenko.

Alexander I. Ginzburg is a distinguished human rights leader—an inmate of the Gulag Archipelago with Aleksandr Solzhenitsyn—and is the administrator of the fund established by Solzhenitsyn to sustain political prisoners and their families.

Physicist Yuri Orlov, a long-time member of the Moscow human rights movement, is a founder of the unofficial U.S.S.R. group monitoring compliance with the humanitarian provisions of the Helsinki Final Act.

Mykola Rudenko, Ukrainian writer and member of Amnesty International, is head of the Ukrainian committee monitoring implementation of the Helsinki agreement.

There is some talk that the arrest of these three human rights leaders is a deliberate test of the will and staying power of President Carter. This may be so; and if it is, the President made a good start in his press conference response this week. The President's determined follow-up will be of central importance.

There is also the fact that the Soviet Union is seeking to throttle the Soviet citizens who are trying to promote the observance of the humanitarian articles of the Helsinki agreement. June 15—the date for the opening of the Belgrade session of the CSCE [Conference on Security and Cooperation in Europe]—is approaching. These human rights defenders have been exercising their internationally affirmed right to freedom of opinion and expression, informing the government signatories to the Helsinki agreement, as well as the public at large, of cases of flagrant violation of the human rights articles. The Soviet authorities hear this criticism and comment, and they hope to have it silenced before the Belgrade meeting gives the truth a world audience.

The U.S.S.R. has bound itself to respect the exercise of the right to freedom of opinion and expression for its citizens by becoming a party to the Universal Declaration of Human Rights, the International Covenants on Human Rights, which it ratified, and by the Helsinki accords, which reaffirm these earlier international undertakings.

Indeed, Secretary Brezhnev himself said, less than one month ago in a speech at Tula:

> Standing now in the center of European politics is the task of fully implementing the accords reached by 35 states a year and a half ago in Helsinki. We regard the Final Act of the European Conference as a code of international obligations aimed at ensuring lasting peace. Of course, all its provisions should be fulfilled and that is our daily concern.

It is precisely in the name of these freely accepted international obligations that I call upon Secretary Brezhnev to release these three heroic human rights leaders and permit them and their colleagues to exercise their simple, elementary rights.

19
Terrorism as a Weapon
in International Politics

Jerusalem Conference on International Terrorism,
Jonathan Institute, Jerusalem, Israel
July 1979

Senator Jackson welcomed an invitation to address the 1979 Conference on International Terrorism, sponsored by the Jonathan Institute in Jerusalem. The Senator had been stirred by the heroism and
death of Lt. Col. Jonathan Netanyahu in the rescue of the Israeli
hostages at Entebbe. A conference sponsored by the institute named
for Jonathan had a special appeal.

The invitation focused Jackson's mind on developing what became
his comprehensive statement on the growing menace of international
terrorism. Given as the keynote speech of the Jerusalem Conference,
it set the tone for the proceedings and heavily influenced the Conference findings, which were widely circulated in the community of
Western democracies. Not unexpectedly, the Senator continued again
and again to present the analysis and advocate the lines of remedy
developed in this address.

Individual acts of bombings, hijackings, and assaults on innocent
civilians were abhorrent. But, in Jackson's view, the great threat came
from the highly organized groups, connected and supported internationally, which relied on terrorism as a political weapon against
democratic societies. He had in mind, for example, the Basque and
Puerto Rican terrorists; the notorious European terrorist groups; the
Palestine Liberation Organization (PLO), with its assaults on airliners
servicing Israel, its operations in Lebanon, and its attacks against
moderate Palestinians and other moderate Arabs who might be motivated to back the Egyptian-Israeli peace agreement. With modern
technology at their disposal, supported and encouraged by Soviet
and East European connections, such groups worked their deadly
mischief across the international borders of the free nations.

What could be done?

AS WE GATHER HERE THIS EVENING OUR THOUGHTS TURN to Lt. Col. Jonathan Netanyahu. We recall the quality of his personal character, his inner devotion to the public good, his voluntary performance of the most demanding duties that the defense of democracy entails, and the sacrifice consummated in the heroic rescue at Entebbe. Jonathan's heritage is an unpurchaseable treasure of the spirit that moth and rust cannot consume nor thieves break through and steal.

When in George Bernard Shaw's play, they tell Joan of Arc that they are going to burn her at the stake, she foresees the effect upon the people. "If I go through the fire," she says, "I shall go through it to their hearts for ever and ever." So Jonathan went through the Entebbe fire to our hearts for ever and ever.

I believe that international terrorism is a modern form of warfare against liberal democracies. I believe that the ultimate but seldom stated goal of these terrorists is to destroy the very fabric of democracy. I believe that it is both wrong and foolhardy for any democratic state to consider international terrorism to be "someone else's" problem.

If you believe as I do, then you must join me in wondering why the community of liberal democracies has not banded together more effectively to oppose these international murderers and to loudly and vigorously expose those states which cynically provide terrorists with comfort and support. One of the great coverups of this century is the effort by Western governments, who know better, to muffle the facts about Soviet bloc support for international terrorism.

I'm not talking about individual acts of madmen. I'm talking about highly organized groups with international connections and support who systematically rely on major acts of violence as a political instrument. I'm thinking of the Basque and Puerto Rican terrorists, the European terrorist groups, and the PLO attacks, or threats of attack, against moderate Arab states which might be motivated to support the Egyptian-Israeli peace agreement. I have in mind the PLO attacks against moderate Palestinians—the murder of a moderate leader in the Gaza is a recent brutal example. I am reminded of radical

Palestinian terrorist attacks on airliners servicing Israel. I'm thinking of the Palestinian operations in Lebanon and the activities of Turkish terrorists. Such acts of terrorism are part of a broad campaign aimed at the disintegration of democratic societies through undermining the confidence of their citizenry in their governments.

International terrorism is a special problem for democracies. To a totalitarian regime like the Soviet Union, it is mainly a nuisance. The government applies whatever force is needed to liquidate the group and its members; borders are closed to unwanted entry or exit; individual rights are held subservient to "law and order"; publicity can be denied by fiat. The biggest difference between the Soviet Union and such states as Libya, Iraq, and Iran is that these governments are not as efficient—yet.

A democratic government, on the other hand, rests on the consent of the governed. It is responsible for assuring the democratic freedoms of speech, assembly, travel, press, and privacy. These conditions, obviously, facilitate terrorist operations, directed against a particular government or as the battleground for opposing terrorist groups. When the PLO and Iraqi terrorists were at war, they chose to fight it out in Europe, not in the Middle East.

Terrorism is not a new phenomenon. What is new is the international nature of the terrorism. Today's terrorists have modern technology to help them, permitting rapid international communications, travel, and the transfer of monies; they can work with others of like mind across the international borders of the world's free nations.

More important, however, these groups receive extensive support from the Soviet bloc. Most terrorists use Soviet or East European weapons; they have been trained in the Warsaw Pact countries, or in such Middle East countries as South Yemen and the PLO-controlled areas of Lebanon; they generally flee for protection and rest to East Europe or to such countries as Libya. The primary supporters of international terrorism are the Soviet Union and those states which the Soviets support: the Warsaw Pact and the radical Arab camp.

Modern terrorism is a form of "warfare by remote control," waged against free nations or against nondemocratic but moderate states which dare to sympathize with freedom. In this kind of war, the totalitarian regimes see little risk of retribution directed at them.

What can be done?

First, and foremost, liberal democracies must acknowledge that international terrorism is a "collective problem." Everything else follows from this. When one free nation is under attack, the rest must understand that democracy itself is under attack, and behave accordingly. We must be allied in our defense against terrorists.

The cooperative effort of Western European countries to combat terrorism in Europe is a major step in the right direction. But we must go further. Terrorists must know that when they operate against any liberal democracy, they will receive no sanctuary and no sympathy in any free nation. By not making our position crystal clear, we allow fanatic groups to think we tolerate policies like those emanating from Iran concerning the Shah, members of his family, and certain others. I quote an Iranian announcement:

Anyone who wants to assassinate these people in Iran or outside [could be] free anywhere to carry out the order of the court. They cannot be arrested by any foreign government as a terrorist because they will be carrying out the order of Iran's Islamic revolutionary court.

And let me emphasize two propositions whose truth should be evident to all democracies. To insist that free nations negotiate with terrorist organizations can only strengthen the latter and weaken the former. To crown with statehood a movement based on terrorism would devastate the moral authority that rightly lies behind the effort of free states everywhere to combat terrorism.

Secondly, every free nation must work against Soviet and radical state efforts to define away terrorism. The idea that one person's "terrorist" is another's "freedom fighter" cannot be sanctioned. Freedom fighters or revolutionaries don't blow up buses containing noncombatants; terrorist murderers do. Freedom fighters don't set out to capture and slaughter school-children; terrorist murderers do. Freedom fighters don't assassinate innocent businessmen or hijack and hold hostage innocent men, women, and children; terrorist murderers do. It is a disgrace that democracies would allow the treasured word "freedom" to be associated with the acts of the terrorists.

Third, we must turn the publicity instrument against the terrorists, and we must expose Soviet and other state support of terrorist groups whenever we identify it. When PLO terrorists toss a bomb into a marketplace or murder a holy man or shoot rockets randomly at a village, each and every democracy in the world should stand up to condemn those radical Arab states and the Soviet Union who train, arm, finance, harbor, and encourage them.

When an act of terrorism occurs, and the odds are it will occur in one of the free countries, democracies should unite in sponsoring resolutions in the United Nations condemning the act. Where we have evidence of support for the terrorists by some other state, this support should be censured in the strongest terms. If the Soviet Union, its allies, and the radical Arab and Third World states want to vote against such resolutions, let them. Let's educate the whole world as to who opposes and who tolerates international terrorism.

I am convinced that this will make a difference; I am convinced, for instance, that the exposure of East European support for European terrorism has contributed to the lessening of this support and to the signs of some cooperation to combat terrorism between these countries and the nations of West Europe.

Fourth, liberal democracies must work together to apply sanctions against countries which provide sanctuary to international terrorists. The Bonn Anti-Hijacking Agreement is a good start. It is ironic that the pilots and the airlines, and not our statesmen, provided the leadership which led to this agreement.

We can do more. For instance, is it moral to trade openly and freely with states who use the profits from such trade to finance the murder of innocents? Why should those who conduct remote control warfare against us rest easy that we will contribute to financing our own destruction?

Fifth, within each of our own countries, we must organize to combat terrorism in ways consistent with our democratic principles and with the strong support of our citizens. Israel has long done this. And the nations of Western Europe are moving in this direction. In my country, we are making some progress in organizing federal, state, and local agencies to deal more realistically with terrorist threats. A number of my colleagues in the U.S. Senate are working to improve our counterterrorism capacities. As I see it, the best means to cope with terrorism is to structure national programs to reinforce the capabilities of local authorities. Local police and governments know their area; they know their people; they are the primary link between citizens and government.

Now this final word:

In providing for her own defense against terrorism, Israeli courage has inspired those who love freedom around the world. The Entebbe rescue was a classic lesson for all free nations that terrorism can be effectively countered with strength, skill, and determination. These are qualities in short supply in many countries where freedom comes more easily. Indeed, the great need in the world today is for men and women who stand in the tradition of Jonathan Netanyahu—strong, dedicated, courageous, dependable.

My friends, I know that we shall return home from this historic conference more determined and better prepared to do what we can to combat the menace of terrorism and to defend the freedom of us all.

VI
Technology Transfer Control

20
Technology Transfer
to Soviet Bloc Countries

United States Senate
11 June 1974

In 1973 Senator Jackson became chairman of the Permanent Subcommittee on Investigations (Committee on Governmental Affairs). In the course of his chairmanship he addressed another core policy issue: the neglect and mismanagement in the transfer of security-sensitive technology to the Soviets and other Warsaw Pact nations. Subcommittee studies and public hearings identified deficiencies of the export control system, and Senator Jackson brought them to executive branch attention in repeated communications. But reforms moved at a snail's pace. Jackson decided on a concrete legislative move.

The licensing of exports was primarily administered by the Department of Commerce, well known for its enthusiasm for East-West trade. Moreover, that Department was not staffed or otherwise equipped to analyze and evaluate the military and security implications of high-technology transfers, and in the era of so-called détente, it was less than ever motivated to do so. Why not enhance the role of the Defense Department and ensure that a national security perspective would be present early in the licensing process? An amendment to the pending defense procurement bill could serve the Senator's purpose.

On 11 June 1974 Jackson's amendment, with only minor modifications, was accepted by the Senate. His introductory statement in the debate on the Senate floor gave the clear signal that he intended to keep pressuring the executive branch until there were decided improvements in technology transfer controls.

MR. PRESIDENT, THE AMENDMENT (NO. 1405) WE ARE PROposing to the defense procurement bill has a simple purpose: to assure that adequate weight is given to the requirements of our national security in the complex process of assessing and approving export licenses to the Soviet Union and the Eastern bloc countries. The amendment accomplishes this purpose by enabling the Secretary of Defense, in those cases where he finds that the granting of an export license would significantly increase the military capability of the recipient, to disagree to the issuance of any export license presently required by law.

The amendment provides that all actions undertaken by the Secretary of Defense pursuant to this section shall be subject to a final determination by the President of the United States, subject, in turn, to congressional review. This later provision, that of congressional review, will help to assure that the Congress will play its rightful role in making the final determination in those cases serious and controversial enough to be brought before it through the procedures outlined in subsection (j).

In recent years, Mr. President, we have seen a dramatic increase in the number of requests for export licenses for the transfer of high technology to the Soviet Union and the Eastern bloc countries. There are, at this very moment, some 200 cases awaiting action in the computer area alone. The existing procedures weight the determination to grant an export license heavily on the side of commercial interests. The principal control function is exercised in the Department of Commerce, where, despite the enormous increase in the number of license requests in recent years, the number of personnel involved in this crucial work has actually declined, just as, ironically, the number of personnel engaged in promoting the sale of goods and technology to countries controlled under this amendment has increased considerably.

In the Department of Defense, which is consulted on these matters, the direct staff reviewing applications for export permits consists of three full-time officials, two of them senior, and the part-time assistance of a fourth. These dedicated and able individuals have to deal with a very large number of cases —some 3,300 for the years 1972–1974. Despite the resources elsewhere in the government on which they are able to draw, they lack both the authority and the staff to give to each request the careful scrutiny that I believe this sensitive national security matter requires. Given more authority in this area, as we do in this amendment, I am confident that the requisite staff support can be organized within the Department of Defense.

In my judgment, Mr. President, commercial considerations ought to be subordinate to considerations of national security in the granting of export licenses—particularly in the area of high technology—to the Soviet Union and the Eastern bloc. It is only logical, therefore, that the decisive authority to pass on these requests ought to lie in the department that is best able to assess the military implications of proposed exports. That, clearly, is the Department of Defense.

SOVIET INTEREST IN IMPORTING TECHNOLOGY

The Soviets have made it plain that their interest in importing technology lies not so much in buying our products as in buying our know-how and production capability. The Soviets do not lack ability in basic science. It is in turning basic scientific and technical ideas into production line items that they lag far behind us. It is the products, techniques, and manufacturing facilities which represent our highest technology in which the Soviets are principally interested. Agriculture is one of these, but I shall concentrate my attention here on those which have more direct military significance. Wide-bodied jets, computers, and integrated circuitry are three good examples of the kind of thing I have in mind.

We have an overwhelming technological lead in these areas. When I speak of our lead I do not refer to basic scientific understanding—though we lead there also—but rather to the ability to mass-produce these items.

WIDE-BODIED JETS

First, consider wide-bodied jets. There are only three companies in the world who produce long-range, wide-bodied jets: Boeing, Lockheed, and McDonnell-Douglas. The Soviets have asked all three of our wide-bodied jet manufacturers to build a large-capacity aircraft-manufacturing complex for the quantity production of wide-bodied transport aircraft. This aircraft manufacturing complex would be more advanced than anything in the United States. It would produce in one place everything from the airframe and the engine to the fasteners. No such integrated aircraft-manufacturing complex now exists anywhere in the world. The aircraft it would produce would be 60 percent faster, carry 25 percent more, and fly 20 percent farther than the world's now-largest wide-bodied jet, the 747. The production rate of this plant would be approximately equal to the total annual production of all three of our wide-bodied jet manufacturers.

The military implications of such a plant are obvious. It is the opinion of our best analysts that the Soviets have no need for so many long-range jets of such large capacity and high speed for commercial purposes. Nor are they likely to develop such a need in the foreseeable future. They might, of course, be planning to export these jets to the world market, which would deeply injure our own aircraft industry and remove the biggest industrial hard currency earner we have.

But the Soviets do have a clear military need for such aircraft. They have previously based military transports upon prior civilian transports. The AN-12, for example, their most common military transport, was produced from the AN-10, a civilian transport. While the Soviets have a considerable cargo-carrying capacity in their present military transports (although as we have seen in the recent Arab-Israeli conflict, it is not up to our own), they lack suitable aircraft for moving large numbers of troops over long distances. They have their forces dispersed in two large groups: one in Western Russia and Eastern Europe, the other in the Far East along the Chinese border. They very much need the capability to move troops from one of these areas to the other rapidly, surely, and efficiently. In addition, the capability for Soviet military intervention in other areas of the globe, such as we recently were faced with in the Middle East, would be enormously facilitated by superheavy, very long range, high-speed, wide-bodied jets. Moreover, since what the Soviets wish to purchase are not aircraft but an integrated production facility, it could also be used to make any sort of long-range, high-speed aircraft, including other types of military transports, airborne tankers, and very large bombers.

COMPUTERS

Let me now turn to the area of computers. Computers perform vital functions throughout the entire structure of our defense establishment. It is not only the speed of a computer that is important but also its flexibility of function, its ability to input and output data, the number of independent users it can simultaneously serve, and the amount and type of software which is, or can be made, available to use on it. The most current estimate by the Commerce Department's own independent technical advisers is that we are at least *ten years* ahead of the Soviets in computer capability and that they show no signs of closing the gap. Five years ago they were also ten years behind us. The Soviets have produced in quantity only one large computer, the Bessem 6. This computer, which is still in production, is based on technology which is 15 years old. It is made of individual transistors and tubes, each hand wired into place by workers with soldering irons.

In the middle 1960s the Soviet Union decided to move into third-generation hardware by building the RYAD family of machines based on the architecture of the IBM series 360 computers. By 1969, most of the countries of Eastern Europe had joined the program under Soviet pressure. The original Soviet goal was to begin production in 1970 and to produce twelve to fifteen thousand RYADs during the ninth five-year plan (1971–75). The only RYAD model in current production is the small ES-1020, and probably no more than one hundred of these machines were built by the end of 1973. The expansion of 1020 production and the series production of the other models suffer primarily from serious difficulties in the production of sufficient quantities of reliable integrated circuits and to a lesser degree from a lack of modern production technology. It seems clear that the Soviets' original goal of several thousand RYADs per year by 1975 is unobtainable. Without Western assistance this goal may prove difficult even by the end of the 1970s.

The Soviets are making every effort to close the gap in computer technology in the only way that is possible for them: to get us to give it to them. Their efforts have not been without success. Recently one of our largest computer companies signed a Protocol of Intent with the Soviet Union which calls for the joint development of the next generation of large high-speed computers. In addition, this protocol calls for the American company to create a plant for manufacturing this new computer and for manufacturing the most modern peripheral devices. This plant, in the usual Soviet style, would be one of the largest in the world. This venture, if allowed, would not only create, full-blown, a most serious competitor for our overseas computer sales, but it also would, by moving the Soviets ten years into the future, enormously upgrade their military potential across the board.

INTEGRATED CIRCUITRY

Finally, integrated circuits are critical components in almost all of our high-technology military systems. As a matter of fact, integrated circuits were first developed for the Minuteman missile program, largely with research and development funds appropriated for the Air Force in procurement bills such as this one. Until 1967 the vast majority of all integrated circuits produced in this country went into military systems. In addition, they play a fundamental role in the production of modern computers. As I indicated earlier, the most important factor holding up the new Soviet line of computers is their difficulty in the production of sufficient quantities of reliable integrated circuits. The technology of integrated circuits lies not in the circuits themselves but in the production line by which they are produced.

One of the countries of the Soviet bloc, not long ago, signed a contract with one of our largest manufacturers of integrated circuits. This contract calls for the American company to set up a complete turn-key production line to make integrated circuits for hand calculators. It also calls for this American company to transfer any new knowledge and techniques that it develops for the production of these circuits within the next five years. The production of integrated circuits for hand calculators sounds like an ordinary commercial transaction. But it has implications far beyond that. Because the technology lies not in the circuits but in the production line, such a production line, with at most minor changes, can produce almost the entire range of circuits used in military applications. If this production line is built, we will have transferred a large part of our national integrated circuit technology. This is particularly true since, with the very large amount of cross-licensing in this industry, the technology available to this company includes most of the technology in the industry as a whole. If this contract is allowed to go through, we will have removed the largest single problem the Soviet bloc has in the production of modern computers and enormously upgraded the military potential of our adversaries. All this for less than $20 million, and most of that on very low cost loans.

SUMMARY

We and our allies, Mr. President, have gone down the road of unimpeded free trade for a quick buck with our totalitarian adversaries before. The scrap iron we sold to Imperial Japan before the Second World War came back on battlefields in the Pacific. The Rolls-Royce Neve jet engines the British sold to the Soviet Union after the Second World War were copied and went into the MiG-15s, which flew against us and the British in Korea, and the MiG-17s, which have flown and are still flying against our allies today.

The mistakes we are in danger of making today are far more serious. The Soviet Union has more men, more planes, more tanks, and more of almost every other kind of armament than we do. It is only the quality of our weapons that allows us to maintain the military balance. The higher quality of our weapons is almost solely based on our more advanced technology and manufacturing know-how. If we do not *give* the Soviets our most advanced technology, I do not believe, given the nature of our two societies, that they will ever catch up. Indeed, I believe they will fall constantly further behind. If we do give them our most advanced technology, if we design for them the world's most advanced wide-bodied jets and supercomputers and then build them the world's largest plants to manufacture these and other high-technology products, we will earn the all-time record for shortsightedness.

This amendment is a step in the right direction. It gives the Secretary of Defense, under the President, the right to disagree to the issuance of an export license to the Soviet Union and Eastern bloc if doing so would significantly increase the military capability of the recipient. The Commerce Department is ill-equipped to understand all the military implications of high-technology areas. It is essential that the Department of Defense be brought into this process in a fundamental and statutory way to protect us from the sort of dangers I have outlined. And it is sound and prudent to provide for ultimate congressional review.

21
Technology Transfer Policy— The High Stakes

United States Senate
11 February 1982

From 1974 into the 1980s, technology transfer continued high on the agenda of the Permanent Subcommittee on Investigations, with Jackson and Senator Sam Nunn working together closely. (Senator Nunn succeeded Jackson as chairman of the subcommittee in 1977.) In 1979 the two Senators secured adoption of amendments to the Export Administration Act which further strengthened the role of the Defense Department in licensing and control-list determinations. When the Soviets invaded Afghanistan, President Carter took some steps to tighten controls. But there was no convincing follow-through. Meanwhile, the evidence was overwhelming that the continued loss of our technology to the Soviet Union and its East European allies was improving Moscow's military systems, its economic leverage, and its intelligence capability.

Senator Jackson hoped President Reagan would give this problem a higher priority, and so wrote the President-elect on 14 November 1980. The new President did speak up for effective export controls, but fourteen months into the administration, there were still few signs of the hard work Jackson had hoped for, and thus he took his case to the floor of the Senate.

The effort helped to buttress the role of the Defense Department in policing strategic trade, and the Reagan administration managed to implement a number of important policies to restrain the leakage of technology to the Soviets, notably prevailing upon our allies to work more closely with us. But Jackson's challenge to do much better still stands.

MR. PRESIDENT, AS MY COLLEAGUES ARE AWARE, MY CON- cern for the flow of security-sensitive technology to the Soviet Union and its allies is of long standing. For several years, the Senate Permanent Subcommittee on Investigations, which I chaired, demonstrated through its studies and hearings that our policies in this area have been seriously flawed. Moscow and its associates have acquired the West's latest technology and thereby significantly enhanced their military-industrial capabilities. I and several others have repeatedly pressed for tighter controls on technology transfer.

NEED FOR A CLEAR, COHERENT POLICY

On November 14, 1980, I wrote President-elect Reagan calling his attention to this problem and suggesting several measures that merited his prompt consideration. I noted the lack of a clear and comprehensive policy regarding technology transfers, which had led to inadequate technical analysis, weaknesses in export controls, serious imbalances in East-West exchange programs, inconsistent governmental decisions, uncertainty for U.S. exporters, and a weakening of COCOM [Coordinating Committee on Multilateral Export Controls]. I urged that he act quickly to strengthen the government's work on critical technologies, foreign availability assessments, national security safeguards in exchange programs, cooperation with allies, and enforcement.

In the fifteen months since that letter was sent, events have reinforced my earlier conclusion: there is much we can do, if only we will. But we have a long way to go.

There is no longer doubt that our technology has materially aided Soviet expansion. It has improved Soviet weapons, intelligence devices, and economic leverage. We are still much too far away from a vigorous program to effectively meet the danger.

MOSCOW'S GAS PIPELINE TO EUROPE

As proof, Mr. President, we need only consider the administration's handling of the Siberian gas pipeline project.

In my November 14, 1980, letter to President-elect Reagan and my enclosed letter of October 1, 1980, to Secretary of Defense Harold Brown, I questioned the policy of excluding the oil and gas industry from the list of strategic defense industries and the policy of presuming that licenses would be granted for the export of oil and gas equipment. I urged the new administration to reassess this position as part of an overall national security assessment of the world energy situation.

Yet the administration started off by approving a first shipment of Caterpillar pipelayers to the Soviet Union. It is claimed that these pipelayers will not be used on the West Siberian pipeline, a generous supposition given Soviet practice of violating end-use representations. More importantly, in licensing this equipment, the administration sent the signal that in principle the export of technology and products relating to oil and gas production and shipment are not considered strategic items.

President Reagan at Ottawa made known U.S. concerns with the West Siberian pipeline, but the administration didn't get itself together for an effective follow-up. It took the crackdown in Poland to energize the government. And even now high officials are talking about the decision regarding U.S. technology and the pipeline in terms of "weighing the damage to the Soviet Union against the damage to the alliance."

What accounts for the confusion and the foot dragging?

Because this pipeline project is supposed to be a strictly economic arrangement? Nonsense. If it is, why have the Germans so steadfastly rejected serious consideration of any alternatives to dealing with the Soviets? The United States has offered some alternatives, and a pipeline to exploit Norwegian gas was also proposed. The price of Siberian gas promises to be quite high. Furthermore, the deal requires an enormous amount of Western credit, at a time when the German government is joining many others in complaining about the price of money.

Only on the surface is this deal an economic one, whereby the Western allies provide funding and technology in exchange for Soviet natural gas. Both sides, in fact, are fully aware of the significant political relationships involved. The pipeline deal will provide Moscow with a substantially increased flow of hard currency and political leverage for years to come, and we would be reckless to gamble that these resources will not be used against us and our European allies. For one thing, Moscow's revenues from the pipeline will facilitate acquisition in the West of sophisticated technology useful in strengthening the Soviet military. Even without direct Soviet action, the project creates the possibility that significant portions of allied economies and societies could fundamentally shift away from the West toward the Soviet Union. There would be massive diversion of energy-related capital, talent, and effort away from Western economic development.

What we should be doing is quite plain.

First, we should recognize the strategic importance of energy supplies and treat technologies and end products related to them accordingly. Procedurally, this means giving the Secretary of Defense the same review over exports of oil and gas equipment that he now has over strictly military exports.

Secondly, we should recognize that in talking about energy self-sufficiency for the industrialized West we are talking about *protecting* the alliance, not *damaging* it. The administration should immediately prohibit the use of any American technology in connection with the pipeline. It should promptly convene meetings at the highest allied level to develop alternatives for Western European energy. It should provide substantial assistance in developing such alternatives, including technological and financial measures. And it should provide strong incentives for our allies to develop Western energy supplies rather than Soviet ones.

RECENT IMPROVEMENTS

Mr. President, certain developments of the past months encourage me to hope that some effective steps will be taken, both on the Siberian pipeline and for broader issues of technology transfer.

Most importantly, key assumptions about the importance of trade to détente are now critically questioned. During the past decade, three administrations acted on the assumption that increasing economic ties with the Soviet Union would moderate Soviet behavior in ways that would improve our security and build a peaceful world order. With this assumption came a consistent effort to relax controls on strategic trade with the East and to define quite narrowly what we meant by "strategic" trade.

Today, we can view those years as a costly experiment. The results included an increasingly adverse military balance, both strategic and conventional; renewed Soviet military expansionism; increased Soviet subversion in the Third World; a sharp escalation in the anti-U.S. Soviet political offensive around the globe; and a dramatic increase in Soviet espionage and clandestine operations against the West. Our technology, acquired and exploited by Moscow, contributed to each of these developments. There is now a growing awareness that our technology in Soviet hands is a threat to our security.

Also of importance, there is a broader appreciation that the Kremlin is determined to try to get our technology by any means available. The public press, as well as government reports and defense estimates, have reported how Western developments in design, materials, components, and production have been acquired by our adversaries. The techniques have included classical espionage as well as the evasion of export controls through diversion, retransfer, and the use of foreign-owned but U.S.-chartered front corporations. The result has been weapons aimed at us that are higher in quality, greater in quantity, more lethal in effect, and quicker in the field than would likely have been the case if Moscow had to rely solely on its own technical/industrial base.

The present administration has begun some remedial action. The Department of Defense is taking the export control problem more seriously than before and is beginning to improve its ability to evaluate and control critical technologies. There seems to be more awareness in licensing decisions about the need to safeguard national security as well as to advance commercial interests abroad. And the intelligence community has sharpened its awareness of this threat and has begun implementing new procedures to monitor, evaluate, and report on technology transfers and developments.

CONTINUING SHORTCOMINGS

Mr. President, these new beginnings are a fragmentary start. What is needed is a clear, comprehensive government-wide policy that frontally addresses the hard, central issues of technology transfer and loss. To date, the administration has lacked the top-level conviction and participation needed to shape such an overall policy.

Time Perspective

For one, it is not yet clear that the administration's efforts have deeper roots than a concern to impose sanctions. They should. Technology transfers involve vital long-term issues of our national security, and they should not be turned on and off for foreign policy considerations of the moment. It may be appropriate to use normal commercial exchanges of butter and grain to reward and punish Soviet behavior. But national security concerns must be protected in times of cooperation as well as strain, and judgments about the wisdom of transferring certain technologies should be separate from the prevailing winds of foreign policy advantage. I am not sure that we yet have a firm national conviction on this matter, and I am worried that our recent efforts will not outlast the current sanctions resulting from events in Poland.

National Security Perspective

In this regard, it is important to emphasize that national security involves more than strictly military considerations. The notion of "strategic" trade needs a much broader interpretation than it received in the past ten years.

The Siberian gas pipeline is a salient example.

Even purely civilian/commercial transfers can indirectly help increase the Soviet threat to our security. By acquiring and exploiting Western technology, Moscow has been able to fill selectively gaps in its industrial base and to profit from the modernizing effects of, for example, Western microelectronic and computer technologies. It has been able to concentrate funding and manpower on other priority projects and to alleviate consumer dissatisfaction. By taking Western "proven designs" as road maps, Soviet research and development activities have saved funds and important developmental time. The point is not that all trade should be stopped on national security grounds. Many of our exchanges with the Soviets are only remotely linked with security threats, and the level and quality of such exchanges are the appropriate province of commercial and foreign policy considerations. But the fact that a particular exchange involves nominally commercial/civilian technologies does not ipso facto mean that national security is unaffected. The key here is informed judgment. The United States needs to examine carefully the possible effects of each proposed transfer.

Dual-Use Technologies

This is particularly true for transfers involving "dual-use" technologies, items proposed for sale for civilian/economic purposes but which could readily find military applications as well. There is now a clear pattern of such diversions once Western technologies are in Moscow's hands. The U.S. government allowed American business to build the Soviets a truck plant at Kama River, somehow assuming that only civilian trucks would be built there. As we all know, that plant builds military vehicles as well, some of which carried Red Army units into Afghanistan.

Our experience with several other cases is similar. For example, American bearing grinders licensed for sale to the Soviet Union contributed greatly to various Soviet military programs. In other cases, we have seen that there is no real control over the use to which a computer is put once it is under Kremlin control; that another "truck" plant supported by American technology produces missile launchers; and that Soviet plants to produce farm machinery also produce weapons.

But requests for U.S. export licenses are still processed under a system that is biased against protecting national security. The political pressure exerted by commercial interests together with our government's structure and system for processing such licenses effectively creates a presumption of license approval. The onus of disapproval then falls on small, underfunded governmental units that are asked in effect to prove that such transfers will be diverted to military ends—definitive proof that is often only available once our security has in fact been breached. Experience suggests reversing this approach—the risks of diversion are high, and great caution is necessary.

Allied Cooperation

I am also concerned that we have not achieved more progress toward effective controls with our allies in COCOM. Recent discussions led to several agreements in principle which appear to promise more vigorous cooperation in the future. But it is particularly true of these matters that the "devil is in the details." Alliance-level mechanisms for oversight and harmonization of national efforts on technology transfers are still inadequate. National-level procedures are also still quite weak; among our allies, only France has a national approach to export licensing similar to ours in providing formally for military advice and review.

At the same time, the inadequacy of COCOM measures has helped corrupt our national control systems. Arguments based on the "foreign availability" of even dual-use technologies are repeatedly and successfully pressed within our government to permit transfers. There is little sense in permitting transfers that could threaten our security merely because the items could be obtained elsewhere; logic like this would have parents supplying heroin to their children. A punitive unilateral approach, however, risks creating a system of penalties that would have the effect of driving high-technology firms abroad. Dealing effectively with this type of problem requires strong allied cooperation, which the administration should do much more to encourage.

Other Measures

Furthermore, there is too little recognition of the fact that problems of technology transfer and loss require more than effective export controls. Moscow's campaign to acquire our technology is sophisticated, diverse, and well-coordinated. Opportunities are fully exploited: visits and exchanges, exploratory contract discussions, academic meetings and programs, public information services, and applications under the Freedom of Information Act. Covert and clandestine methods, however, have virtually become the method of preference for the Kremlin, apparently because they are so effective. A host of espionage techniques are involved, including intercepting communications, suborning or otherwise recruiting personnel, and theft and black-market operations. And all of these techniques are in addition to the methods I noted earlier to avoid and evade our export controls: illegal diversions, front and dummy corporations, and foreign retransfers.

ACTION NEEDED

Specifically, Mr. President, I urge the following improvements and innovations in government programs:

First, the role of the Defense Department needs to be considerably strengthened. Responsibility for defense concerns with technology transfer should be centralized in a policy-level office with adequate resources to discharge the Department of Defense's responsibilities regarding license applications as well as intelligence monitoring and cooperation with our allies. In previous years, the Department of Defense failed to fund its technology transfer offices adequately to perform its statutory role. Congress should consider this need specifically in reviewing the fiscal year 1983 budget and earmark funds for it, preferably by establishing a separate line item.

Second, the role of the intelligence community should also be strengthened. The Senate Select Committee on Intelligence, of which I am a member, has been particularly interested in problems of technology transfer and loss. Initiatives to improve our intelligence process in this area have recently been undertaken by the administration, and we will look carefully at their budget requests and performance. Here again, earmarked funds might prove helpful. Particularly important is the structuring of the policy process so that coordinated, current intelligence from the community as a whole can be brought to bear on policy judgments about technology transfer and loss. Sound information and analysis cannot alone ensure prudent policy decisions, but it will help considerably. Third, all U.S.-Soviet exchanges and agreements need to be carefully reviewed for full reciprocity—not just on paper but in practice. Academic exchanges, for example, should involve people of comparable professional level and interests as well as simply equal numbers. It is particularly important that we keep in mind the difficulties posed by such exchanges and agreements for our foreign counterintelligence programs and that we strive to reduce the exploitation of our political freedoms by hostile intelligence services. Here, too, Congress should investigate how legislation could help to accomplish genuine reciprocity in our dealings with the Soviet Union and its allies. An important part of full reciprocity would be requiring the disclosure of ownership for Communist-owned U.S.-chartered commercial entities.

Fourth, more far-reaching public awareness programs need to be implemented. The FBI and Defense Department have begun awareness programs of the hostile intelligence threat for U.S. defense contractors, and various concerned officials have been cooperating with the press in bringing this story to the public. Much more needs to be done, however, particularly to make the academic community aware of the threat from hostile intelligence agencies. Information and awareness are more secure safeguards than censorship.

Fifth, consistent and determined U.S. leadership is required to forge an effective consensus on these matters within COCOM. Sustained evidence of a serious U.S. conviction to control transfer and losses is the key to effective allied cooperation. Both our government and the governments of our allies can be victims of "union-busting" pressure from large commercial interests. Congress should undertake hearings and investigations aimed at reducing this and other obstacles to improving COCOM's effectiveness.

Sixth, strategic trade policy should include credit controls. The Soviet lack of hard currency means that a great deal of the hemorrhage of our technology might be restricted if the Soviets and their allies had to pay for their acquisitions in cash at time of purchase. Today the debt of the Warsaw Pact countries to the West is about $80 billion. Poland is unable to service its $26 billion share of that debt, and there are increasing signs that Moscow's hard currency shortages are mounting. The export of Western capital through extensions of credit permits the Soviets to fortify their military-industrial system every bit as much as the transfer of technology. The United States, in concert with its allies, should begin now to develop a multilateral approach to comprehensive controls on credit to the Soviet Union and its allies. This might be done under the aegis of COCOM.

Seventh, technology transfer control considerations should be incorporated into the design and production of sensitive advanced products. For years, the United States government and others have struggled with the problems of controlling loss of selected technologies by political and diplomatic means. Many of these problems could be obviated at the engineering stage. Semiconductors and integrated circuits, for example, could be coated with commercially available substances that would preclude reverse engineering of the products, thereby improving both national and proprietary security. Counterintelligence considerations should be incorporated more systematically at the earliest stages of product development.

Eighth, the contribution of business to effective export controls should be strengthened. The export business community has long played an important role in the formulation of export control policy. Their advice is sought on technological advances and types of controls. In the course of the critical technologies studies conducted by the Department of Defense, representatives of our nation's leading aerospace, electronics, and other high-technology have made a substantial contribution.

In at least two other ways business can make a broader contribution. One is in the area of foreign availability. I urge business to aid our government's efforts in developing effective allied controls. In effect, I am inviting American businessmen to "blow the whistle" on companies that put greed above Western security.

Second, I urge exporters to develop voluntary procedures to further the aim of national export controls. Recent Soviet practices in this country make it especially desirable now that American businesses know their customers and the ultimate use and destination of their products. Perhaps Congress can help here by legislation requiring some form of identity and end-use certification for purchasing agents of foreign nations.

Mr. President, what I said on April 30, 1980, about the post-Afghan strategic trade policy of the Carter administration is still applicable: "The flaws in our export controls are due to an absence of conviction, not of resources; it is within our capacity and that of our allies to remedy them. It is still possible to improve our export controls. But the time is long overdue to translate rhetoric about our tough new policy into effective action."

VII
American Policy
in the Middle East

22

The Jackson Amendment
and the Security of Israel

United States Senate
1 September 1970

A humane concern for the persecuted and homeless remnants of European Jewry prompted Senator Jackson's interest in the new State of Israel created to receive them. His steady support for Israel over the years, however, arose from two convictions that dominated his public life: his belief in open democracy and its civilized values along with his conviction that democracies must work together to deter and counter external threats. He viewed Israel as both a strategic asset to the West and a bulwark of democracy and freedom in the Middle East. Jackson time and again gathered and led the bipartisan congressional coalitions to provide support for the safety of Israel.

One example is his amendment (section 501) to the 1971 Defense Procurement Act. By the summer of 1970 the Foreign Military Sales Act authorizing U.S. aid to Israel and other nations was indefinitely tied up in the labyrinthine processes of the Congress. Meanwhile, the Kremlin was increasing its involvement in the Middle East, including military aid to Israel's adversaries. The Senator introduced an amendment to the 1971 Defense Procurement Act reaffirming the long-standing American policy to help maintain the military balance in the Middle East by furnishing Israel with the arms required for defense. His amendment then authorized the President to implement this policy.

Adopted by the Senate Armed Services Committee, the Jackson amendment was opposed by Senator William Fulbright, chairman of the Foreign Relations Committee, who devised an amendment to the Jackson amendment that would have nullified the Jackson initiative. The challenge had been anticipated. Senator Jackson's defense of his amendment on the Senate floor carried the day.

MR. PRESIDENT, THE ISSUE BEFORE US IS A SIMPLE ONE: will the Senate now provide the President with the authority he needs to implement our long-standing policy in the Middle

East, a policy based upon support for the security of Israel and the maintenance of a military balance in the Middle East? That there exists a consensus among us as to the wisdom and importance of this policy is a certainty affirmed by five Presidents and more than three-fourths of the current membership of the Senate.

The distinguished chairman of the Foreign Relations Committee has said that his amendment is nothing more than an effort to protect the jurisdiction of his committee. To the people of Israel, and to the citizens of the world whose security rests on the avoidance of war in the Middle East, the Senator's amendment is more than that. It would deny or delay the absolutely essential authority upon which we can provide, on favorable credit terms, the aircraft and other equipment necessary for the defense of Israel and for the stability of the Middle East.

Section 501 of the Defense Procurement Act contains a policy statement of great importance. It is a policy statement that echoes the sentiments of eighty-one Senators who have expressed themselves in letters to the President or the Secretary of State. Section 501 would enable the President to respond positively to their expressed view and to give effect to their collective request.

Mr. President, most Senators are realists. Had we proceeded to attach this amendment to the Military Sales Act, it would have failed utterly to aid Israel, because some of us were aware that this particular act, the Military Sales Act, was going to be tied up indefinitely. I was aware of this; and when I offered my amendment in the Committee on Armed Services, I did so for the purpose of trying to get action, so that the President of the United States would be in a position he needs to grant the aid. I think that events since then have clearly sustained my position.

Mr. President, if the Fulbright amendment prevails and the Foreign Military Sales Act, or similar legislation, were to be enacted into law, section 501 would die at once. The result would be to deny to the President the authority he needs to carry out our policy of providing Israel with the tools she needs to provide for her own defense. If, on the other hand, the Foreign Military Sales Act fails to be enacted into law, the effect of the Fulbright amendment would be to delay to a date uncertain the authority contained in section 501. Either result is undesirable; neither has any redeeming value, save as a senseless obstruction to important legislation that is supported by the administration, the Congress, and the American people.

I am hopeful, Mr. President, that the House and Senate conferees will achieve a compromise in their deliberations, and that they will thereby prepare the way for the Foreign Military Sales Act to be enacted into law. I am convinced that the interest of the Senate in seeing its version of the Foreign Military Sales Act emerge from conference is adversely affected by the Fulbright amendment. This is so because the Fulbright amendment provides that if the conference does produce agreement, Israel will have available to it only the severely limited credits contained in the Foreign Military Sales Act, rather than the adequate credits available under section 501.

I believe, Mr. President, that the Foreign Military Sales Act is inadequate for the purpose of assisting Israel to maintain the military balance on which her survival—and our vital interests in the Middle East—is based. There are several reasons why this is the case and why, therefore, section 501 is vital:

First, the total authority to appropriate in the Foreign Military Sales Act is only $250 million for each of fiscal 1970 and 1971, a sum small in itself and one which must serve the credit needs of approximately thirteen nations. The Israeli share of these funds is but a fraction of the total and has been negotiated for the purpose of meeting Israeli obligations for equipment agreed to in earlier years. In fact, Mr. President, there are no funds available to Israel under the Foreign Military Sales Act to meet the sharply increased requirements arising out of recent Soviet aid to the Arab States.

Moreover, Israel has outstanding obligations to make repayments on prior arms transactions that today constitute a severe burden on an economy already laboring under a defense budget that consumes more than a quarter of her GNP, the equivalent of a $300 billion U.S. defense budget. In addition, Mr. President, total immediate Israeli needs are several times greater than the entire authorization for Israel in the Foreign Military Sales Act, and these needs are subject to rapid increase as the military balance in the Middle East is in a state of continuous adjustment.

Finally, I am bound to say that I anticipate additional Israeli requirements for credit aid. The repeated violations of the cease-fire—each time they occur—raise the costs to Israel of maintaining an adequate defense. This financial burden on Israel is matched, I believe, by an equal burden on the United States to provide, on favorable terms, the equipment necessary to offset the effects of clandestine military activity to which Israel is now unable to respond as a result of their adherence to the terms of the cease-fire. We can never offset the price in Israeli lives that may have to be paid to restore the deteriorating military balance. The provision of adequate credit aid is the very least we can do.

Second, section 501 would be necessary even if the authority contained in the Foreign Military Sales Act were substantially greater than it in fact is. This is so because the terms under which credits are made available through that act are wholly inappropriate to pressing Israeli needs. Repayment, for example, must be completed within ten years. There can be no departure from this statutory provision. Moreover, it is standing practice under the Foreign Military Sales Act to charge rates of interest equal to the prevailing cost to the Treasury. Both of these conditions, in the present case, are prohibitive. Israeli foreign exchange reserves are such that it is impossible for them to meet their defense needs on a cash sale basis. Ten-year and cost-to-the-Treasury terms are only a marginal improvement, given the serious state of the Israeli economy.

It is for these reasons that I introduced section 501, with the intention that credits be made available to the extent necessary to effect the policy stated in section 501. Moreover, I anticipate that my intention to have credits made available on substantially more favorable terms has proven essential and will be so regarded by the executive branch. I have in mind a period for repayment on the order of twenty-five years or more and rates of interest that would be negligible—and certainly concessionary.

It was also my intention that the executive branch should place a broad interpretation on the terms "equipment necessary to use, maintain, and protect [such] aircraft" so that equipment such as ordnance, ECM [electronic countermeasures], maintenance and repair facilities, reconnaissance devices, defensive missiles and the like are included, as well as vital advanced aircraft. This is in recognition of the fact that the security of Israel is dependent upon the unchallenged superiority of the Israeli Air Force.

The Israelis have said that they will not be another Czechoslovakia and we alone are in a position to help them restore and maintain the military balance. I might add that the fate of Czechoslovakia in 1938 is as real to the Israelis as the fate of Czechoslovakia thirty years later, in 1968.

We cannot escape the fact that the Soviets have manifested an interest in the Middle East since czarist times, and they would be involved there today even if Israel did not exist. Moscow is aggressively exploiting the tragic conflict between Arabs and Jews to strengthen the Soviet position in the Middle East and to destroy Western influence in the area. We must recognize the threats to our own security that result from Soviet designs in that region. The Mediterranean is of crucial strategic interest to all NATO nations, including the United States. The Middle East is a gateway not only to the Persian Gulf but to the Indian Ocean and North Africa. We have important political interests in the Middle East, where we have good friends, including Israel and a number of nations in the Arab world. We, and especially our NATO allies, have vital interests in the area.

Mr. President, the chairman of the Foreign Relations Committee has expressed the view that, were it not for the fact of cultural and sentimental relationships between the United States and Israel, the question of who controls Israel would not involve a direct threat to the United States. For the reasons I have just suggested, I simply cannot agree with this view.

But I wish to add, Mr. President, my deep belief that the cultural and sentimental ties of which the Senator speaks are a tribute to the open identification of the American people with the ardent desire of the Israeli people for freedom, peace, and security. Far from lamenting the fact that we as a nation are moved to a common bond with this liberal democracy in the Middle East, I am proud that our sentiments lie with the impulse to democracy and justice wherever in the world these values are to be found. So long as we retain our determination that free men desiring to remain free and independent will strike the sentiments of the American people, we and the free world will survive and flourish.

Mr. President, I, for one, could not find it in my conscience to ask the Israelis to allow another day to pass, while they continue to support our peace initiative at great risk to their survival, without assuring them that we will stand by our commitment to help them maintain the military balance in the Middle East. Section 501 offers such assurances by granting the President the authority he needs. Seldom in the history of our country have the dictates of national prudence and honor been so congruent. Seldom has an issue so clear and direct been within the power of the Senate to resolve.

23
Reassessing the Middle East

American-Israel Public Affairs Committee,
Washington, D.C.
14 April 1975

Following the failure of Secretary of State Kissinger's shuttle diplomacy between Israel and Egypt in the spring of 1975, the Ford administration announced a reassessment of policy in the Middle East. This sounded innocent to some, but not to many Members of Congress. Among them was Senator Jackson, by that time fully aware of the administration's ongoing campaign of secret meetings, background briefings, and anonymous leaks to the press designed to blame Israel alone for the failure. The Senator had followed the course of the Egyptian-Israeli negotiations. He knew what had happened. He was fully aware of the Kissinger practice of saying one thing in public and quite another in private. Without a basic honesty and openness in the conduct of our foreign affairs, he believed the American people were denied the truth that made possible sound judgments.

An invitation to speak to the American-Israel Public Affairs Committee (AIPAC) gave him a chance to outline his own assessment of the American Middle East policy. And he had no intention of sparing an administration that he considered dangerously wrongheaded. As he put it at one point in his speech: "A genuine and reciprocal improvement in East-West relations is to the advantage of all peoples in the world. But we must not ask our friends to pay the price of the administration's illusions about détente."

IN RECENT DAYS THE NEWSPAPERS HAVE BEEN FILLED WITH commentary about the relationship between the tragedy in Indochina and the failure of the Kissinger mission to the Middle East. But somehow the most profound connection between these two distant situations has been overlooked. It is this: negotiated settlements that do not include movement toward a genuine peace are certain to fail. Without starting the process of political accommodation, cease-fires and disengagements that alter only the military situation cannot lead to lasting peace. In the search for peace, a change of line is no substitute for a change of heart.

This is the bitter lesson of the Paris accords. And if the Israelis have learned from it, if they have concluded that they would rather understand history than repeat it, who can hold them at fault?

ASSESSING THE SHUTTLE DIPLOMACY

Unhappily and unwisely, the end of shuttle diplomacy has been followed by a campaign of background briefings, meetings, and leaks to the press calculated to imply that Israel alone was responsible for the failure to reach an accord. Partly as a result of this campaign and because the Secretary of State returned to Washington from Jerusalem, some people concluded that the talks had failed when Israel rejected an Egyptian compromise proposal. The truth is otherwise; and the record should be clear on this point. Dr. Kissinger departed Jerusalem when President Sadat of Egypt refused even to consider an Israeli compromise proposal that sought to provide a basis for continuing negotiations.

The American people must judge for themselves whether Egypt was justified in breaking off the talks. Unfortunately, their task in fairly considering the issue is complicated by the administration's one-sided characterization of the course of the negotiations. So perhaps it would be useful to review for a moment the two proposals that proved, in the end, to be irreconcilable.

In exchange for an Egyptian statement of nonbelligerency and some concrete political and economic steps along the road to peace, Israel offered to give up the strategic Sinai passes and to return the oil fields at Abu Rudeis to Egyptian control. Egypt, for its part, refused to make a pledge of nonbelligerency or to take concrete steps that would begin the process of peace and reconciliation. Instead, Egypt insisted on a deep Israeli withdrawal, well beyond the passes—a withdrawal that would seriously and immediately worsen Israel's physical security. It is hard to resist the conclusion that Israel was searching for the road to peace while Egypt sought the road to Tel Aviv.

To break the impasse, Israel then proposed to withdraw from the western half of the passes and to permit land and sea access to the oil fields which were to be returned to Egyptian control. In return she asked only that Egypt agree to refrain from the use of force, a very partial—some would say marginal—step toward peace. Egypt declined the Israeli compromise, refused to receive Dr. Kissinger in Aswan, and the negotiations came to an end.

ARGUING FROM DIFFERENT PREMISES

Samuel Pepys once observed two women arguing across a back fence. "They will never agree," he remarked. "They are arguing from different premises." So it was in the Middle East. Israel's premise in the negotiations was that withdrawals from strategic positions in the Sinai should be matched by commensurate progress toward a genuine peace.

The Egyptian premise was quite different. Sadat regarded a second disengagement agreement as an essentially military arrangement. Thus he sought a deeper Israeli withdrawal, a more advantageous disengagement line, unaccompanied by real political concessions.

My own view is expressed in remarks I made on December 17, 1973. It is this:

> Peace must be more than a word, more than a mere document that can be torn up when it suits the convenience of aggressive governments to go to war again. It must be something concrete. It must exist in the daily lives of men, for only then can it eventually come to exist in men's minds as well; and only then—finally—can it be secure. It is naive to imagine that the enmities of decades will vanish with the stroke of a pen. But for a peace treaty to be more than just a scrap of paper, it must do more than simply move the walls that separate Arabs from Israelis to a new location. It must permit Arabs and Israelis to work together, to trade with one another, to talk with one another, to see for themselves the truth about their neighbors.

THE NEGOTIATIONS AND THE ADMINISTRATION

Surely the inflexibility of the Egyptian position reflected President Sadat's belief that Israel would yield to administration pressure and settle on Egyptian terms. An anxious Washington, Sadat believed, and a dependent Israel would lead to irresistible pressure. In such circumstances there was little incentive for Egypt to compromise, and a predictable ultimatum resulted. In any case, Sadat must have reasoned, a failure of the talks would drive a wedge between Israel and America.

Well, Sadat was wrong. He was wrong about Israel and he was wrong about America. Israel resisted the temptation to make unrequited concessions, and it did so with remarkable unity. And America will not allow a wedge to be driven between our people and the people of Israel. The administration knows that the American people will not permit it to pressure Israel into withdrawals that prejudice her security and increase the risks of war. That is why we find the administration saying one thing in public and quite another in private. Thus in public the administration urges the view that no useful purpose is served by assessing blame for the failure of the negotiations; while in private Israel is held to have been responsible. Well, the time to end that unwise charade is long past. The American people have a right to an administration that says what it means and means what it says. They have a right to read in the morning papers that remarks attributed to "a senior official traveling with Kissinger" are in fact the words of the Secretary of State. They have a right to know who it is that is speaking in their name. For without candor and openness in our foreign policy, in the Middle East and elsewhere, the American people are deprived of the right to make their judgments felt.

THE ADMINISTRATION'S REASSESSMENT

There has been much talk by the administration of a reassessment of its Middle East policy. I hope and trust that it will be thoughtful and deliberate. Above all it must be fair. It must not be marked by the petulance that marked its inception.

In my judgment the first conclusion to which any sober re-assessment should come is this: the idea that a stable peace can be achieved by pressuring Israel to diminish her physical security without a political reconciliation with her neighbors is dangerous and unwise.

Second, the reappraisal should return to UN resolutions 242 and 338 by recognizing that a real peace must involve direct negotiations among the parties in which Israeli withdrawal to secure and recognized borders is matched by an end to the state of belligerency. The last round of shuttle diplomacy, by departing from the hopeful formula of these resolutions, did much to subvert what I believe to be the most promising prospects for peace.

Third, a fair reassessment will reaffirm the soundness of the long-standing American policy of helping to maintain the military balance in the Middle East. Some of you may recall that we wrote that policy into law in the 91st Congress. We said then that it was the policy of the United States to maintain the military balance in the Middle East by furnishing Israel with the arms she requires for her own defense. And I mean to see that we continue to adhere to it because it is essential to any realistic hope for peace.

Finally, any clear-sighted reassessment will include a reap-praisal of the role of the administration's détente in promoting peace in the Middle East. Détente didn't inhibit the Soviets from sending the arms that started and then sustained the Yom Kippur war. It didn't restrain the Soviets, who first in-cited other Arab governments to join forces with Egypt and Syria and then urged OPEC to use the oil weapon against the West.

A reassessment of the administration's détente will reject the dangerous illusion that underlay the ill-fated Paris accords on Indochina. I am referring, of course, to the idea that we can *count* on Soviet cooperation—or even restraint. Détente didn't save Cambodia and it won't save Vietnam, despite the fact that we and the Soviets are coguarantors of the Paris accords. And that, by the way, is something to keep in mind when one hears that we and the Soviets should replay the international guarantee game in the Middle East.

A genuine and reciprocal improvement in East-West relations is to the advantage of all peoples in the world. But we must not ask our friends to pay the price of the administration's illusions about détente.

Finally, let me conclude with this thought. In their frustration at the seemingly intractable conflict in the Middle East there are those who are tempted to fashion a piece of paper into a paper peace. To yield to such temptation would be a mistake of historic proportions. I am confident that we will not so yield; that in the end we will summon those resources of courage and vision that are the best hope for a lasting peace.

And let me just say to our friends overseas that America is not about to withdraw from the world. In adversity we have always found strength. And the conviction of the American people that America must remain strong is undiminished in these difficult times.

24
A New Marshall Plan for the Middle East

United States Senate
12 October 1978

From the first, Senator Jackson welcomed President Anwar Sadat's historic peace initiative. He believed the Camp David Israeli-Egyptian Agreements could be a significant step toward a stable peace in the area. But that depended on the follow-up. What might be done to use the opportunities created by the agreements to fashion new cooperative political relationships in the region?

Long troubled by the poverty, illiteracy, disease, lack of economic opportunity, and endemic instabilities of the region, Jackson sensed the chance for a cooperative partnership of the Egyptians and Israelis for the common economic development of their countries, working with the United States and other Western nations and in time including other nations in the region. Why not a Marshall-type plan for the Middle East?

The Senator presented his idea before a number of American audiences and in conversations with Prime Minister Menachem Begin in Jerusalem and President Anwar Sadat in Egypt. Buoyed by the responses, he introduced a nonbinding sense-of-the-Senate resolution in the Congress on 12 October 1978 designed to encourage President Carter to take the lead by inviting Egypt and Israel to explore with us and other Western industrial nations the possibilities for a Marshall Plan for the Middle East. President Carter did not follow Jackson's counsel. But the idea of a Marshall Plan for the Middle East is still a live option, and the effort to root the Middle East peace process in a cooperative Israeli-Egyptian relationship continues.

MR. PRESIDENT, I WISH TO INTRODUCE ON BEHALF OF MYself, Senator [Frank] Church, Senator [Jacob] Javits, Senator [Clifford] Case, and Senator [Richard] Stone a resolution expressing the sense of the Senate with respect to developing a new Marshall Plan for the Middle East. This resolution affirms the sense of the Senate that the President of the United States should take the lead in inviting Egypt and Israel to explore with our government and with the governments of other Western industrial nations the opportunity for a new Marshall Plan for the Middle East, leading to a full economic partnership with the Israeli and Egyptian people and all those in the Middle East who are willing to live in peace.

Mr. President, the representatives of Israel and Egypt today open their negotiations at Blair House to complete the historic Israeli-Egyptian peace treaty initiated at Camp David. At this time, the Camp David Agreements remain a political framework—a foundation—for the construction of a new political relationship.

The Middle East, with the exception of Israel, and despite vast oil revenues, remains plagued by poverty and instability. While a fourfold increase in the price of oil has enriched a small minority in a few countries, the great mass in the Middle East continue to suffer the burdens of inadequate food and shelter, high unemployment, and a dismal future. A major factor in the tensions that have produced a generation of political instability in the Middle East has been the desperation that afflicts all but a handful of rich and privileged individuals.

For example, the Egyptian people, some thirty-eight million and growing over a million a year, live from hand to mouth. In Cairo, where six million people are crowded together, hundreds of thousands of urban poor live—without water, plumbing, or electricity—inside the tombs of the ancient cemetery area. Ten percent of the infants born each year die in infancy. In the Upper Nile, and in farming areas generally, the parasitic disease schistosomiasis contributes to Egypt's male life expectancy of fifty-four years and condemns millions to internal bleeding, debilitation, and suffering. Professionals and skilled workers emigrate in droves, for there is no work for them in Egypt.

This can and must be changed. The potential resources are rich and plentiful. With peace they can be developed, and with peace one can foresee a fruitful partnership of unprecedented proportions between Israel, Egypt, and the United States.

In helping to alleviate poverty in Egypt and elsewhere in the Middle East, there is a great and historic role for the United

States, a role we once before filled in the reconstruction of postwar Europe.

As was the case with the Marshall Plan, it is essential that any such program for the Middle East be based on a full partnership with the Israelis and Egyptians. They should work with us and with other Western industrial nations for the common development of their countries and, eventually, the region as a whole. Among them, the countries possess all the potential resources: capital, ingenuity, management skills, labor, and, with Western nation involvement, technology and markets. Together we can do much to reverse the misery of centuries, to make the deserts bloom.

The resolution we introduce today is intended to encourage President Carter to take the lead by inviting Egypt and Israel to explore with us and with other governments of Western industrial nations the opportunities for a new Marshall Plan for the Middle East. The American government can and should let all the countries of the Middle East know that there is a path to the realization of their peaceful dreams along which we are willing to accompany them. And at the same time we must make it plain that those who are unwilling to join with us and Israel and Egypt will lose out on the economic and other benefits of such cooperation and mutual assistance.

The Camp David Agreements are, we trust, a significant step on the road to a stable peace in the Middle East. But for the peace to last it must be more than a peace among armies and diplomats, more than an official peace. It must come to occupy a place in the daily lives of Arabs and Israelis alike. There must be movement across once-fortified borders that can now become gateways to the development of social, economic, and political relations—first among the Israeli and Egyptian people and in time among all those in the Arab world who are willing to live in peace.

SENATE RESOLUTION

Expressing the sense of the Senate with respect to developing a new Marshall Plan for the Middle East.

Whereas the Camp David Agreements have established a political framework for the construction of a new political relationship between Israel and Egypt which can be a significant step on the road to a stable peace in the Middle East;

Whereas a major factor in the tensions that have produced a generation of political instability in the Middle East has been the poverty and desperation that afflicts the great mass of people in the area;

Whereas the potential resources of Egypt and other countries in the region are rich and plentiful and can be developed in peace and in partnership through cooperation and mutual assistance;

Whereas in helping to alleviate poverty in Egypt and elsewhere in the Middle East, there is a great and historic role for the United States, a role we once before filled in the reconstruction of postwar Europe:

Now, therefore, be it

Resolved, That it is the sense of the Senate that the President of the United States should take the lead in inviting Egypt and Israel to explore with our government and with the governments of other Western industrial nations the opportunity for a new Marshall Plan for the Middle East, leading to a full economic partnership with the Israeli and Egyptian people and all those in the Middle East who are willing to live in peace.

Sec. 2. The Secretary of the Senate shall transmit a copy of this resolution to the President of the United States.

25

Iran and the Middle East: Past and Present

American Professors for Peace in the Middle East,
George Washington University, Washington, D.C.
25 February 1979

For Senator Jackson, comprehending—and applying—the experience of history was the basis of wisdom in national decision making. Never reluctant to try to clarify a policy issue by viewing it in its historical context, he accepted a February 1979 invitation to address the American Professors for Peace in the Middle East.

The Shah of Iran had fallen. Iran had moved from an ally of the United States and friend of Israel to a posture of radical Islamic fundamentalism. For Israel, for Egypt, and for the United States this strategic shift raised profound policy questions.

How, for example, would the Soviets benefit, or try to benefit, from the momentum started by the revolution in Iran? Since Jackson's 1956 visit to the Soviet Union—at which time he had left by way of Afghanistan—he had been an avid student of Russia's historic approach to its southern border, including its periodic drive for a warm-water port.

WE HAVE SEEN IN RECENT MONTHS A SHIFT IN THE BALance of power and influence in the Middle East of historic proportions. The passage of Iran from a Western-oriented power, closely allied with the United States and opposed to Arab radicalism, to a fundamentalist Islamic and potentially radical state has profound implications for Israel, for Egypt, and for the Western world.

However much we may hope that it will not fully develop, we must, on the basis of what has already happened, assume that Iran will become a base for operations of the PLO and a significant source of strength for radical Arab regimes. This momentous shift means increased danger for Israel, increased pressure on President Sadat, and a decrease in the security of oil supplies for the United States and its allies in Europe and elsewhere.

THE HISTORICAL CONTEXT

It is remarkable how an atmosphere of crisis can obscure, even obliterate, the historical context in which contemporary events are rooted. Knowing of the high standard of scholarly work that the American Professors for Peace in the Middle East and its members have brought to bear on the problems of the Middle East, I know that this audience shares my concern at the failure to assess current political events in their historical context. So I want to say a few words today about the history of Iran and how that history may bear on the further evolution of events there and in the Middle East generally.

The Iranian constitutional revolution of 1906 aroused great hopes; but it also created great dangers. The alliance of forces which had imposed its will on an autocratic shah soon broke up into its component parts, and a weakening of authority at the center gave free scope to the age-old separatist and particularistic traditions in the various Iranian provinces. This situation, then as perhaps now, provided a new opportunity for Russian penetration and expansion.

Russian expansion at Persian expense had been going on for a long time and had brought great territories to the east and west of the Caspian Sea under Russian control. Two Russo-Iranian wars, from 1804 to 1813 and from 1826 to 1828, resulted in the Russian acquisition, partly from local dynasties and partly from Iran, of the territories which now form the Soviet Republics of Armenia and Azerbaijan.

Russian acquisition of the northern half of the Iranian province of Azerbaijan proved very profitable, principally through the discovery of oil. The first drilling took place there in 1842. Thereafter the development of the oil industry in Russian Azerbaijan was roughly contemporary with American oil field development in Pennsylvania.

Successive Russian governments and regimes pursued two basic objectives: first, the extension of their influence from northern to southern Azerbaijan on the road towards the Persian Gulf and the Indian Ocean and, second, a defensive interest in the protection of their Muslim subject-provinces from possible contamination by ideas and movements originating in the still-independent Muslim countries to the south.

In the confusion following the 1906 revolution, conflicts occurred between nationalists, constitutionalists, centralists, and separatists, in the course of which the Russians advanced their forces into northern Iran, where they occupied a number of places, including Tabriz, in 1909. Attempts were made to persuade them to withdraw their forces, but they refused; and in 1911 they reinforced them considerably. In 1912 Russian forces suppressed an uprising in Tabriz (the site of great turmoil today). In northeastern Iran, they bombarded and invaded the sacred shrine in Mashhad. By 1914 Russia controlled most of the northern provinces of Iran, and Russian nationals were acquiring land in Iranian Azerbaijan.

IRAN AND THE SOVIET UNION FROM WORLD WAR II

The revolution and civil war in Russia brought a weakening of Russian power and a withdrawal of Russian troops. They returned, however, in 1941 and immediately reestablished themselves, especially in Iranian Azerbaijan and Kurdestan, in both of which they tried to set up separatist regimes under Russian auspices. The Soviets were also active in the northeast, for example, in Mashhad. In a revealing incident in 1945, Communist demonstrators harangued a crowd while Russian machine gunners made sure that Iranian security forces did not interfere. The two lines of Russian action were, first, the encouragement of separatism in the areas under their control and, second, Communist subversion in the remainder of Iran.

The Soviet occupation of Iran in 1941 had been undertaken as part of a joint Allied operation for military purposes against the Axis. British forces entered at the same time from the south and were later joined by some American units. The ending of the war against the Axis removed the reason and the justification for the presence of these foreign forces. The

United States had withdrawn its forces by the end of 1945 and the British followed in March 1946—both within the time agreed by treaty. Russia, despite repeated requests by the Iranians and pressures from the Western allies, not only failed to withdraw but actually reinforced her troops in Iran. It was only after the strongest pressure from President Truman that Stalin was induced to remove Soviet troops in 1946.

THE CURRENT SITUATION

The recent developments in Iran show striking similarities to the course of events earlier in this century. The alliance which held together long enough to overthrow the Shah is already beginning to break up in its component parts. A period of conflict now seems inevitable—possibly even civil war, whether full scale or in the limited Lebanese style. The leftist elements in Iran are well armed, well disciplined, and led by competent professionals who certainly made a substantial contribution to the victory of the revolutionary alliance. They are now, not surprisingly, beginning to assert themselves. The weakening of authority at the center is already giving scope to separatism in the provinces. Iran is of vast extent, with very strong regional traditions. When the central authority is weak, for whatever reason, separatist regimes of one sort or another appear in the provinces.

A likely development at the present time is the emergence of a series of military regimes based on fluctuating alliances of religious, nationalist, separatist, and leftist elements with local support. Remember that Iran is a country of great ethnic diversity. In addition to the Farsi-speaking Persians, who constitute the dominant authority (but probably not much more than half the population), there are many other ethnic groups.

In the northwest there is Azerbaijan, with some ten million people, Shiite by religion, speaking a form of Turkish and with a common historic and cultural identity with their brothers to the north in the Soviet republic of Azerbaijan. There are already reports of steady fighting with serious loss of life in Tabriz. The emergence of a separatist regime with Soviet sponsorship is probably being prepared.

Immediately to the south of Azerbaijan lies Iranian Kurdestan, also the scene of an earlier Soviet exercise in controlled separatism and an excellent base for subversion among the Turkish and Iraqi Kurds. Here separatist manifestations among the Iranian Kurds have already been reported.

Continuing southward there are different tribal groups always ready to throw off the control of the central government. In Khuzistan, a major oil-bearing area, there is a minority of about a million Arabs already affected by Arab radicalism and the subject of irredentist claims. To the south there are Baluchis linked with their brothers in Pakistani Baluchistan and with a separatist movement of their own. The whole of eastern Iran is open to penetration from Afghanistan, where, almost unnoticed, a pro-Soviet regime was installed by a coup d'etat last April.

In the past, Russian incursions into northern Iran were contained or limited by British power in India. Sometimes by agreement, sometimes in conflict, the two major imperial powers in Asia, Russia and Britain, somehow balanced each other. But Britain has gone and Russia remains alone. In the absence of a countervailing force, there seems nothing to stop the Russians from extending their influence—this time not merely through northern Iran but through the whole country.

The consequences of this would be far-reaching. Turkey would be outflanked on her eastern border; Iraq would, for the first time, be directly linked by land with a pro-Soviet regime. The countries of the Persian Gulf—Kuwait, Bahrain, the Emirates, and, above all, Saudi Arabia—would be within easy striking distance for sedition, sabotage, or direct military action. There would be no need for the Soviet government, or even for what Iranian government may emerge in the future, to take any overt part in such actions. The PLO and some parallel organizations stand ready and available. We have already seen Yassir Arafat reveling in his occupation of offices formerly belonging to the Government of Israel; and we have heard him boasting of the PLO's services to the Iranian revolution through the provision of arms and training. And already there are signs that the PLO is preparing to bestow on Iran the blessings they have already brought to Lebanon. They would, of course, have better and more pressing reasons to do the same in the countries of the Arabian peninsula, and especially in Saudi Arabia.

THE SPILLOVER FROM IRAN

Now we are faced with the vexing question of the larger spillover effects of the situation in Iran. Turkey is surely in danger. So is Pakistan. And the oil-producing states of the gulf could be forgiven if their fears persist despite the recent visit of Secretary of Defense Harold Brown. The fact is that we have been witnessing for some time now an effort by the Soviets, through the use of proxies and surrogates, to encircle the oil-producing countries on which the West depends.

A reasonable test of how far Soviet influence has spread is found in reviewing the list of the fifteen or so countries that have recognized the pro-Soviet puppet regime recently installed in Cambodia by the force of Vietnamese arms. In addition to the Soviet satellites, the list includes Ethiopia, Mozambique, Afghanistan, Angola, and South Yemen.

Saudi Arabia, like Iran before it, is in the process of being encircled by friends of the Soviet Union. The danger that the Soviets and their friends will gain control over the nine and a half million barrels of oil that the Saudis ship daily to the United States and its allies is real—and growing. And the Soviets, who understand the connection between military and political power, have begun to make overtures to the Saudis, overtures that the Saudis would prefer to reject if they could be certain that the West is in a position to protect them, if they could be certain that we have the power and the will to underwrite their security.

THE UNITED STATES AND THE MIDDLE EAST

Yet the United States must appear weak and vacillating to the Saudis—and the Egyptians and Israelis as well. It is hard to believe that in their conversations the Shah of Iran has sought to persuade President Sadat that the United States was a firm and reliable ally. It is hard to believe that our friends in Israel have been reassured either by the post–Camp David pressure that was brought to bear on them or by our indecision and weakness as events unfolded in Iran. One can only hope that despite the calamity in Iran a peace settlement will emerge between Israel and Egypt.

Such a settlement cannot be safely and responsibly "comprehensive." Indeed, had we not sought to turn the promising beginning at Camp David into an unpromising general settlement that neither Israel nor Egypt desired, we would, in all likelihood, have had an initial peace by now. Upon such a peace one could hope to nurture a de facto alliance among Israel, Egypt, and Saudi Arabia—countries with a common interest, heightened by the events in Iran, in a stable and secure counter to the growth of Soviet influence in the Middle East.

There can be no doubt that the Soviets have benefited, and hope to benefit more, from the revolution in Iran. Clandestine transmitters in southern Russia, to say nothing of Radio Moscow, were deeply involved in fomenting turmoil in Iran and in functioning as the communication network for the political and religious opposition in Iran. Infiltration of Soviet agents across the Afghan border provided organizing cadres to coordinate demonstrations and strikes. The Soviet Union was the ultimate source of the weapons that appeared when militant forces in Iran were ready to administer the coup de grace to the fledgling Bakhtiar government. Whether the Soviets and their agents and surrogates succeed in capturing the momentum that the situation in Iran has started, and spreading disorder to the rest of the region, will depend importantly on whether we realize the danger and act in time to meet it.

It remains within our power to fashion an alliance of states prepared to resist the encroachments of the Soviets and their friends. But it will take more understanding than we have thus far demonstrated, more will than we have shown, and more imagination than we have evidenced. It is time to stop repeating the silly cliché that we "cannot be the world's policeman" and to begin to think about our future in a world without a cop on the corner.

VIII
U.S. Relations with China

26
New Directions in the Pacific Area

Rotary Club of Seattle, Seattle, Washington
5 November 1969

Because of his roots in the Pacific rim and his geopolitical perspective on the world, it is not surprising that Senator Jackson had a special interest in China. Clearly, however, it was the Vietnam War that concentrated his attention on U.S. relations with Beijing.

In the tradition of rallying behind a President in a foreign policy crisis, Jackson supported President Kennedy when he sent his Green Berets and President Johnson when he deployed follow-on U.S. forces to help resist the subjugation of South Vietnam by North Vietnam. Once U.S. troops were committed in the field, the Senator worked to help sustain bipartisan support for the undertaking. As the conflict wore on, and on, with the mounting human and domestic political costs of a war of attrition, Jackson focused his efforts on achieving a negotiated, mutual cease-fire that would permit a staged withdrawal of U.S. troops. In his words: "As I see it, American disengagement from Vietnam must be phased and orderly, or our foreign policy problems will become more difficult and more unmanageable than ever."

Meanwhile, the Senator had moved toward the view that China was not the chief aggressor in the conflict—that Hanoi's interests coincided more with Moscow than with Beijing. He became convinced that trying to end the Vietnam War on stabilizing terms and trying to achieve constructive relations with Mainland China were separable problems. By 1966 the Senator was bent on drawing public attention to the issue of working out in the years ahead a livable relationship with the Chinese communists.

Given so contentious an issue in American politics and with Mainland China convulsed in the terrors and chaos of Mao's Cultural Revolution, Jackson moved deliberately, signifying in occasional speeches and conversations his concern for a fresh approach to U.S.-China policy. When in 1969 the new Nixon administration embarked on the policy of Vietnamization, which had Jackson's support, and American participation in the Vietnam conflict was waning, the Senator saw his chance to step out front in developing American policy for a post-Vietnam Asia. Thus, well before President Nixon's 1970 "ping-pong diplomacy" and Henry Kissinger's secret China mission of July 1971, Senator Jackson was at work to help fashion an opening to China.

As it turned out, Vietnamization did not work; the South Vietnamese forces were not strong enough to resist those of North Vietnam, which overran South Vietnam and Laos and then Cambodia. The Senator had anticipated that if the despotic North Vietnamese leadership won out, there would be brutality, massacre, and terror in the region. But the wholesale tragedy of Indochina was even greater than he expected.

THREE TIMES IN THE PAST GENERATION THE UNITED STATES has found itself involved in costly wars in the Pacific area. If this painful experience has any lesson for us today, it is that peace and stability in that area depend very heavily on what the great powers do, and notably on the coherence and rationality of our own foreign policies.

In the Pacific Northwest, we have always felt close ties to the countries of the Western Pacific. Our economic and cultural relationships have special significance. At a time when much of our policy in the Pacific is in a state of flux, I am persuaded that we can make a contribution in attempting to think, and think hard, about our policies and develop new, forward-looking approaches for the years ahead.

I believe it would contribute to peace and stability in the Western Pacific if Communist China, comprising over seven hundred million people, could begin to reenter the international community and place its international relations on a more normal stable plane. Whether the Peking leadership is seeking opportunities to move in this direction remains an open question.

The Peking regime a few weeks ago commemorated its twentieth anniversary. At present the Chinese people appear to have weathered the worst of the Great Proletarian Cultural Revolution. The Red Guard excesses and the chaos that characterized the period from mid-1966 to late 1968 have given way to some modicum of internal order and stability, albeit under military control. While the Peking regime has continuously aided and abetted Hanoi in South Vietnam, there is evidence that the regime's own military policies remain cautious and of a low risk nature. The refrain is constantly reiterated, "We shall not attack unless we are attacked."

Also, there are some indicators of a new preoccupation in Peking with its diplomatic posture. The Chinese have recently entered into discussion with the Soviet Union regarding the border issue that only a few months ago was leading toward a major Sino-Soviet confrontation—and which may yet end up that way. As for its attitude toward the United States, the Mainland government has evidenced some downgrading in its estimate of the nature of the so-called threat from America. Hints persist of a revived interest on the part of the Chinese in reopening the bilateral ambassadorial talks with us, which Peking broke off in February this year.

Meanwhile, there is the continued progress of the Chinese in developing a nuclear missile capability. The Chinese detonated two nuclear devices in late September—one underground and one above ground. In fact, Peking's decision to develop nuclear weapons may well be proving counterproductive in that it has encouraged some other governments in the area to consider the indigenous development of nuclear weapons and has made public acceptance of such weapons more tolerable. These are not developments which would be welcomed by any leadership in Peking. Time may well see a changing attitude on its part toward arms control arrangements. It is pretty obvious that sometime, somehow, the Mainland Chinese regime will have to join in the negotiations on arms control if it and the rest of the world are going to have peace and security.

In any event, as far as United States policy toward Mainland China is concerned I believe we should get it on a less-rigid, more-sensible footing. The U.S. government has already taken a few hesitant steps to ease exchanges between the Chinese and American peoples. But more are possible, and these may in turn contribute to a more substantive exchange between our respective governments. We cannot guarantee that a favorable response will be the case; we cannot predict how Mao Tse-tung or his successors will respond to U.S. overtures. But a new U.S. policy, which, while respecting American treaty obligations in the area, leaves open the way for a positive Chinese response, should increase the chances of more normal relations between our two governments if not in the immediate future, at least over the longer term.

I propose that we take two steps immediately. One, we should renew the invitation to the Peking regime to join in the twenty-five-nation arms control meetings in Geneva. Negotiations on arms control are going to be long and difficult. This isn't the sort of thing that can be negotiated in a month or six months or a year. But we shouldn't have to waste any time talking about the desirability of Mainland China's participation in such efforts.

Two, we should press Peking for the reopening of the bilateral U.S.-China ambassadorial talks, either in Warsaw or at another agreed site. At the reopening of the ambassadorial talks the United States ought to be prepared to make constructive suggestions for discussion and negotiation. As I see it these suggestions should include the start of mutual U.S.-Chinese exchanges of reporters, scholars, scientists, and cultural performers; the regularization of postal and telecommunication problems; the improvement of trade relations between U.S. and Mainland China, including the mutual reduction of barriers to trade; the subject of Mainland Chinese participation in the United Nations and other international bodies on terms that would not exclude the Republic of China on Formosa.

The approach I am proposing is in the interest of the United States. But it is also in the interest of Mainland China. It is time that both the Americans and the Mainland Chinese recognized that they have a mutual interest in, and a mutual responsibility for, peace and stability in the Western Pacific area. Furthermore, I believe this approach would have a broad appeal internationally and would be supported by our allies and others in the Asia-Pacific area. In effect, we would be signaling United States willingness to explore with Mainland China directly and with greater concreteness than before the possibilities for peace and stability in the Western Pacific.

In recent months, significant steps have been taken to start winding down the Vietnam War and to reduce American casualties. We are all intensely concerned that progress toward peace in Vietnam be continued in the months ahead. The question at issue in the debate over Vietnam is not whether to end the Vietnam War. Everyone I know wants to do that. The question is *how* to do it?

Many Americans are now preoccupied with the problem of getting out of Vietnam. But we have to be concerned with more than that. We have to be concerned with the kind of world we will be living in after we have withdrawn and with the effect of *how* we withdraw on our ability to deal with the problems of the post-Vietnam world.

As I see it, American disengagement from Vietnam must be phased and orderly, or our foreign policy problems will become more difficult and more unmanageable than ever. A precipitous withdrawal, a disorganized and haphazard retreat in the face of the recalcitrance we have met at the negotiating table in Paris, would have fateful consequences for the future of this nation and of individual liberty. President Nixon described those consequences in his speech this week. Our adversaries would figure they have us on the run, and they would not hesitate to take advantage of it by pushing their luck in other trouble spots in Asia, in the Middle East, and in Europe. A hasty retreat in Vietnam would disconcert and destabilize other countries to which we have made commitments—for example, South Korea, the Philippines, Japan, not to mention our partners in NATO. And a disorderly withdrawal would not bring peace in Vietnam. Fighting, doubtless bloodier than we have yet seen, would go on and on.

The key to peace in Vietnam is a careful, deliberate, and phased replacement of U.S. troops by those in the Army of the Republic of Vietnam. If the South Vietnamese are better prepared today to defend themselves, it is because we have secured for them time in which to build a trained and organized and equipped self-defense force with which to meet the challenge from the north.

In spite of our best efforts, of course, we cannot, from the other side of the world, guarantee the future of the people of South Vietnam. What we can and should do is everything possible consistent with our national interest to leave in the hands of the South Vietnamese the capacity to determine their own future, in short, self-determination.

27

The 1974 Visit
to the People's Republic of China

Press Conference Statement, Washington, D.C.

8 July 1974

Once Senator Jackson had taken on the task of helping develop ties with China, he tackled it with energy and enthusiasm, soon becoming one of the Senate's most informed and influential members in the debate on American policy on China. When a 1974 invitation came from the Chinese side to visit China, Jackson seized upon it. In a private meeting with a very ill Premier Zhou Enlai in his hospital room in Beijing, Jackson discussed the need and possibilities for Sino-American cooperation. The Senator often spoke of this talk as one of the most moving and instructive conversations of his life. The Senator also had lengthy meetings with China's senior leader Deng Xiaoping in which they covered geopolitical and bilateral issues with remarkable frankness. During the course of these talks, the two seasoned, pragmatic politicians came to respect each other. Their continuing relationship over almost a decade proved an unusual and significant channel in the development of U.S.-China relations.

The Senator made four official trips to the People's Republic, in 1974, 1978, 1979, and 1983. He met with Deng Xiaoping and other high officials in Beijing and visited different regions of China to learn more about the history, the cultural variety, the economic issues, and the strategic problems facing the Chinese. Each trip was followed by a public, printed report to the Senate and one or more press conferences. On his return to Washington, D.C., in 1974 from his first trip, the Senator made this statement to the press.

MY VIEW THAT THE CHINESE THINK REALISTICALLY ABOUT the geopolitical situation on the Eurasian landmass has been strongly reinforced by my talks in Peking. I found that there are many areas in which American interests parallel those of the Chinese. Even though we use different language to express our positions and even though we start from different premises, there are a range of matters in which the national interests of our two countries are compatible. I found that many of my own positions on vital issues now being debated in America were understood and sympathetically appreciated by the Chinese.

During my stay in China I had over fifteen hours of detailed and frank conversations with Premier Chou En-lai, Vice Premier Teng Hsiao-p'ing, Vice Minister of Foreign Affairs Chiao Kuan-hua, and other high officials of the People's Republic of China. I came away from these discussions with a number of key impressions of the way in which the Chinese view the developing world situation and of some of the problem areas that both we and they face.

At the center of Chinese concern is what they perceive to be the expansionist and unreliable nature of the Soviet Union. While they are convinced of their capacity to defend themselves on the basis of self-reliance, they see Soviet policy as in part directed at the encirclement of China.

It is my judgment that the Chinese recognize the importance of NATO and the danger of any immediate withdrawal of U.S. troops from Europe. Their present position is that the Soviets are "feinting to the East in preparation for an attack on the West." That is, they are concerned about the weakness of Europe and the need for greater unity among the Western allies.

One concern that I perceived is related to Soviet involvement on the Indian subcontinent and in the Persian Gulf, particularly their pressure on Iran and Pakistan. The Chinese expressed concern over their perception of the limited extent of American understanding of persisting threats to the territorial integrity of Pakistan.

Two years have elapsed since the Shanghai Communiqué*

---

*The joint U.S.-China Communiqué of 27 February 1972 was the result of meetings in China between President Nixon and Premier Zhou Enlai. It includes the U.S. commitment not to challenge the contention of both the Chinese and the Nationalist Chinese that "Taiwan is part of China," expresses the desire of the United States for a "peaceful settlement" by the Chinese and we should now be pressing on toward new departures in Sino-American relations, including the establishment of resident correspondents in each country, more substantial programs of cultural and educational exchanges, and the settlement of the assets issue. On the matter of diplomatic recognition, we should try to reverse the location of our embassy and liaison office as between Taipei and Peking.

I was struck by the Chinese spirit of self-reliance, which is manifest in many areas, from security planning to their handling of foreign trade. The American people will welcome the news that trade with China is evolving on a solid commercial basis. Unlike the Russians, the Chinese are not seeking special subsidies.

I was able to explain to the highest Chinese officials the nature of the American decision-making process and the increasing importance of Congress in foreign policy matters. I believe that the U.S.-China relationship must be strengthened by moving beyond contacts between a limited number of personalities to a more institutionalized process and a far wider range of exchanges and other relationships.

To the Chinese, one's word of honor is more important than formalistic agreements on paper, and they profoundly distrust the Soviet Union for failing to act with integrity. The Chinese have learned from bitter experience that their treaties are of little value with the Russians, and they value the frankness with which Americans have spoken with them. I found that while they and I could easily identify a wide variety of issues on which we could agree, they also respected my frankness when we identified matters on which we disagreed. At no point did ideology prove to be a hindrance to precise communication.

I met with Premier Chou En-lai in his suite in a hospital, where he is convalescing. He was alert and keen minded. He was thoroughly familiar with my talks with the other officials and thus we were able to move directly to a discussion of key

---

themselves, and, with that "prospect" in mind, asserts the President's "ultimate objective of the withdrawal of all U.S. forces and military installations from Taiwan."

issues. On leaving he graciously accompanied me out of his suite, where further photographs could be taken.

I must make further mention of how warmly received I was by all the Chinese with whom I dealt, and I particularly appreciate the cordial hospitality of my host, the People's Institute of Foreign Affairs. When I visited Soochow, the birthplace of Mrs. Jackson's mother, the teachers and students at the college greeted us enthusiastically. I also want to thank the American Liaison Office in Peking and particularly my old friend Ambassador David Bruce for their many courtesies.

My trip was short but because we concentrated on working sessions rather than sightseeing, I was able to learn a great deal that hopefully will contribute to better relations and expanding contacts between the United States and China. It is clear to me that in the future there are going to be an increasing number of American policy problems the solution of which must involve considerations of Chinese interests and views. We must grasp this moment in history when geopolitical considerations have brought our two countries closer together to build a web of relations which will promote peace, especially as China moves ahead to become a nuclear and industrial power. I trust my visit has been a significant event in the essential process of expanded and more frank discussions and consultations between Chinese and Americans about world issues.

28

China, Trade, and MFN

United States Senate
22 January 1980

How best to handle relations with China continued to be a contentious issue throughout the 1970s and early 1980s, with Senator Jackson in the middle of the debate. For example, after returning from his February 1978 talks in Beijing with Deng Xiaoping and other senior leaders, the Senator stressed to President Carter the importance of complete normalization of Sino-American relations for enhancing America's strategic position in the world. Full diplomatic relations with the People's Republic of China were finally established in January 1979.

By the summer of 1979, the argument was over whether the trade agreement with China, signed in the spring, would be submitted to the Senate for ratification. The Carter administration was divided over whether to proceed with China when it could not simultaneously extend most-favored-nation treatment and government credits to the Soviets. Jackson strongly supported immediate ratification, arguing against "the administration's misguided doctrine of evenhandedness." After all, China, unlike the Soviet Union, had met the conditions in American law for the waiver of the Jackson-Vanik amendment and the granting of most-favored-nation status and official credits.

Following his 1979 talks in Beijing with Deng and seeing the danger of a major deterioration in Sino-American relations, Jackson increased the pressure, issuing a report to Congress, working with allies in the administration, and rallying colleagues on Capitol Hill —making it hard for President Carter to keep delaying on most-favored-nation status for China.

In January 1980 the United States–China Trade Agreement was finally before the Senate for ratification. The Senator used the occasion to make a speech on the Senate floor opposing the fallacious policy of "evenhanded treatment" of the Soviet Union and China and to have recorded in the *Congressional Record* the Chinese assurances on their future emigration policies, so no one could later claim a "misunderstanding."

MR. PRESIDENT, THE TRADE AGREEMENT BETWEEN THE
United States and the People's Republic of China has come
before the Senate at a crucial moment in history. For the first
time in thirty-five years, the Soviet leaders have used their
military forces to invade a country outside the empire they
inherited at the end of World War II. Clearly, the Soviets are
on the move. They may continue beyond Afghanistan, driving
toward control of the Persian Gulf oil and a warm-water port.

The administration's expectation that an accommodation
with the Soviets could be achieved primarily through a policy
of reciprocal cooperation has been destroyed by Soviet aggression. National policy can no longer be based on the illusion
that the Soviets will forbear from adventurism as a reward
for U.S. cooperation and concessions. There has always been
much more to a livable United States–Soviet relationship than
seeking areas of accommodation. What U.S. leaders have overlooked, played down, and, indeed, ignored is the necessity to
maintain our strength in the overall military balance, to continue to convince the Soviets that we would use our military
strength to restrain their aggression when our vital interests
are threatened, and to work effectively with friends and allies
with whom we share common or parallel interests in safeguarding the future of freedom.

A basic difficulty in getting this trade agreement with China
before the Congress has been the position of top administration officials favoring a policy of "evenhanded treatment"
of Russia and China. According to this notion, if we give the
benefits of MFN and credits to China, we must also give them
to the Soviet Union. If China is in conformity with our law and
the Soviets not in conformity, then, it is argued, efforts must
be made to interpret the law to accommodate the country that
has chosen not to conform. In the present case, the country
that has chosen not to conform is the Soviet Union and the law
in question is section 402 of the Trade Act of 1974.

Mr. President, if it was not perfectly clear before, it must
be abundantly clear now—after the invasion of Afghanistan—
that China and the Soviet Union are two very different coun-

tries. They have different interests and ambitions, different associates and allies, and different attitudes and intentions toward this country. They should be treated on separate tracks, and in our own national interest, they cannot be treated alike. I wish I was convinced that administration officers—notably in the State and Commerce Departments—have finally seen the error of their ways in promoting the misguided policy of evenhandedness.

In fact, the United States shares with China a common interest in key strategic areas. The People's Republic is playing a central role in the geopolitical balance of power in the world, including the struggle to deter Soviet aggression and expansionism in critical areas of tension. For example, in Southwest Asia and the Persian Gulf region, China has long understood the threat of Soviet involvement, particularly Russian pressure on Afghanistan, Iran, and Pakistan. China has been the most faithful champion of beleaguered Pakistan. In Southeast Asia, China is resisting Vietnam's effort—undertaken with Soviet blessing and large-scale material support—to dominate Cambodia, Thailand, and other parts of Southeast Asia. In the Far East, Chinese leaders have developed a constructive and helpful relationship with Japan.

Beyond this, the Chinese recognize that their security is affected by what happens in Europe, and they are outspoken advocates of a strong North Atlantic Treaty Organization. They are proponents of an independent Yugoslavia, recognizing that, in this delicate period of transition, it could become a target for another application of the Brezhnev doctrine.

Just four days ago, Chinese leaders indefinitely suspended their normalization talks with Moscow on the ground they are now inappropriate given the Soviet invasion of Afghanistan, which, in their words, "threatens world peace and China's security, creating new obstacles for normalizing relations between the two countries."

The truth is the United States has a significant stake in the continued existence of a strong, independent China. U.S. efforts to aid China in its drive to become a modern industrial state and to work with her where our strategic and bilateral concerns run parallel are in American as well as Chinese interests.

I strongly support the United States–China Trade Agreement now before the Senate. It lays the foundation for the expansion of trade and financial ties between our two countries, with major mutual benefits. China's pursuit of a long-term modernization program calls for ongoing high levels of imported capital goods and technology, and China's leaders are counting on placing substantial orders with firms in this country.

As my colleagues know, section 402 of the Trade Act of 1974, the Jackson-Vanik amendment, prohibits the extension of most-favored-nation treatment and official credits, credit guarantees, or investment guarantees to any non-market-economy country which restricts the right of its citizens to emigrate freely. The President, however, may waive these prohibitions with respect to a particular country, if he reports to the Congress that first, he has determined that such waiver will substantially promote the objective of free emigration, and second, he has received assurances that the emigration practices of that country will henceforth lead substantially to the achievement of the objective of free emigration.

The President has determined that these two requirements have been met by the People's Republic of China, and he has issued an Executive order waiving the application of section 402 (a) and (b). I am pleased to see that the President has based his case for MFN to China both on assurances regarding future emigration practices provided by Chinese leaders in official exchanges and on assurances publicly stated by senior Chinese leaders.

Administration spokesmen have told us that during his visit to this country last January, Vice Premier Deng Xiaoping, in personal talks with top U.S. officials, gave assurances on China's future emigration practices. The administration has also informed us that before the trade agreement was signed last year on July 7, top U.S. Embassy officers discussed Chinese emigration policy and practice with the Ministry of Foreign

Affairs in Beijing in light of the legal requirements of the Jackson-Vanik amendment. The Chinese were fully apprised of these requirements, including the requirement that assurances regarding future emigration practices be given, and at that time senior Chinese officials provided the assurances the law requires. There is a written record of these official exchanges, on the basis of which administration officials have informed the Senate Finance Committee regarding the substance of these assurances.

On several occasions, Chinese leaders have publicly given assurances regarding their government's future policies on emigration. For example, in a Washington, D.C., speech before the National Association of Chinese Americans & Overseas Chinese in the United States on January 30 last year, Vice Premier Deng Xiaoping said:

> Many of you may have relatives living on the mainland of China and wish that they may come over for a family reunion, and others may wish to go back to China to visit their relatives. This is quite natural and understandable. The Chinese Government will treat these legitimate wishes favorably and with sympathy and will adopt effective measures to satisfy these wishes. You may rest assured on this score.

For another example: On the occasion of the formal establishment of the Embassy of the PRC in the United States in March of last year, Ambassador Chai Zemin gave the following public pledge:

> Among the Americans and overseas Chinese residing in the United States who have relatives living in China, some may wish to have their relatives come to the U.S. for family reunion and some may wish to visit relatives in China. This is quite natural and understandable, and is in accord with the interest and desire of the two peoples and is also beneficial to the enhancement of mutual understanding and friendship. Now that relations between our two countries have been normalized, the movement of people between the two sides will certainly increase significantly. I avail myself of this opportunity to solemnly declare: Our Government will adopt positive and effective measures to satisfy the reasonable wishes of people who wish to visit their relatives or reunite with them.

Of all the individual liberties contained in the UN Declaration of Human Rights, we in Congress have particularly emphasized the right to emigrate. It is the touchstone of all human rights. As cosponsor of the Jackson-Vanik amendment, I—and its host of supporters—can take satisfaction as our amendment encourages greater respect for freer emigration.

Mr. President, I urge the Senate to move expeditiously to pass Senate Concurrent Resolution 47, the resolution to approve this promising agreement on trade with the People's Republic of China.

Again, I commend my distinguished colleague Senator Ribicoff, who has worked long and arduously on this matter, ably assisted in all this, in a truly bipartisan effort, by the Senator from Delaware [Mr. Roth].

29
The United States, China, and the 1980s

School of International Studies, University of Washington,
Seattle, Washington
9 February 1980

In the final decade of Senator Jackson's public service, China had
become a central factor in his view of the world—its power and potential making its orientation crucial to world stability. He had also been
increasingly persuaded that the wise management of the U.S.-Sino-
Soviet relationship was the key to the future of world peace and personal freedom. And for him, the chances that American policymakers
would skillfully manage U.S. interests in this Washington-Moscow-
Beijing triangle depended on their understanding the history of Russia and China and of Sino-Soviet relations, as well as being informed
on current leaders and policies.

The Senator had long been a strong advocate for the School of
International Studies at the University of Washington, with its special
focus on research and teaching in Asian and Soviet bloc affairs. During the last years of his life he redoubled his efforts on the school's behalf. He delighted in visits to the campus and the chances to speak to
students and faculty. This is the school that now appropriately bears
his name—the Henry M. Jackson School of International Studies.

In an address at the school in February 1980 the Senator
talked about the Sino-U.S. relationship, highlighting questions about
our policy on China that he believed needed the urgent attention of
both scholars and policymakers.

I HAVE ALWAYS BEEN PROUD OF THE UNIVERSITY OF WASH-
ington's achievements in Asian and Slavic studies. Washington
was a pioneer in this field starting with the founding of a Department of Oriental Subjects under Herbert Gowen at the
turn of the century, and continuing to build an international
reputation during the quarter-century after World War II
under the leadership of George Taylor.

The achievements of this university are widely appreciated.
Last summer, when we visited the University of Inner Mon-

golia, the Rector expressed delight at the work that had been done at the University of Washington in Chinese and Mongolian studies. I understand that the new Chinese language program at Beijing University, to be opened this summer for American students, will be directed by Professor Brandauer. I also understand that in the recent competitions for federal support of Asian and Russian studies this university ranked among the top four or five in the country.

To maintain and build excellence in these fields requires a partnership of state, federal, and private support. As many of you know, I have taken a personal interest in the development campaign undertaken by the School of International Studies. We are particularly pleased that Eddie Carlson and Harold Shefelman are chairing this effort, ably supported by T. Wilson. Private giving, like the Chester Fritz one-million-dollar endowment for Chinese studies, can provide the extra margin required to sustain a record of distinction. I am delighted that corporations, foundations, and individuals are joining in support of this campaign. Our friends here from Harvard and Michigan have comparable drives under way. In particular now, we want the new Center for the Study of Sino-Soviet relations to get a vigorous and productive start.

We meet today at a supremely critical moment in history. The expectation that has animated American policy toward the Soviet Union over the last decade—that an accommodation with the Soviets could be achieved primarily through a series of cooperative agreements—has been swept away by Soviet aggression. National policy can no longer be based on the illusion that the Soviets will forbear from adventurism as a reward for U.S. cooperation and one-sided concessions.

The hard fact is that while we were cooperating, the Soviets were competing; while we were negotiating, the Soviets were doubling their strategic forces and expanding their conventional capability. Moreover, Moscow has not become more accommodating as it has become stronger. On the contrary, it has become bolder, more aggressive, and more determined to satisfy its imperial ambitions.

The invasion of Afghanistan has jolted our nation into asking itself some fundamental questions about what went wrong and where we go from here. It is high time. The longer we wait to arrest and reverse the decline of the 1970s, the more our situation will deteriorate, and the more convulsive will have to be the effort to remedy it.

Even before the Afghan crisis, it was clear that our China policy was entering a new stage. Full normalization of relations is a reality. We have seen the admission of the People's Republic to the United Nations, President Nixon's visit to China and the Shanghai Communiqué, the establishment of Liaison Offices, the lifting of the ban on direct trade with China, cultural and scholarly exchanges, visits by government leaders, the normalization of relations and the exchange of ambassadors, and the coming into force of the U.S.-China Trade Agreement providing for the extension of most-favored-nation treatment and access to official credits.

The Sino-American relationship has come a long way. Today our relations are fully advanced, inclusive, and complex. On the one hand, China is a developing nation which looks to us as a source of strength in order to counterbalance the strength of the Soviets—now their principal adversary. They want from us technology, capital, and expertise to accelerate their modernization. We, on the other hand, are a developed country which looks on China as a counterweight to the Soviet Union, a potentially significant source of stability in Asia, and a likely and alluring market.

No wonder there are difficult choices of policy to be considered in our relations with China. The relatively "easy-to-do" things have been done. Where do we go from here?

We are at a kind of watershed in China policy. Decision makers have run out of the road maps that guided them intellectually over the last decade. It turns out that policymakers in both the executive branch and Congress have more questions than answers. Tonight I want to pose some of these questions. They need ongoing, urgent attention by policymakers and scholars. I thought it would be useful on this occasion to highlight the pressing issues.

First of all, what kind of security relation do we really wish to have with the People's Republic? Do we envision China's strength as supplementary to, or as a substitute for, United States power in the Pacific? What are the implications of the Soviet buildup for U.S. defense posture in the Western Pacific?

These concerns are hard upon us in light of the diversion of United States forces from the Pacific to the Middle East and Indian Ocean area. For the first time in history, there was a period a month ago when the only aircraft carrier in the Western Pacific was Russian. I, for one, do not believe this situation was lost on either our friends or allies in the Pacific.

We need to recognize the benefits our strengths bring to the stability of nations in the Western Pacific. Our presence has been a major factor in the rapprochement of China and Japan. It is important to the stability of South Korea, to the security of all the Pacific islands down through the Philippines, and to the resolve of ASEAN nations [Association of South East Asian Nations] in resisting Soviet pressures.

China has a vital role in the security of the Pacific area. But China's strengths and weaknesses should be clearly understood. We need to explore just what kind of a military relationship makes sense for China and the United States. Whatever the relationship, I believe we must maintain a credible American defense position in the Pacific.

A second group of questions relates to the great power triangle. How do we deal with China in that context? How do we treat the Sino-Soviet dispute with its ramifications on China's northern and southern border? What role can China be expected to play in the Pakistan-India area and in Thailand? How do we handle a closer and improving relationship with China without unnecessarily feeding Soviet anxiety about China? What should be our arms sales policy to China?

As a starter, I suggest we acknowledge once and for all that China and the Soviet Union are fundamentally different countries, with different ambitions and different allies and different intentions toward us. Our interests with respect to each of them differ, and the way we deal with each of them will be distinctive. I stress this point because the administration's handling of the Sino-American Trade Agreement was bedeviled from the start by the declared Presidential policy of evenhanded treatment of Russia and China. Clearly, we should not allow our relations with China to be held hostage to our relations with Moscow. Obviously, also, we should take into account the consequences of our policies with one upon our relations with the other.

As I see it, it is in the American interest that there be an adequate balance of forces between the Soviet Union and China so the disparity does not constitute a temptation to hostile action. Yet over the last decade, the Soviet Union has dramatically increased its strategic and conventional forces arrayed against China, as well as against Western Europe.

I do not think we should at this time become a direct supplier of arms to China. However, I favor providing as much technology as possible to assist China's economic modernization and to strengthen our own balance of payments position. And we should provide some "dual technology" even though it may have a military application, or spinoff, and may contribute to China's military in the long run. Moreover, the United States should not stand in the way of arms sales to China by our European allies.

I object to the notion of the so-called China card. We should not try to use China in some short-term anti-Soviet tactic that cheapens our new relationship. China is already on the front line in North Asia and South Asia. Her leaders are deeply concerned about Soviet expansionism. They are so concerned that they may not choose to be in the vanguard on some issues.

We must treat China with respect. For example, China and the United States share parallel interests in South Asia, in the defense of Thailand, and in the Afghan-Pakistan situation, including the deterrence of India. There are concerns which we share, and there are opportunities to explore jointly, but there are no quick fixes.

A third set of questions relates to our expanding economic relationship with China. How can we advance our mutual interest in the expansion of China's production and export of oil? How do we lodge our new economic relations among ongoing relations with old friends and trading partners in Asia, including Japan, South Korea, Thailand, Malaysia, Taiwan, and Hong Kong?

A key to the success of China's modernization efforts is the pace at which Beijing is able to expand its production and export of oil. Onshore, China will do most of its own exploration, although the way is open to do some work with foreign companies. Offshore, China is relying heavily on American technology for its exploration efforts, and it is in American as well as Chinese interests that these efforts prosper. Although most of this undertaking will be carried out by private companies, I believe the American Government should facilitate these developments where possible. The fact is that future Chinese exports of oil can contribute to easing the worldwide shortage of petroleum. And such exports will help provide China with the foreign exchange it needs to pay for imports of crucial Western technology in other sectors as well.

How do we handle our new ties with China in ways that reinforce our old ties in the area and do not disrupt them? This question goes to the tempo and fashion in which we should allocate U.S. credits and Exim [Export-Import Bank] credits to China and give China access to American markets. One option to consider is whether we could introduce flexibility in quota allocations according to how much a given country purchased from us. Also, we have a trade surplus with China. With Japan and others we have a trade deficit. Should that consideration count in the way we deal with China?

Finally, we face questions involved in developing our bilateral relations with China. Where do we go from here in scientific, cultural, and scholarly exchanges, and in consultations on world problems? What is important to get done, and what is less important? What help should we expect from the Chinese on matters we consider significant?

We already have in place the framework for a full range of cooperative efforts in economics, science, and culture. There are twelve agreed Sino-American protocols or memoranda of understanding that will take many years to translate into reality. We have some good plans on paper. Now we need performance. It is time to establish priorities, focus on the more promising projects, and implement them.

In all this, the essential principle is equality and mutual benefit. The relationship should be genuinely reciprocal, not one-way, and both sides need to recognize that a successful relationship entails mutual obligations.

What should we expect from China in terms of pursuing parallel interests in the maintenance of stability on the Korean peninsula and in countering Vietnam advances in Southeast Asia? More generally, shouldn't we expect China to have a growing role in the search for solutions to critical world problems, including the energy shortage? If China becomes more amenable to arrangements by which international oil companies would finance exploration and development of the oil potential of China's offshore, that development could proceed much more rapidly.

I have found that the Chinese welcome frank and straightforward talk. I believe our relations with China are now mature enough for each side to raise tough issues with the other confident that this will not disrupt the relationship.

The Chinese no doubt will often be demanding of us. We must be properly demanding of them too.

The Chinese are heartened by signs of a new-found resolve in Washington, D.C., to stand up to the Soviet Union. But in conversations these days the Chinese ask: Is it for real, and how long will it last? Will your government's new determination be applied responsibly? Will American rhetoric exceed the capacity or will to deliver?

These are fair questions which we, for our part, must take seriously.

The Kremlin is already trying to rekindle the unfounded optimism of détente and again lull the West into complacency about Moscow's moves. We must have leadership that recognizes the realities of Moscow's intentions and will not be deluded by its now-familiar maneuvers. We must be led without illusions about the nature of the long-term competition with the Soviet Union.

30
The 1983 Visit
to the People's Republic of China

Press Conference, United States Embassy, Beijing, China
27 August 1983

In the first years of the Reagan administration there was a noticeable deterioration in U.S.-China relations, due largely to the President's expressed intention to upgrade ties with Taiwan and the administration's moves to sell to Taiwan an advanced jet fighter. The Senator pressed his criticisms of these policies directly with Secretaries of State Haig and Shultz, Secretary of Defense Weinberger, and the President. In August 1982 the administration came to an agreement with the People's Republic on arms sales to Taiwan. Then, in the spring of 1983, the decision was made to loosen certain controls over technology transfer to Beijing, a step Jackson had long favored.

The Senator decided it was time to visit China again. He could now play a constructive bipartisan role, reassuring Deng Xiaoping and other leaders that President Reagan's basic China policy enjoyed his confidence. He arranged for a letter from President Reagan to the Chinese leaders emphasizing the importance the President attached to Sino-American relations. Jackson personally delivered the letter in August 1983.

Senator Jackson died five days after returning home from this visit. At a press conference held in the American Embassy in Beijing on 27 August 1983, he had addressed the emerging bilateral Chinese-American policy issues as he saw them at the close of his trip. These were the problems he expected to work on when he returned to Washington and which undoubtedly would have become the basis of an early speech.

As it was, in preparing the report to Congress on the 1983 trip, the staff drew heavily on this press conference and included the text as an annex. The full text was also introduced into the *Congressional Record* by Senator Ted Stevens on 14 September 1983.

I HAVE HAD OVER TWENTY HOURS OF DISCUSSION WITH CHI-nese leaders in Beijing and the Northeast. I have visited several communes, factories, including the large Daqing complex in the Northeast. This is my fourth trip; 1974, 1978, and 1979.

I brought with me on this visit a special letter from President Reagan to Chairman Deng Xiaoping which conveys the importance which the President attaches to Sino-American relations.

Here are my five major impressions from this two-week visit:

My major finding is that both sides must intensify their consultations, both on matters of common strategic concern and at the bilateral level as well. A good deal of misunderstanding exists on both sides at present and both sides could pay more attention to the rhetoric about each other. The opportunity is now present to expand our relations. I believe we have weathered a very difficult period, but to seize the opportunities before us requires much more frequent discussions on such issues as arms reductions, the strategic triangle, NATO, the Middle East, Africa, and Southeast Asia and Taiwan.

A second observation: The underlying factors which brought our two countries together remain in place. We have an interest in a strong, secure, independent China which contributes to the peace of the Asia-Pacific region. China now plays an important role in maintaining a global balance of power. China retains an interest in expanding Sino-American relations as a counterbalance against the Soviet Union and as a source of technology.

A third observation: The Taiwan issue continues to complicate our relations with China. The leaders of the People's Republic attach great importance to the reunification of China, and their feelings on this issue, in my judgment, should not be underestimated. It is important that both sides fully implement the August 17 communiqué.*

Fourth comment: I am impressed by the internal changes in China over the past four years. The policies of Chairman

---

*The 17 August 1984 U.S.-China Communiqué on Taiwan provided for the gradual phasing out of U.S. arms sales to Taiwan in response to Beijing's stated fundamental policy of seeking reunification with Taiwan by peaceful means.

Deng and his associates are having a dramatic effect on the economy and I sense an increasing openness to the outside world.

A final observation: Our bilateral relations are at an important stage. President Reagan has made several major decisions to improve relations with China and he is now committed to a one-China policy. The visits of Secretary Weinberger and Foreign Minister Wu, if well planned, can advance our common interests. That concludes my statement. Questions?

QUESTION. In addition to the arms sales to Taiwan issue, what other issues did Minister Deng mention are thorns in our relationship?

SENATOR JACKSON. I believe that the two major immediate issues are indeed Taiwan and the question of the details on technology transfer. As you know, the details are yet to be worked out in depth. However, we have made that strategic decision of moving the People's Republic into a friendly category as contrasted with the previous more restrictive rules and regulations. There are other issues, but those are the two big ones as I see it.

I was especially pleased with the Chairman's view of the world and I think—as it relates to the strategic side—I have not detected any change since I talked with him in 1979 on those fundamental points that relate to the strategic balance.

QUESTION. You said in your statement that President Reagan is now committed to a one-China policy. What specifically made you say that?

SENATOR JACKSON. I was very disturbed when the new administration came to office. I was concerned because the President had made certain statements during the course of the 1980 election. We know, historically speaking, that when Presidents assume authority they have an unusual ability to adjust to reality. I should say that the President has come a long way and I have made this clear to the leaders that in my judgment the President is committed to a one-China policy.

I have talked with Chairman Deng about the letter, which I regret cannot be made public, at least at this time. It expresses a feeling of warmth toward China that the New China News

Agency referred to as being pleasing. But the President and his Secretaries of State and Defense are now in agreement, I believe, on Taiwan.

Speaking personally, I want to expedite the ending of the arms sales [to Taiwan] so that we can at some point indicate when that will come, both from a quantitative and a qualitative standpoint. I want to emphasize that in my view the August 17 communiqué is a long step forward that corroborates what I have just said in terms of a change of policy toward China.

QUESTION. In your discussion about the strategic view did the question of the Sino-Soviet talks or the forthcoming visit here by a Soviet Deputy Foreign Minister come up? How was it handled?

SENATOR JACKSON. I did not, or we did not, get into any specific situations. But let me state in general terms what I see the current situation to be. For some time now the United States and the People's Republic have had certain interests that are parallel. Those interests include a strong and independent China. They include a strong NATO. They, the government, support those two fundamental concepts. The Chinese contribution is enormous because the Soviets have a very large force along their border with China. This ties up a large force that would otherwise be deployed elsewhere in the world. On the strategic side, I see a cooperative American and Chinese adherence to the concept that is as old as time, and that's the doctrine of the balance of power. I see no change in those fundamentals.

Now, you may have problems where we disagree—Middle East, Africa, to name some. And I want to emphasize, too, that I expect that there will be an ongoing expression of differences from time to time. But I want those differences to address collateral issues and not strategic issues in which the peace of the world rests in the balance.

QUESTION. Senator, the members of the House Armed Services Committee were here last week, you're here this week, are these visits in any way related to Weinberger's trip here? Do you anticipate that when he comes here there will be discussions initiated by either side about U.S. arms sales to China, either arms or military technology? Thirdly, what would be the congressional reaction to such sales?

SENATOR JACKSON. May I say that my visit is not related in any manner, shape, or form to the Secretary of Defense visit.

I do believe that Secretary Weinberger's visit is an important one, and I believe a number of useful things can be addressed, especially some of the problems in more detail as pertaining to technology transfer, because technology transfer as you know is a many-sided issue in which both military application and commercial application can be involved with a given transfer. But I do believe that his visit is important and I think there are opportunities for both countries to exchange ideas. But I wouldn't want to go beyond that because the Secretary will be here the latter part of September.

QUESTION. What will be the congressional reaction to a Reagan administration initiative to start pumping a large-scale military-related technology into China?

SENATOR JACKSON. I don't see that happening. I think it's a "supposititious" case, an iffy case.

QUESTION. Did the question of trade come up? Sino-U.S. trade has dropped sharply in the last four or five months. Did Deng say anything about China buying more or wanting to export more to the United States?

SENATOR JACKSON. We do have an issue on the trade side dealing with wheat and corn. Namely, China is committed to purchase this year 6 million tons and thus far they have only purchased 2.6 million tons of wheat and corn. I am certain, or at least hopeful, that they will adhere to that agreement, and I am hopeful that they will move expeditiously to honor that agreement. Failure to do so could cause new tensions and new problems with the United States.

We are delighted, of course, and we saw evidence, that they are having bumper crops. But that means they will have more cash to buy other things—while I don't want to get parochial about my own state—maybe airplanes! And they have a very nice balance of payment situation. I think that up until July, China has over 12 billion reserve in foreign currencies. By the end of the year, this reserve is going to be 18 billion. That reserve is not going to last indefinitely, as they inevitably must increase their purchases abroad. They are going to run deficits if they are really investing in new capital, new plants, new equipment.

QUESTION. Did you get the impression that the Chinese believe that Reagan is pursuing a one-China policy or do they still have their doubts?

SENATOR JACKSON. I can't answer that question adequately. I believe the people that I talked to place substantial credence in that commitment. I pointed out that I am of the opposite political party to Mr. Reagan. I didn't campaign for him; my candidate lost; but I made the point that a bipartisan American foreign policy is absolutely vital to an American President. I believe that President Reagan is committed to that doctrine.

I have been in Congress long enough to know that an American President cannot be effective in this troubled world unless he can elicit the support across the political aisle. That has been my position since the days of Roosevelt, Truman, and on down, every American President from both political parties since the 1940s. I have made and emphasized that point with the Chinese leaders and they seemed to respond in a pleased fashion.

QUESTION. Senator, were you asked specifically what the present congressional sentiment was toward the Taiwan Relations Act?

SENATOR JACKSON. Well, the source of the Taiwan Relations Act is a fact that the nationalists were allies of the United States for a very long period of time, and there continues to this day a residual feeling of support for Taiwan. Americans can be contradictory, you know. On the other hand they say obviously there can only be one China and that policy was established in the Shanghai Communiqué of 1972, when Mr. Nixon was President. I think there are torn feelings about a commitment that we made a long time ago when the problem was, in the minds of many, a bit more simple.

My own personal judgment is that the Congress is moving realistically toward a one-China policy and that means that the two, Taiwan and China, can be reunified peaceably. The strong feelings of the Chennault era, the old China lobby, I see declining very rapidly. But the sentiment toward Taiwan is part of our, I guess, Puritan ethic and that is that we made a commitment. Yet we are the only nation to my knowledge that has any kind of an ambiguous relationship—not in a juridical sense—set up in a way in which no one knows what it means. Sometimes you try and do it that way.

I think the critical thing is that Taiwan is going to exacerbate our relations until we can reach the point where there will be indeed a final resolution on the sale of arms to the Taiwanese, qualitatively and quantitatively. That process is now under way and the August 17 communiqué, of which the administration is a part, makes it very clear that there has to be an ending. As I say, we are going to have to expedite that ending, and Chairman Deng's interview with Professor Yang is rather revealing, and it is certainly an indication how far the People's Republic has been willing to go to reach an accord.

I believe it can be done. China is not interested in beating Taiwan and it is already beginning to become a Hong Kong anyway in terms of trade with the mainland. To China this is an indication of how the market system is working.

QUESTION. Did any question of Hong Kong come up?

SENATOR JACKSON. No.

QUESTION. In terms of reunification?

SENATOR JACKSON. No, it did not.

QUESTION. What are the prospects for Premier Zhao going to the United States and the President coming to China?

SENATOR JACKSON. Well, I think it's very important that the Premier come to the United States after, of course, the visit of the Foreign Minister, which is scheduled in October. It is my personal judgment, and I underline personal judgment, that things are improving for that visit and some time after the first of the year, hopefully, the Premier will be reciprocated by the President of the United States. It is important for our relations with one another, but I detected no hostility on that visit, and on the other hand I detected an openness and a sense of warmth about what might happen from such a visit.

QUESTION. Do you think then that Premier Zhao will be going this calendar year?

SENATOR JACKSON. I would hope so. I think it would not be the wisest thing for the President to come over here right in the middle of an election. That's my personal opinion, because then the charge will be that he's over here in order to aid his own reelection efforts, and I feel the wise course would be for the Premier to be able to visit the United States sometime in November or December. I would like to see that personally and right now I think things are moving, no decision made, but the movement is favorable.

QUESTION. Would that help the President's reelection?

SENATOR JACKSON. Well, my recollection of Presidential history, which is not necessarily ancient [laughter], is that you never lose votes—you have a chance of gaining votes—when you are dealing on issues that especially affect the peace of the world.

The President, I would assume, and I can't speak for him obviously, would like to come to China as we enter into arms control agreement with the Soviets. I think the chances of an arms agreement have improved but we have a long way to go. Several weeks ago, I emphasized that I would insist that any SS-20s taken out of Western Europe not be placed adjacent to China because that would put China in a difficult spot. I was pleased that there is some movement in that direction as suggested in Mr. Andropov's statement.

QUESTION. Did you discuss this with Mr. Deng?

SENATOR JACKSON. I would rather not get into that area. I am not sure that the Chinese view Mr. Andropov's statement in a totally favorable light. They are interested in it but there could be some catches in it.

QUESTION. I certainly share your view about SS-20s being moved to Eastern Europe. That must have come up.

SENATOR JACKSON. They were very pleased with the position that I had taken before Andropov's statement. We do have interests that are parallel and an attempt to simply move the threat out of Europe and into Asia pointed at China would

violate that fundamental concept of parallelism. I believe that
this administration would not be a party to that. I can only
convey to you my own views and I personally will take a very
strong position on it. That would upset the balance that we
have so carefully crafted here between China and the United
States that goes to the peace of the world.

QUESTION. Did you get a feeling from Mr. Deng or anyone
else that you talked to or did they say outright that they are
suspicious about whether or not for political reasons Reagan
might be anxious to reach an arms control agreement?

SENATOR JACKSON. No. No comment on that at all by any of
them. They may have their views but we didn't discuss it.

QUESTION. Did they discuss the U.S. pressure on Japan to
increase its military spending?

SENATOR JACKSON. No. But over the years a strong and independent Japan has been part of that balance and I assume
that that continues to be the policy because there has been no
change in the fundamental elements of the strategic balance
as viewed by the Chinese. Japan is a very important part of
the balance in the Far East.

QUESTION. You think the Chinese feel that?

SENATOR JACKSON. Yes, I think they do. Now you get into the
degree of strengthening Japan, but I think they realize that
they are exposed in the Northeast, and one of the conscious
views that I came away with from the Northeast is that here
is an area that is the industrial heartbeat of China. It is hard
to believe that they produce 80 percent of all the lumber that
is produced, over half of the oil that is produced. They produce a huge amount of light metals, aluminum, and so on—a
long list of industrial products that are vital to the security of
the area. They are conscious of the history of that area, that
Vladivostok until 1856 was indeed a part of China and that
whole area was a part of China.

I have noted a special concern, not overtly, but when you
ask probing questions. The Northeast is an area that is rich
in industrial goods and raw material that is important for the
long haul.

If you don't mind I have really just about come to the end. My voice is going but I don't want to cut anyone off.

QUESTION. The Chinese have said that the latest arms sales to Taiwan violated the August communiqué. Did they bring up that point with you? And what do you sense is the mood in Congress? Do you think they will agree to decrease arms substantially in the next few years?

SENATOR JACKSON. It's not my impression they have said, at least to me, that it violates the August 17 communiqué. The Chinese want to see this thing, the supplying of arms to Taiwan, quantitatively and qualitatively, coming to an end, and they are wondering whether that communiqué is going to be implemented fully. But they support the communiqué; and that Taiwan issue, I want to emphasize, is a pervasive issue as far as Chinese officialdom is concerned.

QUESTION. You mentioned about some hitches being involved in the Andropov statement.

SENATOR JACKSON. I don't want to go into the specifics on it. But I detect that the Chinese have reservations about the meaning of it. It is not one of those cure-alls for their problems with the Soviet Union by any means. I think it would be wrong to assume that this statement or the forthcoming visit by the Soviet Vice Foreign Minister are some new dramatic moves on the part of the Soviets that would change relations between the Soviet Union and China. That would be a mistaken interpretation, in my personal judgment.

QUESTION. How long did your meeting last and can you tell us anything about the Chairman's health?

SENATOR JACKSON. Our visit lasted about two hours and ten minutes. He has a marvelous sense of humor. I was kidding him about his smoking. He is seventy-nine and I explained to him that I quit smoking when I was twelve and he thinks smoking is all right, if it's in the hands of the right person. My friend Senator Jesse Helms ought to try to get a testimonial!

But the Chairman, from everything I can see, appears to be in good health. I'm seventy-one and I hope I'm in that good shape at seventy-nine. That is the only way I can answer that. I mean he is sharp and can maintain a sense of humor. I think that means longevity of service to his native country.

QUESTION. Did he suggest in any way that he would like to give up his reigning position and fully retire soon?

SENATOR JACKSON. I must say I detected no evidence of any desire to retire. That has been bantered around a lot. I invited him to stay at my house in Everett, Washington, when he comes over and he is taking that under advisement. Thank you very much.

IX
Central America

31
Labor and U.S. Central American Policy

Hofstra University School of Law, New York, New York
29 April 1983

Over the years, Senator Jackson joined in many critical debates and votes on Central American issues, including support for ratification of the Panama Canal treaties. His major foreign affairs initiatives, however, had been directed to other areas of the world.

In August 1982, as ranking member of the Senate Energy Committee, the Senator was a main participant in fashioning the international financial emergency package for Mexico, which helped forestall international financial collapse and included prepayment to Mexico for oil to fill the U.S. Strategic Petroleum Reserve. Meanwhile, badly needed legislation to provide economic and security assistance to the Central American area was stalemated in bitter partisan congressional-executive confrontations. In this situation, with continuing Communist-supported insurgencies in the area and the threat of Mexico's economic collapse, Jackson decided to enter the Central American debate and propose a bipartisan commission on Central America. He considered the commission a temporary expedient to help break the rancorous deadlock and reach enough bipartisan agreement to allow the Congress and the President to develop a productive and sustainable U.S. assistance policy.

The Senator chose an American labor movement audience, convened to honor Edward F. Carlough, president of the Sheet Metal Workers International Association, before which to launch his proposal. American labor was firmly defense-minded, yet also deeply concerned at Central America's long history of poverty and social injustice. Jackson believed that American labor, in the tradition of labor leaders like Eddie Carlough, could become the nucleus for achieving a new consensus on Central American policy.

LABOR LEADERS IN GENERAL HAVE AVOIDED ONE-EYED APproaches to international problems. They know that the world is a dangerous and cruel place, and they have championed an adequate defense for the United States and its friends and allies. But labor leaders have also understood the major role economic assistance and the hope of economic opportunity have to play in United States policy towards the developing world. It is not hard to see why.

Individuals like Edward F. Carlough, known for their reliability and effectiveness, were successful because they could look at the world through two lenses. Committed to the welfare of their membership and possessing a deep concern for social justice, they never forgot to take a sober and objective appraisal of the realities confronting them. They had judgment; they knew when to hold the line and when to compromise. They also had hope for the future. They held a deep belief that the world could become a better place, and this hope gave them strength to always be out in front.

The United States government has a lot to learn from such labor leaders about the conduct of foreign policy. In particular, it has a lot to learn about policy approaches toward the current crises in Central America. Today, Central America poses for the United States one of her greatest foreign policy challenges. Again, American labor has been out in front, way out in front.

In El Salvador the American labor movement has been one of the few beacons of light in what has seemed an interminable darkness. Here is a country that has for centuries suffered under tyrannical governments and a small oligarchic class of landowners. It has almost no history of democratic institutions. Even agricultural cooperatives, which can teach people the rudiments of participatory democracy, are scarce. Until the recent effort at land reform, El Salvador was a semifeudal state.

Into this almost intractable situation, where all the policy options seem impalatable, the AFL-CIO, through its American Institute for Free Labor Development, went forward and labored hard to bring about reform. Two of their members, Mike Hammer and Mark Pearlman, were murdered for their efforts. And yet, despite the setbacks, democracy building through the development of free labor unions led to a remarkable accomplishment in early March of this year. Ten thousand campesinos demonstrated peacefully outside the National Assembly demanding an extension of the land reform program. Obviously, El Salvador still faces very serious problems. There needs to be dramatic improvement in the judicial system and concrete progress in the resolution of the Hammer/Pearlman murders and the murders of the four American religious workers. There needs to be progress in unifying the central command over the armed forces and in the titling process of the land reform program. There needs to be a nourishing and extension of democratic political institutions. But the general approach to addressing El Salvador's long-term problems has been charted by the AFL-CIO.

This kind of understanding and perspective needs to inform our policy, not just for El Salvador but for the entire Central American region. And the theme of my remarks today is just this: a sound policy for the Central American isthmus must be based on what the AFL-CIO has known all along—military approaches alone are inadequate.

Clearly, some security assistance is required. The Sandinista government in Nicaragua has evolved into what is plainly a Marxist-Leninist regime. It is suppressing individual liberties and free labor unions; it has imposed press censorship; and it is fomenting revolution in neighboring countries. Nicaragua harbors two thousand Cuban military advisors and has been deaf to all entreaties by her Central American neighbors, as well as by the United States, to negotiate a regional peace settlement.

However, security assistance ought not to be the main focus of national debate, and it ought not to be the foreign policy instrument we emphasize to the rest of the world.

Our security aid to Central America should be given and discussed in one way: it is a shield behind which endangered nations can protect themselves from external threats while they go about the business of building democratic institutions, holding free and fair elections, and working to rectify historical patterns of social injustice. Security assistance should be an adjunct to our Central American policy, not its foundation. We better face it: the shield will crumble unless we address the serious social and economic injustices in the region.

Let me suggest some of the premises on which a constructive regional policy should be grounded.

1. The social and economic crises facing Central America are real, and they arise in large part from long histories of poverty and lack of economic opportunity. Mexico's foreign debt now runs to 90 billion dollars; her agricultural sector is in decline, forcing more and more people to the cities; unemployment hovers near 50 percent; and the middle class is becoming increasingly disenchanted.

2. In much of the region, democratic institutions are weak, if they exist at all.

3. Marxist-Leninist regimes will not offer the people of these countries a democratic future or expanded economic opportunity. The course of events in Cuba and the evolution of the Sandinista government in Nicaragua clearly demonstrate that any such hope is unfounded.

4. The Soviet Union has and will continue to exploit this situation, principally through her proxies in Cuba and Nicaragua.

5. The strategic stakes for the United States are high. The shipping lanes of the Caribbean, so vital to our commerce and to the resupply of our troops in Europe, must be kept open. The stability of the countries in the region, particularly Mexico, needs to be assured.

These premises clearly suggest that America's best minds need to address the problem of security and economic development of the Central American isthmus. Central America must be the focus of a large, long-term effort by the United States and should take a top spot on America's foreign policy agenda.

What kind of effort does Central America merit? It merits an effort of Marshall Plan proportions. I do not make this comparison lightly. After World War II, the United States faced in Europe a serious challenge to her security. We had rapidly demobilized our armed forces while the Soviet Union supported

Communist insurgency campaigns in Greece and Turkey and tried to wrestle control of European unions and European Social Democratic parties from their democratic majorities. General Marshall understood, as did American trade union leadership, that the long-term security of Western Europe, as well as the long-term security of the United States, could be assured only by a program of massive economic assistance. Devastated by the war, Europe needed the aid to bring democracy back on its feet.

The circumstances in Central America, while certainly not identical, have important similarities. The region, like Europe, is vital to our security. Like postwar Europe, Central America is being threatened by Communist insurgency, and its stability can only be assured if the people there have hope for the future and see economic opportunities expanding for them. These are the necessary conditions if the region is to move toward more democratic governments.

Gaining consensus within this country for such a course of action will not be easy. The American people, conditioned by the United States' traditional neglect of Latin America, do not see our interests and security at stake in the region. Similar problems faced those who wanted to embark on a program of European reconstruction after the war. George Marshall, after delivering his speech at Harvard University outlining his program for European recovery, made sure a committee was formed to garner the support of the American people. The Marshall committee, headed by Henry Stimson and drawn from the leadership of all sectors of American society, including trade unions, was more responsible than any other factor for forging consensus in the country to get the Marshall Plan for European recovery through Congress.

Serious consideration should now be given to convening a national bipartisan commission for Central America. Composed of respected leaders of government, business, labor, education, and the Hispanic and religious communities in this country, the commission's charge would be to chart a long-term course of hope for the peoples of Central America. It would function as the instrument to help the American people reach a workable consensus on a long-term, comprehensive policy for this region.

In his remarks to the Joint Session of Congress this week, President Reagan came a long way in recognizing the dimensions of the challenge in Central America. He gave due emphasis to the necessity of addressing the social and economic injustices and the human rights conditions in order to achieve long-term stability and security in the region.

I believe it would be wise for the President to bring in organized labor to play a key role in the formulation and execution of our Central American foreign policy. Labor has led the way. It was there during the struggle for Europe after World War II. It is working now in Central America. Labor's special contribution to American foreign policy has been its compassionate heart combined with its cool head. Its voice needs to be heard now.

32
Toward a Long-Term Policy
for Central America

United States Senate
12 May 1983

As Senator Jackson pressed his idea for a bipartisan commission on Central America, he emphasized one central theme: Military approaches alone to the region are inadequate; unless the serious social and economic dislocations and injustices in the area are also addressed, there is no hope for the long-term stability and security of America's southern frontier.

Jackson was in regular touch with the Reagan White House in his effort to launch the commission. But he decided not to wait for a decision there. The liberal Republican Senator Charles Mathias, Jr., was secured as a principal cosponsor of a Senate resolution calling for the commission. The Jackson-Mathias resolution was then introduced in the House by Democrat Mike Barnes and Republican Jack Kemp, two members on opposite sides of the political spectrum. The strategy succeeded. Before the resolutions had emerged from the legislative process, President Reagan picked up the proposal and appointed a representative commission, along the lines of the Jackson-Mathias resolution. Henry Kissinger was appointed chairman and the four legislative sponsors of the resolution were named counselors.

Just at the start of the commission's work, the Senator died. Its final report was dedicated to him:

> In his life and work Senator Jackson was devoted to the twin goals of national security and human betterment. These are also the goals that have guided this report, and we hope, in this spirit, that it will contribute to their advancement.[19]

MR. PRESIDENT, AS CONGRESS AND THE REST OF THE COUN-try wrestle over U.S. policy in Central America, at least one issue has been settled: The region is of immense strategic importance to the United States. Whatever policy options might be available to us, ignoring threats to the stability of Central

America and refusing to engage ourselves in the problems of the region are not among them.

The commonly cited figures bear a quick mention.

Almost half of our shipping tonnage and imported oil passes through the Caribbean shipping lanes. Sixty-five percent of our supply requirements during a general European military mobilization would be shipped from gulf ports through the Florida Straits.

Controlled immigration through our southern frontier can only become possible with stability in Central America. When one of eight persons born in the Caribbean and alive today resides on the mainland United States, our Southern and South-western States are rightly concerned about preventing a flood of the impoverished and the discontented into this country.

A sequence of crises leading to Castro-type regimes throughout Central America, including Mexico, would have disastrous strategic ramifications, which we all recognize. None of us relishes the prospect of living in a garrison state, unable to meet our commitments to our NATO allies and others, nor do we like to contemplate the threat such a course of events poses to the fundamental nature of American society and her democratic institutions.

Even with the high stakes involved, it is not unexpected that some American citizens and some American politicians harbor wistful thoughts that somehow the United States might not have to engage itself in Central America. The problems in the region are enormous; the policies to address them involve difficult choices; and most important, the problems are not going to go away. There are no quick fixes. Piecemeal proposals and frantic, ad hoc programs are inadequate. The United States faces a profound, long-term challenge in Central America and must devise a set of long-term policies to match it.

The nations of Central America share many differences: different histories, different geographies, different ethnic compositions, different patterns of landholding, and different degrees of democratization. But if we look at the entire Central American isthmus, two facts present themselves. The economic and social crises confronting all of the nations are real, and Mexico, with 79 percent of the total landmass and 76 percent of the population, is a key to maintaining stability in the region.

In good times life was hard, but after almost three years of recession, all Central American nations are hurting and hurting bad. Commodity prices are still too low, interest rates still too high, and servicing foreign debts casts a long shadow over hopes for economic recovery, much less hopes for economic development.

In Mexico, Mr. President, the economic crisis is particularly acute. At the end of 1977, things looked bright: The growth rate was 8 percent, new oil was coming into production and being sold at high prices, employment prospects were improving, and foreign loans fueled a vigorous program of industrial development. But that was five years ago, before the addition of another 12 million mouths to feed, before a persistent worldwide recession, and before the collapse of oil prices.

Now Mexico faces almost $90 billion in combined private and public foreign debt and is attempting to implement an IMF economic adjustment program. Her unemployment hovers near 50 percent, and the agricultural sector is in decline, forcing more and more rural people into the cities, where the middle class is becoming increasingly disenchanted.

The economic problems are not just cyclical but structural. Many of the large industrial projects which were to be financed by the oil money turned sour, unable to be completed because of chronic mismanagement and corruption. And in spite of Mexico's historical commitment to land reform, fully one-third of the agricultural population remains landless, with tremendous inefficiencies in the land under cultivation. With some 40 percent of the labor force devoted to agriculture, that sector produced only 8.5 percent of the gross domestic product in 1980.

Fortunately, Mexico, along with Costa Rica, enjoys political stability under a regime that is more or less democratic. But the institution responsible for Mexican stability since the revolution—the PRI, the Institutionalized Revolutionary Party—has never confronted such a challenging set of circumstances as it does today or is likely to in the near future.

The other nations of Central America face similar economic problems, but suffer under authoritarian regimes of varying degrees of repressiveness. The economic and social injustices abound. In Guatemala, 3 percent of the population owns 70 percent of the land, and until the recent land reform, the pattern of landholding in El Salvador was the same. Adult literacy in Guatemala is under 50 percent, and a Guatemalan army campaign against a handful of subversives has terrorized the Mayan Indians, forcing over 30,000 of them to cross the border into Mexico.

Given the poverty and the unremitting patterns of social injustice in the region, Marxist revolutionary promises of a better future understandably prove attractive to many of the peoples of Central America. But the promises are false. The history of Cuba and the evolution of the Sandinista regime in Nicaragua, not to mention the horrors which have transpired in Indochina since 1975, demonstrate clearly that Marxist-Leninist regimes will not offer the people of these countries a democratic future or expanded economic opportunities. Quite the opposite. Cuba exports her human problems to the United States and requires $4 billion annually in subsidies from the Soviet Union. And in Nicaragua the standard course of Marxist totalitarian control and repression proceeds apace.

How are we then to approach the security needs of the United States in Central America? One thing should be very clear, Mr. President: Military approaches alone are inadequate to deal with the economic crises and social injustices of the region.

Some security assistance will, obviously, be required in the face of armed Communist insurgencies, but our security aid should be understood in one way: It is a shield behind which endangered nations can protect themselves from external threats as they work to rectify injustices, build democratic institutions, and hold free and fair elections. Our security assistance ought not to be the main focus of national debate, for it ought not to be the foundation of our policy toward Central America. The shield protecting Central Americans from Communist insurgency and domination will crumble unless we address the serious social and economic dislocations and injustices in the region.

A second thing should also be clear: America's best minds need to address the problem of security and economic development of the Central American isthmus.

What sort of effort are we talking about? I can best describe it as one of Marshall Plan proportions. The long-term security of our southern frontier is as vital to U.S. interests as the long-term security of Western Europe, and it deserves the same level of American energy and commitment.

Mr. President, I recommend that serious consideration be given to convening a national bipartisan commission for Central America. Composed of respected leaders of government, business, labor, education, and the Hispanic and religious communities in this country, the commission's charge would be to chart a course of hope for the peoples of Central America.

I believe it is high time for the President to bring in the major sectors of American society, particularly labor, to play key roles in the formulation and implementation of our Central American foreign policy. The proposed commission would function as the instrument to help build the necessary consensus on a long-term, comprehensive policy for this region. The commission could communicate to Americans from all regions and all walks of life that their lives are inextricably linked to events in that region—be it the price of coffee, the future of the American labor force, and ultimately the security of their nation.

The commission would consult with governmental and other leaders of Central America, invite their views and receive their recommendations on the policies which would best assist them in their long-range security needs and economic development. The commission could also serve an important oversight role for the nongovernmental international actors that should be a part of an effective U.S. policy for Central America. Labor unions, political parties, churches, and voluntary organizations can often do more to help build democratic institutions than the public diplomacy gestures of governments.

Mr. President, I am convinced that unless the United States works with Mexico and other Central American nations in addressing their chronic economic and political crises, none of the nations of North and Central America can face the future with calm confidence, secure in the inviolability of their borders and assured of maintaining peace with one another. The commission's task will not be easy, and its recommendations will likely require sacrifice from the American people. But over time its work could prove, as the Marshall Plan has proven, to be one of the wisest investments our Nation ever made.

Afterword

Dorothy Fosdick

> The death of Senator Henry Jackson has left an empty
> stillness at the center of American politics. Jackson was the
> symbol, and the last great leader, of a political tradition
> that began with Woodrow Wilson and reached its apogee
> with John Kennedy, Lyndon Johnson and Hubert Hum-
> phrey. That tradition—liberal internationalism—held that
> if democratic capitalism was to have a human face, it had to
> have a big heart and a strong hand.
> —Charles Krauthammer, *Time*, 19 December 1983.[20]

For Henry Jackson there was no period of retirement at the
close of his life. He died on 1 September 1983 at the height
of his powers and productiveness, still in full harness after
serving in Congress for nearly forty-three years. Unlike many
national figures who at some point are emancipated from the
responsibilities of public office, the Senator was on his watch
until the end. There was no opportunity for him to review his
life from the sidelines; no chance to leave behind his first-hand
reflections on an extraordinary career in public service.

Fortunately, important source materials of history are available to students, historians, and others interested in the Jackson era and the Jackson story. The Magnuson-Jackson Papers
Project at the University of Washington Libraries in Seattle
contains not only most of Jackson's speeches for which texts
or transcriptions exist but also the great part of the corre-
spondence, reports, articles, notes, files, and printed hearing
records relating to committee activities, and also photographs
and audiovisual material—all from Jackson's office and personal files. The Jackson papers cover the years 1936 to 1983.

Most depository libraries and many university and college
collections include the three books edited by the Senator and
published by Frederick A. Praeger: *The National Security Council: Jackson Subcommittee Papers on Policy-making at the Presiden-*

tial Level (1965); *The Secretary of State and the Ambassador: Jackson Subcommittee Papers on the Conduct of American Foreign Policy* (1964); and *The Atlantic Alliance: Jackson Subcommittee Hearings and Findings* (1967). Also available is the Senator's short book *Fact, Fiction, and National Security,* published by McFadden-Bartell Corporation (1964).

For the student and general reader there is *Staying the Course: Henry M. Jackson and National Security* (University of Washington Press, 1987), a group of essays—which I introduced and edited—written by people closely associated with Jackson during his congressional career and reflecting their first-hand experience. Also, the memorial addresses delivered by the Senator's congressional colleagues are published in *Henry M. Jackson: Late a Senator from Washington* (U.S. Government Printing Office, 1983).

Not surprisingly, Henry Jackson has been the recipient of many posthumous awards and acts of special recognition. Notable among them was the Medal of Freedom, the nation's highest civilian commendation, presented posthumously by President Reagan at a White House ceremony on 26 June 1984 with these words:

Henry Jackson was a protector of the nation, a protector of its freedoms and values. There are always a few such people in each generation. Let others push each chic new belief or become distracted by the latest fashionable reading of history. The protectors listen and nod and go about seeing to it that the ideals that shaped this nation are allowed to survive and flourish. They defend the permanent against the merely prevalent.[21]

Also of special significance was the decision by the Board of Regents of the University of Washington to name its School of International Studies in Jackson's honor: the Henry M. Jackson School of International Studies. The objectives of the Jackson School are different from those of the schools of government named for Kennedy, Johnson, and Humphrey, which teach skills of public administration and policy formulation. The Jackson School is also distinct from schools of international affairs at Princeton, Tufts, and Johns Hopkins, which traditionally stress the teaching of diplomatic methods and international law. The Jackson School has more than a seventy-five-year record of studying the history, politics, economics, and languages of the world, with an emphasis on Asia, the Soviet bloc, and the Middle East. Senator Jackson believed this historical in-depth area study and advanced scholarship were critical for the training of future leaders and for the conduct of a wise foreign policy. He was proud of the school's achievements. He constantly reminded friends that many of its programs already ranked first and second in the country. Why should it not become the very best? It is clear that he had a deep personal commitment to the school's future.

Another important tribute to the Senator was the establishment in October 1983 of the Henry M. Jackson Foundation by Helen Jackson and longtime friends and colleagues. Its purpose is to commemorate Senator Jackson's national service by encouraging his standards of excellence in government and by pursuing a number of his long-range educational concerns, ranging from national security and foreign affairs to protection of the environment and preservation of the world's natural resources. Understandably, the foundation is giving priority to support for key programs at the Jackson School, particularly those for Soviet and Chinese studies. At the same time, it is moving to assist other educational and public service programs that show promise of contributing to better performance in the public policy arena. Today, in its seventh year, the foundation is emerging as a resource of national significance.

The great philosopher Alfred North Whitehead once said it is the business of the future to be dangerous. Henry Jackson understood this. But this prospect did not dishearten him. He had a great hope for America and a great faith in the young people who would be moving into positions of public responsibility.

Speaking to them, as he so often did, he liked to quote Teddy Roosevelt: "We see, across the dangers, the great future . . . and we rejoice as a giant refreshed, as a strong man girt for the race. . . . The greatest victories are yet to be won, the greatest deeds yet to be done." [22]

Notes

1. George P. Shultz, "U.S.-Soviet Relations in a Changing World," remarks before the Henry M. Jackson School of International Studies, Seattle, Washington, 5 February 1988, Jackson Papers, University of Washington Libraries, Seattle.

2. David Remnick, "Sakharov Warns Soviets on Threat of 1-Man Rule," *Washington Post*, 2 November 1988, sec. A., p. 1.

3. Reinhold Niebuhr, *Christianity and Power Politics* (New York: Charles Scribner's Sons, 1940), p. 104.

4. Sam Nunn, tribute on the floor of the Senate, in *Henry M. Jackson: Late a Senator from Washington* (Washington, D.C.: Government Printing Office, 1983), p. 206.

5. Dean Acheson, "The Past and the Future," in *The Atlantic Alliance: Jackson Subcommittee Hearings and Findings*, ed. Henry M. Jackson (New York: Frederick A. Praeger, 1967), p. 75.

6. Elie Wiesel, "Henry M. Jackson," in *Henry M. Jackson: Late a Senator from Washington*, p. 188.

7. Henry M. Jackson, "Labor and U.S. Central American Policy," address to Labor Law Conference honoring Edward Carlough, President, Sheet Metal Workers International Association, Hofstra School of Law, Hempstead, New York, 29 April 1983, Jackson Papers.

8. Henry M. Jackson, "A Time to Stress Excellence," commencement address, Carroll College, Helena, Montana, 6 May 1973, Jackson Papers.

9. George F. Will, "The Finest Public Servant I Have Known" (6 September 1983), in *The Morning After: American Successes and Excesses, 1981–1986* (New York: Free Press, 1986), p. 410.

10. Daniel Patrick Moynihan, remarks at the memorial service for Senator Henry M. Jackson, National Presbyterian Church, Washington, D.C., in *Henry M. Jackson: Late a Senator from Washington*, p. 422.

11. J. Bennett Johnston, tribute on the floor of the Senate, in ibid., p. 63.

12. Peter Jackson, remarks at the family memorial service for Senator Henry M. Jackson, First Presbyterian Church, Everett, Washington, in ibid., p. 260.

13. Thomas S. Foley, remarks at the family memorial service for Senator Henry M. Jackson, First Presbyterian Church, Everett, Washington, in ibid., p. 264.

14. Henry M. Jackson, "Introduction," in *The National Security Council: Jackson Subcommittee Papers on Policy-making at the Presidential Level,* ed. Henry M. Jackson (New York: Frederick A. Praeger, 1965), p. xiii.

15. Senate, Subcommittee on National Security and International Relations, *The Atlantic Alliance: Basic Issues,* study submitted to the Committee on Government Operations (Washington, D.C.: U.S. Government Printing Office, 1966).

16. Richard N. Perle, "The Senator and American Arms Control Policy," in *Staying the Course: Henry M. Jackson and National Security,* ed. Dorothy Fosdick (Seattle: University of Washington Press, 1987), pp. 97–98.

17. Senate Committee on Armed Services, *Military Implications of the Proposed SALT II Treaty Relating to the National Defense,* 96th Cong., 2d sess., 1980, S. Rept. 96-1054.

18. Henry M. Jackson, private letter to Ronald R. Reagan, 24 March 1981, Jackson Papers.

19. National Bipartisan Commission on Central America, Report, 10 January 1984.

20. Charles Krauthammer, "Whatever Became of the American Center?" in *Cutting Edges: Making Sense of the 80's* (New York: Random House, 1985), p. 98.

21. President, *Weekly Compilation of Presidential Documents,* Remarks on Awarding the [Presidential] Medal [of Freedom] to the late Senator Henry M. Jackson (Washington, D.C.: Office of the *Federal Register,* National Archives and Records Service, 2 July 1984), Ronald R. Reagan, 20:941.

22. Henry M. Jackson, "Across the Dangers, the Great Future," commencement address, Whitman College, Walla Walla, Washington, 22 May 1983, Jackson Papers.

Index of Names

DOROTHY FOSDICK is a member of the Board of Governors of the Henry M. Jackson Foundation and of the Visiting Committee of the Henry M. Jackson School of International Studies, University of Washington, Seattle. From 1955 to 1983 she served as adviser to Senator Jackson in a succession of positions. She earned her Ph.D. in 1939 from Columbia University. Her books include *What Is Liberty? A Study in Political Theory* (1939) and *Common Sense and World Affairs* (1955).

JAMES H. BILLINGTON was sworn in as Librarian of Congress in 1987, after serving as director of the Woodrow Wilson International Center for Scholars since 1973. He received his D.Phil. in 1953 from Oxford University, served on the faculty of Harvard University, and was professor of history at Princeton University from 1964 to 1974. His books include *The Icon and the Axe: An Interpretive History of Russian Culture* (1966) and *Fire in the Minds of Men: Origins of the Revolutionary Faith* (1980).